Playing for Their Nation

Playing for Their Nation

*Baseball and the American Military
during World War II*

STEVEN R. BULLOCK

UNIVERSITY OF NEBRASKA PRESS

LINCOLN & LONDON

⊗

Portions of this book were previously published in
"Playing for Their Nation:
Baseball and the American Military during World War II"
in the *Journal of Sport History*
(spring 2000), 67–89.

Library of Congress Cataloging-in-Publication Data
Bullock, Steven R.
Playing for their nation : baseball and the American military
during World War II / Steven R. Bullock.
p.   cm.
Includes bibliographical references and index.
ISBN 0-8032-1337-9 (hardcover : alk. paper)
1. Baseball—United States—History—20th century.
2. United States—Armed Forces—Sports—History—
20th century.   3. Baseball players—United States—
History—20th century.   I. Title.
GV863.A1 B84 2004
796.357'0973'09044—dc22
2003016945

Contents

Illustrations

Acknowledgments

Although it would be impossible in this limited space to recognize everyone who has aided me in the completion of this project, I feel compelled to mention several of the most important. First of all, my wife, Drlynn, helped motivate me to finish the work and always showed the understanding essential for someone living with an individual compiling a work of this size. Secondly, both my son John, who was born while I was in the process of putting words to paper, and my son Alex have provided me with the inspiration I needed to put the finishing touches on this book. Also, without question my mother, Jo Ann; my grandmother, Marie; and my father, Donny, have all aided me financially and emotionally during my quest to reach my ultimate goal, this book. To them, I extend my ultimate thanks. Furthermore, I must acknowledge the members of my committee, Kenneth Winkle, Parks Coble, Kenneth Price, and especially Benjamin Rader. Dr. Rader has allowed me to pursue my intellectual curiosities under his direction and provided superior instruction and advice throughout my years at the University of Nebraska–Lincoln.

Introduction

On October 6, 1941, the New York Yankees concluded the Major League Baseball season by defeating the Brooklyn Dodgers 3–1 in the final game of that year's World Series. It was a Fall Classic short on offense—both teams combined for only twenty-eight runs in five games—but certainly not short on drama. With the Dodgers trailing in the series two games to one, Brooklyn catcher Mickey Owen committed one of the most infamous gaffes in big league history during the pivotal fourth game. Owen dropped what should have been the third strike and final out of the game in the ninth inning with the Dodgers leading 4–3. The Yankees proceeded to take advantage of their good fortune, scoring four runs and eventually winning the game for an insurmountable three games to one lead in the series. Just two months later, with the World Series a distant memory, the attack on Pearl Harbor brought the United States directly into a war that had been raging around the globe for several years.

The 1941 World Series capped what had been a truly amazing baseball season filled with outstanding individual performances and records that stand even today. Most notably, Yankees centerfielder Joe DiMaggio embarked on a hitting spree that spanned more than a third of the season and eventually reached an astonishing fifty-six games. Across the nation, Americans became captivated by the feats of the Yankee Clipper as the number of consecutive contests in which he hit safely rose above thirty, forty, and eventually fifty. Even individuals not normally interested in the sport of baseball asked, "Did DiMaggio get a hit today?" While baseball fans focused on DiMaggio during the heart of the summer, by the final weeks of the season attention had turned to Boston, where arguably the best pure hitter to ever play the game was flirting with the magical .400 barrier. In a tale that has become part of baseball lore, before the final day of the 1941 season Red Sox left fielder Ted Williams had compiled an average that rounded off to exactly .400. Red Sox manager Joe Cronin, not wanting to see his young star miss an opportunity for such an achievement, suggested to Williams that he sit out a season-ending double header. Never one to evade a challenge, Williams refused to take the day off and promptly tallied six hits in eight at-bats to finish the year with a .406 batting average—the last time the .400 barrier has been broken in the Major Leagues.

In stark contrast to the magical 1941 baseball season, Hitler's Germany had overrun most of continental Europe the year before, and militaristic Japan was threatening Asia and the South Pacific in an ever-increasing global war. Although the United States did not officially enter the conflict until December 1941, the specter of American involvement had long haunted most citizens' minds, especially when it became evident that Germany and Japan were bent on world domination. When the United States finally did join the fray, Americans fought for various principles and institutions, one of which, for many, included the national pastime.[1] From the turn of the twentieth century to the beginning of World War II, the American people enjoyed an unusual and unprecedented fascination with the game of baseball. To some, baseball was "America's anchor"; it personified the nation's values and helped to unify an increasingly diverse population. Historian Benjamin Rader has correctly stated that "until the 1950s no other team or individual sport seriously challenged baseball's supremacy" in the sporting consciousness of the American people.[2]

Early in the war, the revelation that the Japanese also maintained a rabid fascination with baseball threatened to undermine to some extent the assertion that the game embodied America's essence. Editors at *The Sporting News*, the premier baseball publication of the day, attempted to resolve the issue in the inflamed rhetoric typical of the time: "[The Japanese] may have acquired a little skill at the game, but the soul of our national game never touched them. No nation which had as intimate contact with baseball as the Japanese could have committed the vicious, infamous deed of the early morning of December 7, 1941, if the spirit of the game ever had penetrated their yellow hides."[3]

Because the war years were such a unique time, not only for the United States, but also for professional baseball, this book is not the first investigation of the national pastime during this pivotal era. Authors such as William Mead, Bill Gilbert, Harrington Crissey, and William Kashatus have produced largely undocumented works concerning aspects of the game during World War II. General histories by Harold Seymour, David Quentin Voigt, and Benjamin Rader focus primarily on the impact of the war on Major League Baseball but give only brief attention to a larger connection between the game and the American military.[4] Others, such as Robert Creamer and Frederick Turner, have focused on the seasons immediately preceding or following the conclusion of hostilities, and hence used World War II as a backdrop for their accounts.[5] All of these studies, however, fail to adequately address the ways in which the game manifested itself within the military and the inseparable link between the national pastime and the war effort on a variety of levels throughout World War II. Therefore, the principal goal of this work is to provide a more comprehensive view of baseball and the American military during the war years.

The first chapter of this study focuses primarily on the sheer prevalence of the game within the armed forces both domestically and abroad. Because of the popularity of baseball among soldiers and sailors, military commanders often used the game as a vital tool for supplementing morale through, first of all, participatory athletic programs. Virtually every significant military installation around the world boasted formalized athletic teams and leagues designed to soothe the anxieties of combatants and to physically prepare them for battle. Officials also sponsored hundreds of exhibition baseball contests involving both military and civilian teams as well as tours by Major League stars primarily to entertain servicemen and elevate group morale. Furthermore, military authorities often disseminated literature, such as *The Sporting News*, which centered largely on the national pastime. Even the most widely read military publication, *Stars and Stripes*, regularly featured a prominent sports section that updated servicemen on both civilian and military baseball along with other athletic events.

The second chapter investigates the financial contribution the national pastime made to the war effort, primarily through monetary and athletic equipment donations. Professional baseball organizations, in particular, bolstered military coffers and war-related charities throughout the conflict, despite the fact that attendance, profits, and the quality of play dipped well below prewar standards until the 1946 season. Team owners and executives donated millions of dollars in cash subsidies as well as baseball equipment worth millions more to each branch of the American military both to ensure victory and to illustrate the devotion of the national pastime to servicemen around the world.

The next two chapters of this study revolve specifically around the manifestations of baseball within the armed forces. Chapter 3, for example, details the individual catalysts who promoted, organized, and supervised military baseball programs around the world, often amid perilous conditions. A particular concern is the way in which the American military operated and supported baseball programs in the absence of charismatic leadership. Because none of the branches of the armed forces maintained a reliable strategy to ensure uniform athletic participation domestically and abroad, inconsistencies in the quantity and quality of these baseball programs were clearly evident.

Chapter 4 discusses many of the most impressive military baseball teams that played during World War II. The massive influx of professional talent into the armed forces together with the importance some military leaders placed on creating stellar athletic programs assured that many military installations fielded formidable service teams. Indeed, the talent on several of these squads was so impressive that they often competed quite successfully against Major League competition in exhibition games and all-star contests staged throughout the war. As we will see, these military teams were responsible for, among other things, entertaining servicemen, fostering loyalty and pride, and ensuring bragging rights for officers.

The final three chapters investigate the most visible connection between baseball and the American military during the war—the hundreds of Major League players who eventually served in the fight against fascism. Chapter 5 recounts the military experiences of legendary diamond greats such as Joe DiMaggio, Ted Williams, and Bob Feller, as well as many other lesser-known professionals. By the conclusion of the war, over 90 percent of the players on prewar Major League rosters had served in the armed forces. These individuals garnered headlines and notoriety as they joined in the fight one by one through the waning months of the war, providing vivid proof that America was ready to send its best and brightest to combat enemies abroad. Although competing on military teams was one commmonality shared by most of these Major League players, the nature of their experiences in the service otherwise varied considerably. Although no Major Leaguer active at the time of Pearl Harbor died during the hostilities, a small number of players endured harrowing experiences against enemy forces. Others who were never able to face the enemy directly occupied positions abroad or at home that were either exceptionally dangerous or vital to the war effort. The majority of Major League players, however, because of their status as national icons, served in domestic or secure overseas locales where their officers usually allowed them to remain on the playing field and out of harm's way.

The final chapter investigates the real sacrifices made by the Major League players who served in the armed forces—the curtailment of careers that, even for the most talented, were relatively brief. Upon their return to Major League rosters, players who served in the armed forces witnessed a collective drop in productivity that was directly related to their absence from the professional game. Chapter 6 outlines, through both anecdotal and statistical evidence, the negative impact military service had on both position players and pitchers.

The varied connection that existed between baseball and the military during World War II was deep and extensive, reflecting the important position that the game maintained within the fabric of American culture. To many citizens, baseball represented much of what made America great—equality of opportunity (ignoring, of course, the cruel color line that segregated Major League baseball until 1947), the quest for victory, and cooperation of effort and sacrifice to meet a common goal. For some, if baseball were destroyed the very essence of our nation would be destroyed or, at the very least, irreparably harmed. It should come as no surprise, then, that when America responded to the aggression of totalitarian governments baseball went along for the long and arduous ride.

Chapter 1 **Vitalizing Spirit**

Baseball in Morale Building and Military Training

America's involvement in World War II and the mobilization that it necessitated provided the impetus for an unprecedented explosion in military baseball. In 1939, before many Americans recognized the gravity of the escalating global conflict, the United States Army employed only 175,000 fighting men, and budget constraints necessitated the use of antiquated equipment throughout the armed forces. As the potential for entry into the war increased during 1941, the numbers of soldiers grew tenfold, and the American military machine gradually began to modernize and mobilize at a stunning rate that continued through the conclusion of the conflict. In the end, over fifteen million men and women filled the ranks of the U.S. Army, Navy, Marines, and Coast Guard with the express purpose of ending fascism and protecting American interests everywhere.

Although World War II was a defining point in this nation's history militarily, economically, and socially, it was also cast amid the latter stages of baseball's "Golden Age" in America. At a time when the national pastime was exactly that, World War II interrupted what had been an unprecedented period in the annals of professional baseball. Diamond legends such as Babe Ruth, Ty Cobb, and Walter Johnson were not yet distant memories with an aura of mystery only recognizable in grainy black-and-white photographs. Those individuals, as well as most of the other great players of baseball's "Silver Age" in the first two decades of the twentieth century, still commanded attention and often entered the public eye through charity events, commercial advertisements, and other public appearances. With the dawning of the 1930s, new stars such as Joe DiMaggio, Hank Greenberg, Jimmy Foxx, and Ted Williams replaced the old guard. For a magical period in baseball history the legends of the past coexisted with the last generation of players to dominate the game before baseball lost its status as the true national pastime.

It was within this context that the rapid mobilization necessitated by the war increased the number of soldiers and sailors employed by the American military and brought droves of baseball-crazed men into the armed forces. American leaders quickly recognized the importance of baseball to the majority of fighting men and attempted to integrate the game on many levels within the military lifestyle. Shortly after the Pearl Harbor attack, the War Department identified baseball as the favorite of soldiers and sailors and attempted to ensure whenever possible that the nation's troops had an adequate supply of baseball gear as well as updates on Major League standings and statistics.[1] According to studies conducted by the War Department, approximately 75 percent of American fighting men enjoyed participating in or viewing baseball or softball games, far outdistancing the second-place sport, football.[2] With this information in hand, military leaders began to capitalize on American servicemen's fascination with baseball by utilizing it to elevate morale, primarily by supporting organized participatory baseball programs and informal pickup games. Other methods of augmenting the emotional well-being of fighting men included disseminating baseball statistics, providing radio broadcasts of Major League baseball games, and promoting exhibitions by professional players for military audiences.

Morale among servicemen had long been recognized by the American military as a decisive factor in the efficiency and effectiveness of its soldiers and sailors. Military leaders cited "detailed studies of previous armies and past wars" that revealed the "deep-rooted importance of morale" in the success of an extended military campaign.[3] Military commanders therefore deemed it essential to increase the level of morale both on and off the battlefield to ensure the optimal performance of the American fighting machine. Arguably the greatest military combat commander of World War II, Gen. George S. Patton, for example, often took extraordinary measures to ensure that the men under his command maintained elevated levels of morale.

Not only did he require that attire, hygiene, and personal appearance be maintained to strict standards, he also visited the front lines often and on numerous occasions led his men directly into battle, facing the same imminent danger from enemy fire as the soldiers under his command. His rationale was that only a leader who was visible and willing to risk his life could inspire his men and boost morale during the most difficult situations.[4]

To elevate morale away from the front lines, military leaders, including Patton, often relied upon baseball to placate the athletic appetites of servicemen because of its popularity among them. Although the importance of baseball to each serviceman obviously varied according to individual experiences and preferences, to most soldiers and sailors baseball maintained a prominent place in their lives both before and during the war. During the 1944 invasion of Tulagi in the Solomon Islands, for example, Marine sergeant Dana Babcock witnessed a fascinating scene when he and a few of his fellow, battle-weary Marines found themselves surrounded by the enemy on three sides and the Pacific on the other. Quite unexpectedly, Babcock stumbled upon what looked to be a pickup baseball game amidst the chaos. One Marine had "torn a dead branch from a jungle tree to take the part of a bat," and the players ran the bases, hit home runs, got caught in rundowns, and argued with the umpire, "calling him every name in the book," as Sergeant Babcock watched it all unfold from a distance. When he moved closer, however, Babcock noticed something slightly peculiar—the Marines were indeed playing baseball, but minus the ball! Unable to locate anything resembling a baseball and unwilling to simply abandon their game, the Marines proceeded to employ a "ghost" ball, which the umpire earnestly called a ball or a strike as the "pitcher delivered his phantom pitch." To Sergeant Babcock, the exhibition he witnessed illustrated that baseball was "deep in the hearts" of American servicemen, providing a bit of sanity in an atmosphere rife with insanity.[5]

Even German and Japanese fighting men recognized how ingrained baseball was in American culture, particularly among male servicemen. In Europe, soldiers routinely lamented that German bombing missions targeted a disproportionate number of baseball diamonds. In the Pacific, Japanese troops often attempted to demoralize American servicemen by defaming their baseball idols. Reports that

Japanese soldiers charged into battle with war cries such as "To hell with Babe Ruth" infuriated many, not least of all Ruth himself. When questioned about the Japanese invoking his name for nefarious purposes, Ruth commented that he hoped "every Jap that mention[ed] my name gets shot."[6]

Brooklyn Dodger fans, a notoriously loyal and often disappointed bunch, were not even safe from harassment from Japanese soldiers, some of whom apparently had an intimate knowledge of the American professional game. In an unidentified location in the China-Burma-India theatre, a lull in action and an unusual silence prompted a Japanese fighting man, "speaking perfect English," to harangue any fans of the "Brooklyn Bums" within earshot by commenting, "Hey Jonesy, did you hear the Giants blasted Dem [sic] Bums today, 15 to 2?" According to reports, "it took strict orders from their officers to keep the Brooklynites from coming out swinging."[7]

Aside from these passionate Dodger fans, Marine major Roscoe Torrance wondered "if the folks at home realize the hold baseball" had on the majority of other men donning American uniforms. Torrance explained that baseball helped relieve tension and displace the trauma experienced by the men in battle.[8] To many soldiers and sailors, only one thing was better than the game "as relaxation and a morale builder"—a letter from home.[9] Likewise, according to Phil Rizzuto, the Hall of Fame Yankee shortstop and Navy enlistee, while in the service he "never met anyone who didn't like baseball." Among the uncertainties and unfamiliar surroundings associated with the military lifestyle, the game served to "bring [servicemen] together," Rizzuto noted, and elevate morale.[10] Similarly, Marine corporal George Paulson stated unequivocally that there was "no question" that baseball was extremely important to most servicemen and was a part of the American way of life for which soldiers and sailors were fighting.[11]

The most beneficial and direct way in which baseball bolstered soldiers' and sailors' morale was through the participatory baseball programs that flourished on bases and camps around the globe during World War II. One of the outstanding proponents of military baseball, Capt. Robert Emmet of the Great Lakes Naval Training Station, attested to the importance of such programs to incoming sailors: "They're facing the job of adjusting themselves to military life, in addition to undergoing intensive routine. A game of baseball is a genuine incentive for wholesome thinking. They'll discuss the plays and the players of the exciting game for days after the last out. When a man's mind is alive with interest and enthusiasm, there's no room in it for homesickness or depressive thoughts."[12]

As Captain Emmett knew, for many soldiers and sailors acclimating themselves to the military lifestyle was a significant obstacle, particularly for young men away from home for the first time with "all parts of [their] former life missing."[13] No longer could newly inducted servicemen come and go as they pleased and enjoy the rights and privileges of American civilians. Officers instructed fighting men as to when they would eat, sleep, shower, shave, and, most importantly, train. Psychologically, this proved difficult for many to accept, and uncertainty, depression, and anxiety among soldiers and sailors naturally emerged as significant concerns for American leaders. Recognizing the problem, military officials searched for methods to ease servicemen's transitions into military life, including incorporating various facets of their civilian culture into military-sanctioned events. Thus, military leaders often sponsored the organization of participatory baseball programs for soldiers and sailors, especially during the first few months after their inductions. Maj. Leon T. David, who eventually supervised all Army Special Services operations in the Mediterranean region, was one of many who testified to the importance of military athletics. David insisted that the state of a unit's athletic programs was an adequate barometer of that unit's morale level. An increase in the numbers of and participation in athletic programs would presumably benefit morale directly.[14]

Both the Army and Navy, in fact, believed that ample athletic programs were instrumental to maintaining morale and subsequently integral to a victorious military campaign. The Army maintained a program for officers at Fort Meade (Maryland) for the sole purpose of training them in the proper methods for organizing, promoting, and sustaining athletic programs around the world. The Navy created a similar curriculum under the direction of former heavyweight boxing champion Gene Tunney, most notably at Norfolk Naval Training Station (Virginia). Tunney supervised the instruction of enlisted men and officers, many of whom had been professional athletes as civilians. These individuals then dispersed to various naval installations around the globe to orchestrate athletic and recreational activities for sailors.

Thus, under the assumption that athletics and morale were closely linked and with its men trained to supervise such activities, the American armed forces supported a wide array of programs designed to physically stimulate the millions of soldiers and sailors who served during the war. These athletic programs were most prevalent during basic training and during the time, if any, that was spent waiting for shipment overseas. In some cases, during the early phases of a serviceman's military stint participation in baseball and other athletic programs was not even voluntary. Many officers strongly believed that high participation rates in athletic programs correlated directly with increased morale and thus promoted "unit sports with mandatory attendance."[15]

Aside from easing the transition from the civilian to military lifestyles, baseball also provided a practical solution to the problems caused by the inevitable periods of inactivity. Awaiting shipment overseas, units occasionally stood fast for weeks after their training had been completed, and restlessness and irritability often followed. Even units in combat areas earned furloughs and had significant periods of idle time when they were not engaged directly on the front lines. Although extra training was a possibility during these down times, officers ran the risk of overtraining their men, which predictably eroded morale. In fact, the down time soldiers and sailors spent away from combat were arguably the most difficult situations in which to control morale. As the famous war correspondent Ernie Pyle noted, after weeks of combat during which time they might not bathe or, in some cases, even change socks, men often had to return from the front lines and participate in the "drab, hard work of supplying" their replacements before receiving any type of break in their military duties.[16]

Once they did gain some time for themselves, servicemen tended to want to do as little as possible before the return to the front lines. Long before the outset of World War II the U.S. military had realized, according to historian Wanda Wakefield, that the "idle soldier was the most likely to get into mischief, become homesick, or brood about the dangers he faced."[17] The War Department surmised that inactivity was directly associated with a rise in AWOL cases, decreased levels of efficiency, and increased incidences of venereal disease.[18] Regarding venereal disease, in particular, military leaders hoped that "sexuality could be sublimated through athletics," with sports such as baseball helping to reduce the numbers of infections and consequently improving the health and efficiency of America's armed forces.[19]

Military officials recognized that baseball could "break down [the] monotony" that inevitably arose with the military routine and alleviate the "weeds [that] choke good morale."[20] Baseball executive Branch Rickey insisted that competing on baseball teams provided soldiers and sailors with an "outlet for the abundance of [their] surplus energy and emotion." Through baseball, soldiers and sailors could be kept focused more on hits, errors, and runs rather than on the horrors of war, if only for brief periods. Special Services officer Maj. Leon T. David held team sports such as baseball in high regard for their ability to discourage idleness and negative thoughts and to direct service men's attention from solitary, often destructive activities, to more productive group activities.[21]

The American military promoted, in particular, organized team sports within its ranks because of their ability to provide "validation" to servicemen. Military leaders determined that informal, pickup contests might not establish the cohesive solidarity that arose out of more structured activities.[22] Also, some officials insisted that baseball provided "healthful exercise" that prepared men for the "rigors of combat conditions" without having to incessantly drill them to the point of exhaustion, which might threaten group morale.[23]

As the war progressed, sports became an increasingly integral part of military life around the United States, and to a lesser extent in overseas locales. At Fort Huachuca in Arizona, for example, one officer in the Ninety-second Infantry Division recalled that athletics there received a "lot of attention" and participation was extremely high.[24] After completing basic training and supplemental instruction in various camps throughout Texas in 1944, Army private Art Primer recalled playing baseball on a number of occasions. While awaiting notification of his point of embarkation to the battlegrounds of Europe, Primer experienced significant "down time," which he filled by competing on the diamond for a military team. The games, which stretched on for hours, were "a lot of fun," he said, and had a positive effect on his mental well-being.[25]

By promoting athletics and specifically baseball, military officials attempted to also instill within servicemen the perception that the American athlete was a superior breed. According to American leaders, this perception of superiority would then transfer to the combat arena by boosting morale and confidence, ensuring success for America's fighting men. Maj. Leon T. David asserted that organized team athletics developed "leadership, aggressiveness, initiative, and the will to win, all qualities essential to the soldier."[26]

On most military bases at home and abroad, baseball was one of the most popular choices for athletic activities, both by servicemen and by military leaders determined to utilize athletics to improve the quality of the American fighting man. The director of the Army's Athletic and Recreational Division during the war, Col. Theodore Bank, insisted that sports such as baseball were "not a supplement to [the Army's training] program; they [were] a basic part of it."[27] As early as 1922, no less an authority than Gen. Douglas MacArthur remarked: "Nothing more quickly than competitive athletics brings out the qualities of leadership, quickness of decision, promptness of action, mental and muscle coordination, aggressiveness, and courage. And nothing so readily and so firmly establishes that indefinable spirit of group interests and pride which we know as morale."[28]

Furthermore, proponents of military baseball emphasized other important benefits for soldiers and sailors who engaged in the national pastime. The widely held assumption, for example, that Americans were more skilled than other nations' soldiers in the art of grenade-throwing led to the conclusion that this was a result of "their ball-tossing background."[29] The editors of the premier baseball publication of the day, *The Sporting News*, expanded on this connection between baseball and battlefield performance by asserting that the game instilled a "sense of co-ordination that is important in modern warfare." The sports weekly concluded that this "sense of co-ordination" led directly to military success by enabling American fighting men to become more efficient, flexible, and innovative during the pressures of combat.[30] Marine captain O. W. Todd, whose civilian duties included supervising the operations of the Pacific Coast League's San Diego Padres, expressed similar sentiments by observing that the baseball played by most American servicemen was "paying off in the Pacific by [making Americans] better fighters."[31]

Likewise, Maj. John L. Griffith, commissioner of the Big Ten Conference, expressed his satisfaction that the majority of American servicemen played baseball at some point in their lives and that many continued to do so while in the military. Griffith pointed to instances during World War I in which Americans displayed unique leadership qualities during difficult situations that he attributed directly to the game of baseball. According to him, German soldiers often became disoriented and discouraged by unplanned disruptions in their operations, such as when an officer was killed, whereas Americans improvised, persevered, and maintained high levels of morale under similar circumstances. Griffith attributed this primarily to the fact that the Germans had utilized calisthenics and mass exercises to maintain the fitness of their armies while the American armed forces incorporated a program of team athletics such as baseball. For Griffith, such sports instilled camaraderie, leadership qualities, and quick, decisive thinking in soldiers and sailors.[32]

Despite the apparent physical and psychological benefits of participating in baseball programs, athletic injuries incurred on the playing field sometimes threatened to detract from the positive aspects of diamond competition. At the Special Services Branch School at Fort Meade, Maryland, officers training for duties, which included supervising Army sports programs, received instruction in minimizing athletic injuries. Care was to be "taken to see that games involving physical strain shall be participated in under close observation" and that men were not "subjected to tests, which are beyond their present athletic condition."[33] Although the majority of athletic injuries suffered by soldiers and sailors resulted from contact sports such as football and boxing, baseball presented its own hazards. A hard ball traveling at high speeds, thirty-five-inch bats, and various slides, tags, and throws all were capable of inflicting serious injuries and deactivating an individual for days or weeks.

In some cases, however, military officials actually incorporated baseball within the framework of traditional training. In one unique situation at Fort Custer (Michigan) military officials scheduled a game between two service teams, one of which was the Chemical Warfare Division located at the installation. Officers required members of the team to compete in the game while wearing gas masks to accustom the soldiers to the equipment. Likewise, at the Mare Island Marines Barracks in California, in a more typical marriage between training and the American pastime, officers used baseball as a means not only to entertain soldiers but, most importantly, to keep the players in "tip-top physical condition."[34]

In spite of the great importance some proponents placed on base-ball and other team sports as tools for increasing the efficiency and morale of the American military, Wanda Wakefield has observed that athletics could not "serve as a total replacement for other types of mil-itary training."[35] Becoming skilled in executing a sacrifice bunt or a rapidly turned double play did little to educate the American fighting man in the nuances of warfare or the vagaries of his military equip-ment. Recalling the war years many years later, Navy draftee and Cleve-land Indian Gene Woodling implied that his early months in the ser-vice could have been better spent. Woodling remembered receiving quite a bit of instruction in organizing athletic programs, though his actual military training was not exceptionally extensive. During his time in the Pacific on the island of Saipan, the site of fierce fighting in summer 1944, Woodling spent most of his time before the island was completely secure hiding from the Japanese. He cited his lack of ex-pertise in weapons and combat as one of his primary motivations for avoiding the enemy.[36]

Nevertheless, most officers encouraged soldiers' and sailors' fas-cination with baseball and made substantial efforts to accommodate their desire to stay connected to the game whenever possible, primar-ily through participatory programs. Organizing baseball programs, however, was not always feasible, particularly in combat locations over-seas. Ensuring high levels of morale during the critical first weeks of military service was not the only reason that servicemen experienced most of their participation in organized military baseball early in their stints. There were also practical reasons. For many reasons, which we will discuss in chapter 3, once shipped overseas, soldiers and sailors had a much more difficult time playing the national pastime.

Marine corporal George Paulson insisted that there were "very few [Marines] that didn't play baseball" during the time he was sta-tioned on the home front. While fighting in the South Pacific, how-ever, combat conditions limited their opportunities to compete on the diamond as much as they would have liked, though they were not completely absent.[37] Another veteran of the Marines, Charles Maier, recalled similar circumstances. Maier had also played baseball while stationed on the West Coast during basic training and afterward when he awaited shipment overseas. As with Corporal Paulson, as soon as Maier arrived in the Pacific combat zones concerns for safety and military schedules prohibited Marines from participating in athletics on a regular basis.[38]

Similarly, during sailor Richard Nowak's early months of naval training in San Diego, he and his fellow servicemen enjoyed many organized games. Although there were occasional equipment shortages, Nowak believed that these games "helped a lot" in easing anxieties. However, once he entered active combat areas in the Pacific, recreational possibilities were naturally limited by the days or weeks his vessel often spent at sea. But, Nowak and other members of his crew did not let their situation completely dictate their activities. On many trips throughout the Pacific, he and his fellow shipmates kept gloves and balls close at hand and were able to at least engage in spirited games of catch until they docked.[39]

Army veterans of World War II experienced similar limitations in their ability to play baseball overseas. Army colonel Earl Peak recalled that while on the domestic front, many soldiers participated in baseball programs designed to improve morale and instill cohesiveness. Overseas, however, combat conditions and a lack of adequate equipment rarely gave soldiers the luxury of spending time on the diamond.[40] This held true despite the fact that morale was especially important in combat areas, and athletic programs there would seemingly have benefited soldiers more than on the domestic front. Nonetheless, when conditions and equipment supplies allowed, Colonel Peak's superiors often required officers in his area to "participate in athletics at least two hours a day, rain or shine," thus ensuring a large number of participants.[41]

Even in the absence of participatory baseball programs soldiers and sailors found other ways to maintain a connection with the game. In many cases, this connection manifested itself through idle conversation, reading newspapers, or listening to radio broadcasts. Marine veteran Chuck Maier recalled that he and his fellow Marines spent many nights in the barracks "shooting the breeze." Because many of his fellow recruits were from different regions of the country and had diverse ethnic and religious backgrounds, few topics were as universally acceptable as baseball. Maier insisted that servicemen used discussions about the game as a way to relate to one another and also as a therapeutic method to distract themselves from the horrors of war. When asked if baseball banter helped servicemen form a cohesive bond, Maier acknowledged that he definitely "saw some of that."[42]

Because the majority of U.S. soldiers and sailors were fans of Major League Baseball, most American leaders, including the president, supported the continuation of the game during the war. Franklin D. Roosevelt was not alone in championing the benefits of baseball, however, as many prominent Americans rallied to support the perpetuation of the game. World War I ace fighter pilot Eddie Rickenbacker stated that "when there is no more reason for self-reliance in this country, then and then alone will there be no more reason for baseball." New York mayor Fiorella LaGuardia echoed Rickenbacker's sentiments when he commented, "our people don't mind being rationed on sugar and shoes, but those men in Washington will have to leave our baseball alone." One of those men in Washington, Sen. Albert "Happy" Chandler of Kentucky—the future Major League Baseball commissioner—heeded Mayor LaGuardia's call: "I'm for winning the war, and for keeping baseball. . . . We can, and must, do both."

The most influential man in Washington, however, provided the pivotal support for the survival of the game during the war. In January 1942, President Roosevelt issued his famous "green light" letter to Major League Baseball commissioner Kenesaw Mountain Landis: "I honestly feel that it would be best for the country to keep baseball going. There will be fewer unemployed and everybody will work longer hours and harder than ever before. And that means that they ought to have a chance for recreation and for taking their minds off their work even more than before. Baseball provides a recreation which does not last over two hours or two hours and a half, and which can be got for very little cost. And, incidentally, I hope the night games can be extended because it gives an opportunity to the day shift to see a game occasionally."[43]

Roosevelt's "green light" letter, although instrumental to the endurance of the game during the hostilities, was a product of careful negotiations and questionable conflicts of interest. The most sensitive issue involved the mutual dislike between Roosevelt and Landis. Landis, a staunch conservative, considered Roosevelt and his socialistic programs to be extremely dangerous to American society. As a result, the commissioner, "was not welcome at the White House" because of his open disdain for the president. After the outbreak of the war, the question then arose who would represent Major League Baseball in convincing President Roosevelt that the game was invaluable to the American people. Two prominent figures then emerged—Washington Senators owner Clark Griffith and postmaster general Robert Hannegan, who was also head of the Democratic National Committee.

Griffith had grown somewhat close to Roosevelt during the president's tenure at the White House primarily because of the yearly ceremonial visits between the two. At the beginning of each baseball season, Griffith greeted Roosevelt with a free pass to the season's games, and the president usually attended at least the opening game in Washington each season. At the beginning of the war, according to the *Washington Post*'s Shirley Povich, Griffith then used his influence to persuade Roosevelt to issue the proclamation encouraging the continuation of Major League Baseball.

The role played by Robert Hannegan was slightly more dubious, however. Hannegan was a "confidant of the president" and very close friends with St. Louis Cardinals' executive Samuel Breadon and St. Louis Browns' executives Donald Barnes and William DeWitt. Hannegan maintained such close ties with professional baseball, in fact, that he became part owner of the Cardinals shortly after the war. According to Dewitt, Hannegan, not Griffith, was the most important individual in convincing Roosevelt to issue the "green light" letter. Because Hannegan was in "great shape with the president" he was able to exert some influence over Roosevelt. DeWitt admitted that the situation could have been viewed as a blatant conflict of interest, and therefore Hannegan's role in supporting baseball's continuation was not well publicized.[44]

Along with the many notable personalities who urged the perpetuation of wartime professional baseball, the nation's preeminent sports weekly, *The Sporting News*, was one of the game's most outspoken proponents. Because its very existence depended upon the popularity and the continuation of professional baseball, *The Sporting News* stressed the importance of the game to the fabric of American society and the integral role baseball might play in providing inspiration for Americans during the hostilities. According to the editors of the sports weekly, baseball had a "special mission" to sustain morale and to provide a "vitalizing spirit" for both servicemen and civilians.[45] To the majority of the American population, male and female alike, *The Sporting News* asserted that baseball was synonymous with the "American way of life." In addition, the popularity of the game allowed the editors to derive a connection between the famous preamble of the United States Constitution, "we the people," and the national pastime by stating that "Baseball is the people."[46]

The other prominent baseball publication of the day, *Baseball Magazine*, expressed similar sentiments immediately following the Japanese attack on Pearl Harbor. The editors of the magazine reprinted an article from World War I penned by a former professional baseball player and a cultural icon, the Reverend Billy Sunday, the last time the continuation of the national pastime was threatened. In repeating Sunday's statements, *Baseball Magazine* noted their relevance to the crisis that faced professional baseball for the second time in less than three decades: "The idea that baseball is a luxury that ought to be postponed until the war is over is ridiculous. It is just as useful to the average spectator as to the soldier. The clerk who is working long hours for small pay needs something like baseball to put a little red blood in his veins once in a while. The American people need it as a mental and physical tonic. And as for the soldiers . . . baseball was made to order for them. The soldiers need just such a healthy influence to guard them against the evils which always lurk around [military installations]. Let's have baseball, plenty of it, all the more because we are at war."[47]

As the war progressed around the globe and the situation became increasingly dire for the Allies, some in the United States began to challenge the wisdom of Roosevelt's "green light" declaration. By the spring of 1942, with the Pearl Harbor attack still fresh in the memories of Americans, the Japanese had already overwhelmed Allied strongholds in the Philippines and other Pacific islands and were seriously threatening Australia. Many Americans even became convinced that the Japanese juggernaut would not be stopped until it reached the West Coast of the United States. Likewise, Germany seemed unstoppable with its firm stranglehold on virtually the entire European continent and Field Marshal Erwin Rommel ravaging Allied forces in North Africa.

In this context, to some Americans it seemed foolish to allow something as relatively insignificant as baseball to continue when greater concerns were consuming the nation. The editors of *The Sporting News*, however, argued vehemently for the continuation of the national pastime. When critics such as Congressmen Andrew May of Kentucky and William Langer of North Dakota questioned the prudence of playing ball during the war, *The Sporting News* was again quick to unabashedly defend the importance of the game to doubters: "Know now, for certain, that those who criticize baseball just don't know what they're talking about."[48] The writer then provided an abundant array of proof that baseball was invaluable to the war effort because of its unique ability to elevate morale. However, that proof primarily came down to *The Sporting News*'s opinion that American servicemen did not want professional baseball discontinued and thus, for their benefit, it should continue.

Nearly every week of the war, quotations supporting baseball from servicemen around the world dominated the pages of *The Sporting News*. Common sentiments included soldiers and sailors lamenting the possible loss of the game as a source of inspiration. Typical solicited responses included pleas from military men "to keep the game going," while others reminded readers that baseball was "symbolic of Americanism" and "for the morale of the soldier and the morale of America itself, keep 'em playing."[49] Reports of soldiers and sailors "aching for some news of the game" were traditional fare for *The Sporting News* throughout the war years.[50] Often, the revelation that servicemen everywhere were fans of the game and were deprived of baseball news flooded the pages of the sports weekly. According to *The Sporting News*, soldiers and sailors wanted not only scores of major and minor league games, but they also desired "to know who pitched, how many hits he gave, what sort of support he had, and most of all, he likes to see the standings of the teams at least once a week."[51]

Early in the war *The Sporting News* even resorted to offering a ten-dollar first prize for the serviceman who penned the most persuasive letter in support of Major League Baseball continuing its operations. Disguised as an unbiased investigation into the true opinions of soldiers and sailors regarding the game, the sports weekly included the winning submission along with several other entries. As one might expect, *The Sporting News* included no critical comments concerning the game, but instead revealed in a complimentary compilation of letters "what [servicemen] actually thought." Dozens of soldiers and sailors chimed in with emotionally stirring accounts of how important baseball was to the morale and well-being of Americans. Pvt. Clifford Mansfield, stationed at Fort Knox, claimed that baseball was his "life blood, as it is so with millions of other Americans." Sgt. Louis Eanes, certainly guilty of exaggeration, stated, "without baseball we would sink back to the dark ages." The winner of the contest, however, Pvt. Wayne Ashworth, was apparently even more emphatic about the value of baseball to the American people: "Discontinue baseball and you remove something from our morale—something only baseball can fill. Even if we haven't the opportunity to attend as many games, we'll be there in 'spirit.' We'll follow the game just as closely through the radio, newspapers and magazines. To us baseball is a morale-booster—a recreation—a source of enjoyment."[52]

For the duration of the war, *The Sporting News* also included numerous other editorials, interviews, and articles that stressed the strong support of American fighting men for the perpetuation of the game. Editorial assertions such as "our servicemen on the battle fronts want baseball to go on" and "[t]hey want their baseball news, wherever they are," were standard comments.[53] Before the war had even reached the six-month mark and shortly after President Roosevelt had offered his support for continuing professional baseball, the editors had no reservations about trumpeting the game's benefits: "Baseball enthusiasts need have no fear about the game justifying its continuance right through the war. The thinking man, who appreciates the value of morale factors, never had any serious doubt about the need of baseball in wartime United States. If he had any lurking misgivings, they have been swept away by action already taken." Quoting a sports columnist from an issue of the military newspaper *Stars and Stripes*, another offering revealed that "most GIs . . . would feel rather let down if the big leagues shut up shop. This goes for the soldier, the sailor, the Marine —and the civilians, both male and female."[54] Similarly, borrowing from an editorial in the Norfolk Naval Training Station newspaper, *The Sporting News* included the opinion that "[b]aseball is part of America, part of what we're fighting for today" and deserved the support of all Americans.[55]

The Sporting News, however, did not advocate continuing baseball at the expense of other, more vital industries and occupations. When Sen. Scott Lucas of Illinois stated that playing ball was not only desirable but absolutely essential in the war effort, even suggesting the possibility of offering draft deferments to professional players, the editors of the sports weekly upbraided him promptly. They praised the senator for acknowledging the importance of the game to both civilian and military morale and the substantial financial contributions Major League Baseball had made to the war effort. Nevertheless, the editors dismissed the notion that baseball was absolutely essential and concluded that "only one thing is absolutely essential—and that is to win the war."[56]

Even if baseball was not "absolutely essential," *The Sporting News* continued to valiantly support the continuation of the game by regularly highlighting favorable comments from high-ranking military men and important civilian leaders. Aside from constantly reminding readers that President Roosevelt's "green light letter" proved baseball's importance, the editors also tapped other sources to justify playing ball. The commander of the Great Lakes Naval Training Station near Chicago, Capt. Robert Emmet, concluded that "baseball [was a] genuine incentive" for soldiers and sailors fighting for America.[57] Likewise, *The Sporting News* included comments from Capt. H. A. McClure, commander of the Norfolk Naval Training Station, who reinforced the editors' stance by stating that baseball and the American way of life were synonymous and ordering Americans to "[p]lay ball!"[58] *The Sporting News* even quoted visionary Brooklyn Dodger executive Branch Rickey for support of the national pastime during the uncertain war years. A winter 1943 article recorded some of Rickey's comments and personal observations on the game, which included the assertion that Major League Baseball need not apologize for playing on during the war. Despite the fact that some took offense at seemingly healthy men competing on big league diamonds when they could have been toting a rifle or manning a battleship, Rickey declared that Major League Baseball filled a "deep need, not only in the matter of home morale, but also in the morale of the service men who are fighting in foreign lands."[59]

To illustrate Rickey's assertions regarding military morale, the editors of the sports weekly, clearly with more than a hint of self-promotion, constantly highlighted the opinions of many military men favorable to the publication. According to the editors, *The Sporting News*, with its in-depth analysis of professional baseball, was servicemen's favorite reading material. Soldiers and sailors around the globe noted that *The Sporting News* "was shared by many of [their] buddies," and the paper was instrumental as a "morale-maintainer." In some areas, military outposts received more copies of *The Sporting News* than any other publication, which indicated to the editors "the importance Special Services back in the States attache[d] to the paper."[60] To further reinforce the importance servicemen placed upon baseball information, the paper ran a weekly advertisement shortly after the outbreak of the war encouraging readers to purchase subscriptions at reduced prices for soldiers and sailors. Variations of the ad ran in the paper throughout the war. According to the advertisement, *The Sporting News* provided fighting men with what they desperately wanted to know—"what's going on in the game?"[61] One editorial cartoon summarized the significance that *The Sporting News* placed upon its accessibility to soldiers and sailors. The animation included two soldiers with an obvious affinity for baseball taking cover in a foxhole while one soldier peered over the top for the enemy with his rifle in hand while the other relaxed with a copy of *The Sporting News*. The caption read: "Knock off that sniper Ernie then I'll continue reading to ya!!!"[62]

Although one might be tempted to dismiss many of these self-referential items as simply *The Sporting News*'s own selective, self-aggrandizing propaganda, this does not seem to have been entirely the case. When one battle-hardened Marine was asked years later if keeping up to date on professional teams and players helped increase morale and relieve some of the tension servicemen endured, he stated that he had personally witnessed just that phenomenon during his time in the service. He concluded that information about the national pastime was very important to the overall mental well-being of his fellow Marines.[63] Although fighting men were most concerned about simply surviving, for many, following baseball did allow them to "have a change of pace in their mind" in the middle of the hostilities.[64] Likewise, one sailor, a rabid baseball fan before the war, suggested that baseball information provided him and his fellow servicemen with something tangible they could connect to. Reading about the Yankees or the Dodgers made the deck of a destroyer in the middle of the Pacific "seem a little more like home."[65]

Whenever possible, the American military also supplied radio broadcasts of important Major League games, such as the World Series, to provide entertainment and sustain soldiers and sailors' morale.

In forward areas where baseball information was scarce, a radio broadcast of a baseball game provided a semblance of order in a chaotic environment. In regions such as North Africa, the South Pacific, and Europe, American servicemen were able to listen to delayed broadcasts of World Series games and other random contests.[66] Even at sea, many sailors were able to follow their favorite teams and players despite being hundreds of miles from land. En route back home for his discharge, Detroit Tiger outfielder and Navy sailor Barney McCosky recalled listening to radio broadcasts of his former team competing in the 1945 World Series, held just two months after the final Allied victory in the Pacific.[67] Gen. Dwight Eisenhower even personally requested that an increasing number of broadcasts be supplied to his men stationed in North Africa. In some cases, Special Services could not supply complete broadcasts of games and resorted to including summarized scores, statistics, and standings for the listening pleasure of troops.[68]

In rare instances, instead of filtering baseball news and information to soldiers and sailors through media sources, military officials actually brought professional-caliber baseball to the men by staging exhibitions with Major League players. Although the American military also enlisted Hollywood figures and other entertainers to make appearances domestically and overseas, for some military leaders sports stars were the preferred form of distraction to raise morale. Army colonel M. J. Meyer noted that actors, singers, comedians, and the like were often difficult to accommodate and not very cooperative, unlike professional athletes. The colonel stated, "we need real troupers here and when we get them the boys appreciate their stuff more than any other kind of entertainment."[69]

Predictably, *The Sporting News* was one of the most outspoken proponents of such direct involvement by professional baseball players. In early 1943, the editors of the weekly stated that serious consideration should be given to staging Major League games overseas during the summer months to raise fighting men's morale. *The Sporting News* observed that several Hollywood stars had already completed goodwill tours and reasoned that baseball should undertake a similar venture. Several months later, *The Sporting News* continued its pitch for a Major League overseas tour by declaring that such an engagement would be a "tremendous opportunity to assist vitally in the war effort" by entertaining the soldiers and sailors who unflinchingly supported the game as civilians.[70]

In North Africa, Lt. Harold Kopp echoed the sentiments of *The Sporting News* by insisting that a big league tour would immeasurably improve morale even if actual contests could not be scheduled. If Major League stars could simply visit different units and "tell 'em baseball stories," Kopp asserted, troops would be ecstatic, and their appetite for baseball would be satisfied, if only for a short time.[71]

Because of scheduling and travel conflicts, however, Major League Baseball was not able to send entire teams for an expedition to overseas military facilities in 1943. A small cadre of Major League players, however, did spend several weeks mingling with American troops in Great Britain, occasionally displaying their diamond skills in exhibitions. *The Sporting News* heaped praise upon Vernon "Lefty" Gomez, Stan Musial, Frankie Frisch, Dan Litwhiler, Fred "Dixie" Walker, and Hank Borowy for "their unselfish answers to the call of our men in the service, who everywhere cry for entertainment . . . from the home sector."[72]

The following year, an almost identical cast engaged in a similar morale-building tour and provided entertainment for servicemen stationed in Europe and North Africa. Although staged several months before the successful D-Day invasion, Allied forces had already secured Italy and most of the Mediterranean and obviously felt comfortable in sponsoring tours by American sports figures. For spectators of such events, it often meant "the fulfillment of a . . . dream" to witness one of their favorite players in action.[73] In January 1944, *Stars and Stripes* reported that "alarming news" was arriving from the tour of Major Leaguers Hank Borowy, Stan Musial, "Dixie" Walker, and Danny Litwhiler. Apparently, most of the GI's "would rather [have] talk[ed] with big leaguers than with Betty Grable or any other dish."[74] This statement may have been somewhat excessive, as Maj. Alfred Brown, stationed in North Africa, noted at the time: "Put yourself in our place! For over a year we've had nothing feminine to observe but Arab women, their bodies completely covered with dirty white robes, their heads and faces covered, with possibly just one eye peeping out. Compare this constant view to that of one squint of Betty's gams. Brother, let's exchange places!"[75]

Despite Major Brown's assertion that ogling Betty Grable's legs might have been more appealing than watching Stan Musial's sweet swing, tours by Major League players remained an annual event during the war. Their impact on overall morale, however, was relatively minimal, primarily because of the modest number of players involved, the limited amount of baseball in which the players actually participated, and the small number of servicemen with whom players actually interacted. Since all of the tours occurred during the winter months, only in mild climes did stars actually compete on a regular basis. In addition, convening large numbers of idle troops to witness exhibitions was impractical and even impossible in most areas, at least until late in the war when the Allied victory was all but assured.

Nevertheless, the key to the success of such tours, at least according to *The Sporting News*, was superior organization. Among the players selected to travel to various outposts to boost morale, it was imperative to have at least one "name player" and several "capable talkers." Since winter was well entrenched in many of the areas the players visited, including the northern Pacific and Europe, these tours often amounted to simple intermingling between servicemen and athletes. Players often discussed some of the most important events of the previous season and gave soldiers and sailors an up-close and personal view of their diamond heroes.[76]

On the home front, military leaders and professional baseball officials also fostered a close relationship so as to increase troop morale and aid the war effort. In most Major League parks, soldiers and sailors in uniform received free admission to games, which increased their attendance levels. Often, teams sponsored military-appreciation days by public acknowledging the contributions of soldiers and sailors and occasionally allowing them down on the field with players. During spring training in 1942, Yankees management chose two GIs to meet and have photos taken with Yankee players, Joe DiMaggio included. The soldiers, both privates, were chosen because they represented "typical rookies." One received a baseball autographed by the entire Yankee squad and the other a photograph with DiMaggio.[77]

Although military leaders encouraged such attempts to bolster the morale through exhibitions, tours by Major League players, and visits to Major League games, after the first few months of the war Uncle Sam had transplanted many of the game's greatest players from the home front's diamonds to the military's. Indeed, by the end of the war, virtually every big league star had spent at least some time in the service. Thus, military officials did not have to search far to find servicemen who had the potential to have an enormous impact on their colleagues' morale. Because of the extensive baseball talent available to the armed forces during World War II, military contests in which some of the game's greats were pitted against one another or against big league teams drew substantial interest from soldiers and civilians alike.

For example, at Illinois's Great Lakes Naval Training Station, the largest of its kind in the world at the time, officials there scheduled many morale-boosting contests involving Major League talent. Capt. Robert Emmet, commander of the Great Lakes Station, was known by naval trainees as the "no. 1 man in baseball." Captain Emmet supervised arguably the greatest military baseball teams during World War II and invited "10,000 to 12,000 men in Naval training to join him as guests for an afternoon of Big Time ball two or three times a week." Because the Great Lakes facility housed 35 percent of all incoming naval recruits, Emmet had access to a continual barrage of Major League talent, such as Johnny Mize, Bob Feller, and "Schoolboy" Rowe. He capitalized on this by scheduling numerous exhibition games for his team against big league clubs and rival bases, all for the entertainment of the Great Lakes sailors.[78]

Elsewhere on the home front, other military officials also orchestrated exhibitions to elevate morale among servicemen. In this regard, however, they were less successful since few of these contests were played where morale was most likely to be suppressed—overseas. The majority of games were staged for soldiers and sailors awaiting shipment overseas. Nonetheless, military leaders determined that such events were imperative to maintaining high morale and scheduled games involving star players in hopes of appeasing the fighting man's athletic appetites.

In May 1943, for example, a "capacity crowd" at the Marine Corps base in San Diego witnessed the Santa Ana Army Air Base team, featuring Joe DiMaggio and future Major Leaguer Ray Yochim, destroy the home squad 22–2.[79] In an exhibition contest later in the year, a West Coast service all-star team, which also included DiMaggio, squared off against a combined contingent of players from the Pacific Coast League's Hollywood Stars and Los Angeles Angels. The "Yankee

Clipper" paced the service squad with two home runs and two other hits in four official trips to the plate, and Major Leaguers Johnny Pesky, Walter Judnich, and Red Ruffing also contributed to the victory. The game was all but decided in the first inning when Chuck Stevens, formerly of the St. Louis Browns, opened with a triple that initiated a three-run outburst. Former big league great "Babe" Herman, attempting desperately to preserve his career by hanging on in the minor leagues at the relatively advanced age of forty, provided one of the few bright spots for the losers, smashing a solo home run. His efforts, however, were not enough as the service team defeated the PCL squad 8–2 in a contest that drew over twenty thousand fans—the most to witness a day game in Los Angeles to that point.[80]

Arguably the most important military baseball extravaganza during World War II, however, was an eleven-game series between an Army select team and a contingent of Navy all-stars in September 1944. Staged in Honolulu, Hawaii, Army lieutenant general Robert Richardson Jr. and Navy admiral Chester Nimitz collaborated on the concept of a "Servicemen's World Series." With the intention of lifting the spirits of the servicemen stationed in Hawaii and determine bragging rights among the two branches of the armed forces, Nimitz and Richardson arranged for the squads to square off in late September, leaving less than a week for both sides to organize their rosters.

Although military leaders in Hawaii viewed this series as very important on many levels, such an organized event was not unprecedented in Hawaii. Earlier that summer, all-star teams from both the Army and Navy played a number of games to entertain servicemen who turned out in numbers as high as twenty-five thousand or more for several of the contests.[81] These games, dominated by the Navy, possibly provided the motivation the Army needed to assemble an impressive array of talent from outposts in and around Hawaii for the "Servicemen's World Series" that September. Unfortunately for the Army club, the "Navy put together—on three days' notice—one of the great baseball teams of all time." According to a reporter for the *Downtown Athletic Club News*, forty-eight hours before the opener, "a Naval Air Transport plane" carrying "a sorely-needed shipment of plumbing equipment" arrived, "supervised by two sailors, one a chief named Dom DiMaggio, the other a bluejacket by the name of Phil Rizzuto." Shortly thereafter, another Navy plane landed in Hawaii, this time with cargo that included "sailors with names like Rowe, Trucks, Walt Masterson, [and] Johnny Vander Meer." Teamed with other naval personnel already stationed in Hawaii, such as Johnny Mize, Peewee Reese, and Barney McCosky, the Navy squad boasted Major League talent up and down the lineup.[82]

The Army contingent, however, was not as fortunate in its recruitment of talent. Although not exactly shabby—it included players such as Joe Gordon, Johnny Beazley, and half a dozen other big leaguers—all-stars Buddy Lewis, Joe DiMaggio, and Hank Greenberg were unavailable for various reasons.[83] Initially scheduled as a seven-game affair, the contests were so popular and widely attended that the clubs played four more to entertain the area servicemen.[84] Predictably, the Navy squad captured eight of the eleven contests, including the first six, with one game ending in a tie.

The series opened with a resounding victory by the Navy, paced by the pitching of Virgil "Fire" Trucks, who shut out the opposition 5–0 and even added two hits to help spark the Bluejackets' offense. The only highlight for the losing squad was the completion of a triple play, started by Yankee star Joe Gordon, that stifled a Navy scoring threat. The second and third games in the series proved to be two of the most exciting, as late rallies decided both contests. In the second tilt, the Navy held a slim one-run lead behind the hurling of Johnny Vander Meer until the top of the ninth inning when the Bluejackets erupted for five runs. The offensive explosion was due in large part to a grand slam by Joe Grace, an outfielder for the St. Louis Browns before the war.

The third game proved to be even more titillating, as stellar pitching by the Navy's Tom Ferrick and the Army's Hugh Casey stifled the offense for most of twelve innings. Former Yankee catcher Kenneth Sears struck the decisive blow for the Navy with a home run in the top of the twelfth inning that resulted in the Army contingent's third consecutive loss. The situation for the defeated Army squad did not improve for the next three games, all losses for the soldiers. Of those three contests, the fifth game was probably the most disheartening for the Army team in that the Navy broke open a close game by scoring all ten of its runs in the fourth inning of a 10–2 victory. The Army contingent finally broke through in the seventh game with their first win, although it was not an easy task. Army first baseman Ferris Fain, who would later star after the war for the Philadelphia Athletics, struck a game-winning two-run home run in the ninth to ensure that the Army representatives would not be whitewashed in the series.[85]

The Army squad went on to narrowly win the eighth contest before being destroyed 11–0 by the Navy all-stars in the ninth game. The humiliating defeat in the series so incensed Army leaders that many far-flung Major League players then assigned to that branch of the service received transfers to Honolulu. All told, official orders relocated dozens of professional players to Hawaii, although they arrived too late in the baseball season to play a substantial role in 1944. With revenge on its mind, the Army attempted to organize another "Servicemen's World Series" against the Navy for the summer of 1945. The Navy, however, had already assigned most of its baseball talent to two primary groups that were dispatched throughout the Pacific to entertain sailors, and thus it declined the invitation for a rematch. Likewise, the Army, realizing that there was no possibility for retribution, sent its rather substantial cadre of professional players around the Pacific to provide a much-needed boost in morale.

Throughout the first half of 1945, the Army and Navy squads from Hawaii independently played dozens of exhibition games for thousands of interested spectators across the Pacific. To the soldiers, sailors, and Marines who had endured some of the harshest fighting of World War II during the "island hopping" stage of the conflict in the Pacific, such productions were a welcome diversion. By early 1945, despite the fact that Japan had virtually no hope of even ending the war on amenable terms, its soldiers, sailors, and airmen continued to fight with utter disregard for their own lives. By that summer, the battles of Iwo Jima and Okinawa had been bitterly fought and won by Allied forces, and the Japanese began the dreaded *kamikaze* attacks that wrought so much havoc on the American Navy. Thus, even though the Japanese military seemed unable to wage an extended campaign, to many the war seemed unlikely to conclude soon. For that reason, the efforts of the professional players then in the military had a substantial impact on the thousands of fighting men then enduring the last desperate measures of the Japanese.

The exhibition games throughout the Pacific drew thousands of servicemen in most locations, especially where adequate facilities allowed for large crowds. Not all of the guests for these exhibitions, however, were invited. On several occasions, unvanquished Japanese soldiers—apparently fans of America's national pastime—emerged from their places of hiding to witness the diamond spectacles. Some even donned American service uniforms in an effort to get close to the action. Major League outfielder Barney McCosky, then in the Navy, recalled seeing MPS "pluck one, two, three, four, five [Japanese] out of the stands" while playing an exhibition game on a remote Pacific island.[86]

Members of the Army teams scattered across the Pacific experienced similar encounters, including one of the most prominent players on those teams, St. Louis Cardinal great Enos Slaughter. Recalling his jaunt around the Pacific many years later, Slaughter noted that he personally saw Japanese spectators apprehended by military authorities on islands such as Guam and Iwo Jima. Slaughter and the other Major Leaguers then in the service took pride in the fact that they played the morale-boosting exhibitions for their fellow servicemen with a great deal of fervor and zeal at a most difficult time during the war. Slaughter insisted that he and the other players "played as hard over there as [we] played here" and on remarkably well-maintained fields considering the situation.[87]

In the European theater, the lateness of the Allied arrival and the instability of the situation prevented large-scale athletic events such as those staged in Hawaii until the final months of the war. Although D-Day in June 1944 had been an unabashed success, Allied commanders had been very cautious in their offensive push into the heart of the continent, fearing that an aggressive assault into German territory might expose the flanks of the invading troops. Moreover, the Allies' progress across France and into Germany had been interrupted by the Battle of the Bulge in late 1944 and early 1945. By the spring of 1945, however, the Allies had all but secured victory, eventually overrunning the German capital and forcing Hitler's suicide in May.

During the summer of 1945, however, with the European conflict concluded and the baseball season just reaching its peak, the attention of many was drawn to the "European Theater of Operations (ETO) World Series" in Nuremberg, Germany. The hotly contested and highly publicized tournament began in mid-summer with dozens of service teams, which were eventually whittled down to the final pair: the Overseas Invasion Services Expedition (OISE) All-Stars and the Seventy-First Infantry Division squad, both Army contingents.

Seemingly outmatched, with only one Major League player, pitcher Sam Nahem, and Negro League stars Leon Day and Willard Brown, the OISE All-Stars outlasted several other talented teams to reach the finals in September. The Seventy-First also dispatched exceptional squads to gain entry into the series, but it could boast a lineup that included Major League stalwarts Ewell "The Whip" Blackwell, Harry "The Hat" Walker, Maurice Van Robays, and several others with big league experience. What appeared to be a mismatch, however, became a thrilling spectacle for the estimated fifty thousand spectators who turned out for each of the series' five games. The Seventy-First seemed destined to overwhelm their opponents with an easy victory in the first game, but Leon Day won the second for the OISE team with a masterful performance in which he allowed only a single run to his teammates' two. Nahem duplicated Day's performance in the third contest, which also ended in a 2–1 count. The Seventy-First rebounded in game four when future Major League pitcher Bill Ayers spun a shutout against the OISE All-Stars. In the decisive fifth game, semipro catcher Lew Richardson laced a base hit off Ewell Blackwell (destined to become a six-time all-star upon his return to the Major Leagues), thereby driving in the run that gave the underdog OISE squad a slim 2–1 victory.[88] Having two Army contingents in the finals of the ETO series did exact some revenge for the Army's horrendous showing against the Navy in Hawaii the previous year and secured bragging rights in that corner of the globe for 1945.

Unquestionably, then, baseball gave American military commanders a suitably indigenous method for improving morale and supplementing training throughout the war. Through participatory programs, exhibition contests, and tours by Major League players, the American military fostered the national pastime on the playing field so as to prepare its fighting men for victory on the battlefield. Because of the game's almost universal appeal among servicemen, baseball was a source of diversion and unity for soldiers and sailors facing uniquely difficult and often chaotic conditions. Thus, the morale-building qualities of baseball alleviated some of the difficulties inherent in organizing such a large fighting force and helped American military leaders assemble an efficient war machine.

Chapter 2 **Your Duty, Our Duty**

Raising Funds for the War and Baseball Equipment

Aside from supplementing conventional military training and boosting servicemen's morale, baseball served another purpose for American military leaders: as a means to raise funds for both the war effort and to offset the sizable expenses of military athletic programs. By staging exhibition games that included both service and civilian teams and accepting gate receipts from other high-profile professional contests, military officials were able to dramatically increase financial contributions to the war effort. Also, by the conclusion of the war the majority of professional players were in the service, which enabled every branch of the armed forces to employ professionals uniquely qualified to help sell war bonds, solicit charitable donations, and recruit new soldiers and sailors. Moreover, Major League baseball teams themselves donated hundreds of thousands of dollars to various war-related organizations and millions of dollars worth of athletic equipment for servicemen around the world.

Immediately after Pearl Harbor, baseball executives began devising scenarios for ways in which the professional game could contribute to the war, even as some were questioning the need for the game's very existence. Owners of professional teams not only wanted to aid the struggle against fascism by elevating Americans' morale; they also sought to prove how financially valuable the game could be during the country's hour of need. This financial contribution in turn would justify, at least in the eyes of the baseball owners, the continuation of the national pastime during the global crisis. The next questions then became how exactly professional baseball organizations could best aid the American military and how much they should donate to the war effort. Famed baseball executive Branch Rickey expressed the opinion that baseball had an obligation to do everything within its power to bolster the Allied cause, even operating at a break-even level if necessary. Baseball, he reasoned, was so deeply embedded in the American way of life that the two were inseparable. For Rickey, professional baseball's fate paralleled the fate of the nation as a whole, and the thus the national pastime should not hesitate to drain its resources to support the war effort.[1]

Rickey's opinion apparently reflected the consensus of Major League Baseball's executives since both leagues together lost over $200,000 in 1943. Donations to the war effort, decreased attendance, and wartime restrictions all made it difficult for franchises to meet operating expenses, let alone generate a profit. The rapid exodus into the military of over 90 percent of Major Leaguers active at the beginning of the war only compounded these challenges. As players began to depart for military service, the quality of play naturally declined, and mediocre talent did not excite fans. During the war years, players committed an average of about 1,500 more errors per year than immediately before or after the conflict. Also, both because of the less lively balata ball introduced during the war and the profusion of less talented hitters, home runs dipped precipitously from 1942 to 1945. In marked contrast to the offensive apex the game had achieved in the decade before World War II, such developments made the game seem boring and stagnant to the diminishing number of fans who attended Major League games.

The lack of talent notwithstanding, throughout the war there were compelling events on the diamond that had substantial fan appeal. In the 1945 season, the St. Louis Browns employed an outfielder named Pete Gray who hit an unremarkable .218 with no home runs. Those numbers might have made Gray just another anonymous Major League player with a brief and undistinguished career if not for the fact that he had achieved them without a right arm! A childhood accident had cost him virtually his entire arm, yet he grew to adulthood with a natural talent for baseball. Defying logic and critics, he hit over .300 several times at the minor league level, albeit with limited power, and was a serviceable defensive outfielder. Gray devised a remarkable technique for throwing the baseball back into the infield that enabled him to rival the speed of his two-handed counterparts. He would field the ball, toss it into the air, pry the glove off his hand with the stump of his right arm, pluck the ball out of the air with his now ungloved left hand, and finally whip the ball into the infield, all in one fluid motion. Unfortunately for Gray, in 1945 the Browns could not repeat what had been a magical season the year before: their first appearance in the World Series in franchise history.

The presence of Gray on a Major League diamond was far from the only unusual occurrence in the war years. In 1944 the Cincinnati Reds employed fifteen-year-old Joe Nuxhall for one game, hoping his precocious talent was mature enough to baffle big league hitters. The experiment proved a disaster as the youngster, who had to obtain a note from his high school principal to play for the Reds, pitched only two-thirds of an inning, surrendering five walks and two hits. After eight years of additional seasoning in the minor leagues Nuxhall did rebound to have a very fine career with the Reds.

Wartime manpower shortages also forced many teams to employ notable players who were long past their primes. Although a number of these veterans had clearly lost the skills generally required of Major League players, some were actually the best available players for their positions and offered the added bonus of a boost at the ticket window. For example, in 1945 the Dodgers signed outfielder Floyd "Babe" Herman, a star for the team in the 1920s and 1930s, who had ostensibly finished his big league tenure at age thirty-four with the Tigers in 1937. As we saw in chapter 1, during the war Herman was struggling to prolong his baseball career by competing in the Pacific Coast circuit (a prominent minor league still in operation today). Surely identifying an opportunity to bring in a "name" player when most of the game's more youthful stars had departed for military assignments, the Dodgers inserted the forty-two-year-old Herman into thirty-seven games as an outfielder and pinch-hitter during which he batted a respectable .265. The war also extended the careers of other aging veterans such as Paul and Lloyd Waner, Jimmie Foxx, and Al Simmons, all Hall of Famers enlisted to win games and, most importantly, to bring fans to the stadium.

Those fans were in shorter supply, as total Major League attendance fell from 10 million in 1941 to a wartime worst 7.7 million in

1943. Though this precipitated an economic crisis, all but one team, the Philadelphia Phillies, managed to weather the storm. Partly because of the poor financial climate, Phillies owner Gerry Nugent declared bankruptcy in 1943 and sold the team to the National League until the league could locate a suitable owner. Eventually, after one aborted sale of the team to a New York gaming figure, a member of the DuPont family purchased the franchise and reinvigorated the club.[2] The financial prospects for professional teams did improve during the final two years of the war, as attendance for 1944 and 1945 grew modestly before increasing dramatically after the war. Adding to the drop in revenues caused by lower attendance were the resource-draining policies instituted by most professional teams. For example, clubs allowed servicemen to attend games for free, "no strings attached," and engaged in numerous charitable activities, discussed next, which quickly eroded profits.[3]

Despite economic hardships, Major League Baseball maintained a steady effort to supplement the war effort generally and support military baseball in particular. Each year of the war, the major leagues donated most or all of the proceeds from the annual All-Star Games and World Series contests to various war-related causes.[4] Allocating funds exactly, however, was often a disjointed and complicated affair. The financial contributions from the World Series, which could last anywhere from four to seven games, proved particularly difficult to reconcile. Baseball and military officials had to consider factors such as teams' travel expenses, parks with varying seating capacities, and four-game sweeps. Moreover, instead of dividing the World Series contributions evenly among several war-related benefactors, officials fell sway to complex tax considerations and assigned certain games' proceeds to certain benefactors. Major League Baseball, for example, determined that the 1942 World Series between the Cardinals and Yankees would benefit both the USO and the Red Cross. Owners of each team received full proceeds from games one, two, and five, and split revenues in games three and four with the two charities. Games three and four were allocated to benefit the charitable groups because they were played in Yankee Stadium, which held almost twice as many spectators as the Cardinals' home park. Major League executives also promised the USO and Red Cross all of the receipts from games six and seven, if played. However, the Cardinals won four straight after losing the opening game, rendering the point moot. The players from both teams also received a small stipend for each World Series game played and had promised to donate their portions for games five, six, and seven if they were held. Because of the brevity of the series, however, the players only had to part with one game's bonus. In total, the 1942 Series produced nearly $365,000 for the aforementioned charities, an amount typical of the other World Series of the war years.[5]

Other examples of Major League Baseball's fervent attempts to justify its existence were its organization of relief games during the first year of the war. These games continued on a structured basis through the 1944 season and then proceeded irregularly during the 1945 season. Weeks before opening day in 1942 baseball executives devised an outline for these games' financial contributions and made the details public to stave off criticism that baseball was an idle amusement unnecessary in such dire times. Each Major League team held at least one regular season relief game from 1942 through 1944, with the gate receipts and additional sums contributing to the war effort.[6]

The first, and as it turned out one of the most profitable, relief games was staged early in the 1942 season between the Brooklyn Dodgers and New York Giants in Brooklyn's Ebbets Field. Because of the teams' close proximity to one another and the fact that they both competed in the National League, the Dodgers-Giants rivalry had historically been a bitter one, setting a perfect stage for the fund-raising event. The action on the field was closely contested, with the Dodgers winning 7–6 on a Dolph Camilli home run. Most importantly, the game drew close to forty thousand spectators and raised just over $60,000 for the Navy Relief Fund.[7]

After such an unabashed triumph so early in the war, *The Sporting News* argued that any criticism of baseball was unjustified: the game had already demonstrated unwavering support of the war effort, both from a morale and financial perspective. Clearly addressing critics of the game, the editors of the baseball weekly insisted that the game had "demonstrated [through relief games] it had a right to live." *The Sporting News* honored Dodger president Larry MacPhail as a "trail blazer in the game's war effort" for his outstanding promotion of the game and implored other owners and executives to follow his lead.[8] Later in the summer, the Giants did just that and hosted the Dodgers in an even more profitable venture, netting over $75,000 for military causes.

On August 23, the New York Yankees hosted the most extravagant relief game of the three full war campaigns and the third such successful contest in the New York metropolitan area during the 1942 season. Despite a cross-town battle between the Dodgers and Giants that same day, a scheduled doubleheader between the world champion Yanks and the hapless Washington Senators, a perennial second-division squad, attracted over sixty-nine thousand fans and raised over $80,000 in donations. The day's competition ended in a draw as the teams split the doubleheader, which included a scintillating 7–6 contest in the first game. The Senators drove Yankee pitcher and future Hall of Famer "Red" Ruffing from the game in the bottom of the ninth and were able to score three runs in the frame to eke out a victory. Due to blackout restrictions enforced by the War Department, the teams were unable to complete nine innings for the second game before darkness enveloped Yankee Stadium. However, the squads did finish six frames—thus rendering the game official—with the Yankees slipping by the Senators 3–0.

The suspension of the second game was a result of the extracurricular activities held between the contests. Players from each team engaged in various skill challenges, such as a sixty-yard dash, an accuracy contest involving throws from home plate toward a barrel at second base, and a fungo-hitting competition. The main attraction, however, were the great Babe Ruth and Walter Johnson who dusted off their spikes to a "thunder of applause." Johnson, fifty-four, had not appeared in a Major League contest in fifteen years, and Ruth, forty-seven, had been out of the game for seven years, yet both men performed admirably in a glorified batting-practice session. Johnson served up seventeen pitches to the legendary Babe who twice drove the ball into the right-field stands, to the delight of the crowd.[9]

Outside of New York during the 1942 season, most other Major League teams, even those with struggling franchises in smaller cities, were able to contribute sizable sums to the American military through relief games. The Detroit Tigers, for example, collected over $68,000 in a June contest against the lowly St. Louis Browns. Also, teams such as the Cincinnati Reds, Boston Braves, Pittsburgh Pirates, Philadelphia Athletics, and Chicago White Sox all raised over $30,000 for the war effort that summer. Other teams, however, were not as proficient in their fund-raising abilities. The St. Louis Browns, Washington Senators, Cleveland Indians, and Philadelphia Phillies all contributed less than $10,000 to war charities, with the Phillies unable even to break the $5,000 mark. Two other teams, the Boston Red Sox and St. Louis Cardinals, also managed relatively paltry sums in comparison to their professional counterparts—neither quite reached $14,000 in donations.[10]

Just as the editors of *The Sporting News* heaped praise upon baseball executives such as Larry MacPhail who relentlessly organized and promoted relief games, so too did they roundly criticize those who failed to do the same. Labeling relief contests "YOUR duty, OUR duty," the editors expressed disappointment that the full fund-raising potential of the 1942 season's early relief games was not realized.[11] Shortly after two of the lowest-grossing relief games of the year, hosted by the Philadelphia Phillies and Washington Senators, *The Sporting News* took the teams' executives to task for failing in their obligations. The editors rationalized the poor showing by explaining that Major League owners often "shrink from forced promotion of their entertainment." The writers then stated their goal—to ensure that the future relief games were not dismal failures. To prevent this, they offered the five-step plan for success MacPhail had utilized in his successful Brooklyn venture. The strategy included saturating the public with advertising for the game, soliciting private companies to purchase hundreds and even thousands of tickets, and gaining the cooperation of local government and law enforcement agencies to ensure that the event proceeded smoothly.

One of the most important factors in the relief games' success, however, were the game dates and starting times. With wartime restrictions limiting the number of night games Major League teams could schedule and baseball under the lights still a novel concept, many owners were forced to sacrifice lucrative day-game dates, and were reluctant to do so, however noble the cause. When the Washington Senators schedule a relief game to start at five o'clock on a Saturday, the editors of *The Sporting News* labeled the result "ruinous." The baseball weekly then praised the executives of the Chicago White Sox for rescheduling their relief game for July to ensure maximum attendance and thus the largest possible financial windfall.[12]

By the conclusion of the 1942 relief game schedule in August, both leagues had donated a total of almost $525,000 to the Army and Navy relief funds. This did surpass the goal set forth by baseball executives before the season of $250,000 for each league and justified optimism for future efforts to bolster the war effort. *The Sporting News* even commented that baseball would "be expected to double their 1942 returns" the following season and that unquestionably "It can be done. And—it will be done!"[13]

Unfortunately, the prediction proved to be erroneous as the totals in 1943 fell almost $200,000 short of the previous year's mark. The 1943 relief games garnered slightly over $325,000 and only witnessed a modest increase in 1944 of approximately $2,000.[14] The relief games of those two seasons were not complete washouts, though the excitement generated during the first full war-year campaign was apparently absent. The New York games again did well, and the Pittsburgh Pirates even raised over $35,000 for the war effort. Across the board, however, the numbers declined in 1943 and remained virtually unchanged the following season.[15] Most of this drop-off surely was the result of the departure of the majority of the era's great players for military service, robbing many of the relief games of their appeal. In 1945, the relief games dwindled even further with interleague contests between city rivals in New York, Boston, Philadelphia, and Chicago providing the bulk of the approximately $245,000 raised during the final year of hostilities.[16]

As the individual relief games lost momentum after the first year of the war, Major League teams searched for other methods to benefit American military charities. Among the most effective were the various techniques for promoting the sale of war bonds. Players for every team spent off-dates cajoling businesses and wealthy individuals to purchase these investments. Baseball executives authorized the erection of war bond booths in stadiums to make it easier for fans to purchase them. On Easter Sunday 1943, the Brooklyn Dodgers even dropped their gloves and circulated through the stands in Ebbets Field to encourage those in attendance to buy bonds. The Dodgers were so aggressive in their "Spring Offensive," as it was known, that, according to the U.S. Treasury Department, the franchise was responsible for the sale of over $75 million in war bond sales.[17] To further generate funds, many teams auctioned off memorabilia from stars past and present. The St. Louis Cardinals capitalized on their 1942 World Series victory by selling gloves, autographed baseballs, and numerous other me-

mentos for well over $100,000 in bonds. In Philadelphia, a signed photograph of the esteemed manager Connie Mack even drew a $16,000 war bond bid.[18]

The most successful effort to promote the sale of war bonds, however, occurred during the summer of 1943 when the New York and Brooklyn chapters of the Baseball Writers Association decided to use their influence and personal connections to promote a bond sale extravaganza. The organization sponsored a unique auction of thirty-six of the most recognizable and popular players from the three New York teams—twelve from each squad. Former New York mayor James J. Walker emceed the affair and sold to the highest bidders the rights to stars such as Mel Ott, Ernie Lombardi, Joe Gordon, Carl Hubbell, Bill Dickey, and "Dixie" Walker. Those who won the bidding pledged to purchase war bonds in the same amount of their winning bid and to add to that amount depending upon the player's performance over the remainder of the season. For every single garnered by a position player, the sponsor promised to part with $2,500, and for each double, triple, and home run the amounts escalated to $5,000, $7,500, and $10,000, respectively. The price structure for pitchers included $35,000 for each regular season win and $50,000 in the event of a shutout.

One of the most popular Dodgers, outfielder "Dixie" Walker, secured the highest bid among the available players. Despite his considerable baseball skill, Walker would lose some supporters after the war for his staunch opposition to integration (at one point, he even started a petition to ban Jackie Robinson from the Dodger squad).[19] However, during the war integration had yet to become an issue, and Walker had been dubbed the "People's Cherce [sic]" by Brooklyn fans for his outstanding talents and genial personality. At the player auction, an organization known as the Brooklyn Club offered an amazing bid of $11.25 million for the Dodger outfielder. While at the podium, the former mayor of New York, seemingly stunned at the amount, inquired as to the exact nature of the club's activities. Representatives informed Walker that they were a "social club," at which point the former mayor retorted, "With that kind of money it's easy to be social." Apart from the Dodger outfielder, one other bid approached "Dixie" Walker's price tag. Brooklyn's Arky Vaughn drew an $11 million pledge, while future Hall of Famers Carl Hubbell and Bill Dickey went in the $3 million range. The baseball writers' war bond drive in New York climaxed later that year when the thirty-six player composite squad squared off against a military team at the Polo Grounds, eventually realizing a total purchase of close to a $1 billion in bonds.[20]

Aside from financial contributions and war bond pledges, Major League Baseball investigated other ways to aid servicemen at home and abroad. Because many servicemen competed in military baseball, the financial cost of maintaining fields, transporting teams, and purchasing equipment was, of course, considerable. With hundreds of billions of dollars being spent to improve the ability of the United States to wage war against the Axis powers, the funds allocated to military athletics were often insufficient to support the large numbers of soldiers and sailors wishing to compete for military teams. Recognizing the situation, professional organizations made a concerted effort to provide funds to servicemen with the necessary baseball gear.

These donations materialized primarily through contributions funneled into an entity known as the Ball and Bat Fund. Major League Baseball owners established the fund shortly after the Pearl Harbor attack, under the direction of Clark W. Griffith, owner of the Washington Senators, and Ford Frick, president of the National League. The fund, which was in operation even before the end of 1941, was modeled after a similar entity created during World War I and, according to *Washington Post* columnist Shirley Povich, it was organized to provide baseball equipment for "every post, on every front, home and foreign."[21]

The Ball and Bat Fund was composed of a committee, headed by Griffith and Frick, who supervised both monetary and equipment dispensations to the fund. Along with straight financial contributions to the fund, which went to purchase tax-free baseball gear, every Major League franchise had arrangements to further bolster the equipment inventory of the Ball and Bat Fund through other means. For example, teams frequently passed on used bats, gloves, and other equipment to the fund's central committee as well as foul balls returned by fans.[22] Once executives had procured the equipment, they then distributed it directly to representatives of the various armed forces who then allocated the materials to soldiers and sailors at home and abroad.[23]

Just weeks after the American entry into the war the Ball and Bat

Fund had already produced sizable donations. By January 1942, the charitable organization had purchased eighteen thousand balls and forty-five hundred bats for use by servicemen. Moreover, before a regular season contest had even been played in 1942, the major leagues had already donated $25,000 to the fund. By June, baseball owners had procured over eighty thousand pieces of baseball equipment for the armed forces, including over two thousand more baseballs. By the end of the year Major League owners had bequeathed over $1 million to purchase even more gear, with nearly every team participating in the donations.[24] By the following year, the Ball and Bat Fund had supplied the majority of the one hundred thousand baseballs, forty thousand bats, thirty thousand gloves, seven hundred bases, and nearly four thousand sets of catcher's equipment available to servicemen in the Mediterranean theatre of operations alone.[25]

Despite the vast contributions of Major League Baseball and the funds allocated to military athletics by the American military, soldiers and sailors often experienced shortages of baseball gear, particularly uniforms. Although entities such as the Ball and Bat Fund aided greatly in equipping service teams, the *Sporting News* noted that often "no provision [was] made for uniforms," which were quite costly.[26] In some cases, officers who supervised recreational programs, such as Capt. Charles Church, the Athletic Officer of the Marine Corps base in San Diego, responded to the scarcity of necessities such as uniforms by simply informing those under his command that new materials would not become available and therefore old gear would have to be recycled.[27]

In several instances, however, professional organizations helped poorly clad military teams obtain adequate athletic attire. During the spring of 1942, for example, future Legion of Merit recipient and former Major League first baseman Zeke Bonura secured a pledge from the New Orleans Pelicans of the Southern Association to donate uniforms for his poorly equipped Camp Shelby (Mississippi) team.[28] That same spring, Bonura also utilized his Major League connections to acquire balls, bats, and other supplies from the Cleveland Indians and the New York Giants when the two staged a contest in Hattiesburg, Mississippi, near his Army headquarters.[29]

Facing a similar predicament, representatives of the Fort Rosecrans (California) baseball squad publicly appealed for relief in acquiring new uniforms. In a letter to *The Sporting News*, the team revealed that their ragged flannels were aged to the point that they had begun falling apart, and the crisis threatened to disband the team. Minor league team owner Bob Ripley, however, rectified the situation by supplying a complete set of new uniforms for the Fort Rosecrans nine.[30]

Professional baseball also contributed substantially to the war effort by scheduling exhibition games with military teams with the specific intent of raising morale and money. Both military and civilian promoters hoped that contests between skilled military squads and Major League teams, with their superior facilities and talent, would excite fans, produce a financial windfall, and help to legitimize the continuation of professional baseball during such a precarious time. One of the first such instances revolved around the 1942 Major League All-Star Game, which was held as scheduled on July 6 at the Polo Grounds but with an additional twist—the winner of the annual contest earned the right to compete against a contingent of service all-stars, many of whom had just recently been plucked from professional rosters.

Plans for the unique exhibition began only weeks after the United States entered World War II. As early as its Christmas Day 1941 issue, *The Sporting News* was reporting that the proceeds from the All-Star game of the following year would go directly toward various war charities.[31] By February, baseball officials had expanded the concept from simply donating funds to the war effort to including the services directly in the extravaganza by scheduling a second All-Star Game involving an elite armed forces team. That executives were somewhat optimistic about the financial success of such a venture was reflected in their unrealistic prediction that approximately half a million dollars would be raised in such an endeavor—several hundred thousand dollars above the eventual figure.[32]

Once the framework was in place for the pair of contests, allocating the charitable contributions then became the key issue. Baseball leaders decided the Ball and Bat Fund would be the recipient for all of the money raised up to $100,000. Any contributions that exceeded that figure were to be delivered to the Army and Navy relief funds, though not everyone was thrilled with this allocation of monies. The Red Cross expressed concern that they were not included on the list of charitable organizations receiving monetary gifts and felt their omission was a serious slight. Several months before the dual all-star games commenced, columnist Daniel M. Daniel, who championed the national pastime ceaselessly during the war, responded in essence that baseball was just beginning to devise strategies to supplement America's war effort and critics of the game should be patient.[33] Commenting on the same topic, an editorial in *The Sporting News* defended baseball's efforts and concluded that, although the professional game might seem to be advancing slowly and deliberately in generating charitable donations, baseball had to "arrange its own house" because "no substantial sums would be expected from efforts poorly organized."[34]

The fruits of the baseball owners' labor began with the traditional All-Star Game, held at the Polo Grounds in July 1942. Although baseball officials had initially scheduled the contest for Brooklyn's Ebbets Field, they moved the affair to the Polo Grounds because of its much larger seating capacity—nearly fifty thousand. The 1942 All-Star Game proved to be a pitcher's duel with the junior circuit slipping by the senior circuit 3–1. Indians shortstop Lou Boudreau opened the game with a home run, and Tiger first baseman Rudy York soon followed with a two-run round-tripper to provide the American League with all the offense it needed. Inclement weather lowered attendance well below the expected fifty thousand and made it impossible to begin the game at the scheduled 6:00 P.M. starting time. The delay threatened to halt the contest before it began since government authorities had given baseball officials until 9:10 P.M. to finish the game in accordance with blackout regulations along the East Coast. A reprieve in the weather and an exemption by the government allowed for the game to be played in its entirety. The final pitch was thrown at 9:28 P.M.— two minutes before the updated deadline.

Since they had won the annual midsummer classic, the American League All-Stars then earned the right to travel to Cleveland for a second exhibition the following night against a conglomerate of service players chosen by future Hall of Fame catcher and then Navy lieutenant Mickey Cochrane. Military officials appointed the former Detroit Tiger and Philadelphia Athletic as the manager of the armed forces representatives and provided him with the authority to fill his roster with the best available players. Spokespersons for all of the services assured Cochrane that every effort would be made to satisfy his requests for desired players, including athletes that were not stationed in close proximity to Cleveland. True to their word, of the twenty-three players coveted by Cochrane, only former Phillies pitcher Hugh Mulcahy was unable to attend the contest because of military obligations.[35] This congregation of players from all branches of the service was not, however, quite the logistical marvel it may seem. Because the game was scheduled only six months after Pearl Harbor, the number of professional players then in the service was relatively small, and virtually all were new recruits. Nearly all the players then in the service were still stationed in domestic locales completing their military training, with former Red Sox hurler Mickey Harris being the one exception. Cochrane named Harris to the military all-star team, and the Army complied with his request by transporting Harris from Panama to Cleveland in time to participate in the contest. Harris did eventually pitch a total of one inning, surrendering two runs.

Aside from the minor hurdle of not having Mulcahy at his disposal, Cochrane was able to assemble a team that would have made many Major League managers envious. His choices included one of the most exceptional pitchers in professional baseball both before and after World War II, Cleveland ace Bob Feller, along with future Hall of Fame inductee Hank Greenberg and numerous other former or future All-Stars, such as Cecil Travis, Buddy Lewis, and Morrie Arnovich. Every one of the twenty-three players Cochrane selected were, in fact, Major League veterans with impressive credentials.

The game itself proved something of a disappointment, however. Feller, the starting pitcher, endured an uncharacteristically poor outing and was knocked out of the game in the second inning. Former White Sox pitcher Johnny Rigney replaced Feller and pitched wonderfully for five innings before relinquishing the mound to former Red Sox hurler Mickey Harris. Little offense materialized during the contest, which the American League won 5–0. Although there were three triples, a remarkably high number for such a low-scoring affair, neither team could manage a home run, and no American Leaguers garnered more than one hit during the contest. Both the All-Star Game at the Polo Grounds and the exhibition with the service team proved to be financial successes, as evidenced by the more than $200,000 they raised jointly for various war-related charities.[36]

The following spring in May 1943, an even more successful event organized by *Washington Post* columnist Shirley Povich transpired in the nation's capital. Povich, a tireless supporter of the national pas-

time, coordinated the events surrounding an exhibition game between the Washington Senators and the Navy's Norfolk Sailors. At the
time, Norfolk claimed one of the best, if not the best, military teams
in any of the armed forces. By 1943, the wartime draft and patriotism-
inspired enlistment had depleted Major League rosters, and Norfolk,
one of the largest naval training stations, had at its disposal a plethora
of big league talent to oppose the Senators. Boston star Dom DiMaggio patrolled the outfield, New York Yankee Phil Rizzuto and Detroit
Tiger Benny McCoy manned the middle of the diamond, and other
Major League veterans such as Jim Carlin, Freddy Hutchinson, and
Charlie Wagner graced the Norfolk roster.

For the price of admission, spectators pledged various amounts for
the purchase of war bonds. Even the owner of the Senators, Clark W.
Griffith, paid $1,000 for his seat at the affair. Eventually, a crowd of
29,221 filed into Griffith Stadium to witness an exciting contest
claimed by the Sailors 4–3. Although play on the field was a bit un-
tidy—the teams combined for four errors—the game was not decided until the final pitch when Senators outfielder George Case hit
a line drive that Dom DiMaggio snared with the tying and winning
runs on base. More important than the game, the war bond pledges it
raised were quite impressive—just over $2 million. In fact, the gate
collected was the second largest ever amassed for a sporting event to
that time, falling a few hundred thousand dollars short of the second
Dempsey-Tunney fight staged more than fifteen years before.[37]

Adding to the excitement of the game itself were the numerous
celebrities and legends who made an appearance. Bing Crosby de-
lighted the onlookers by performing several of his most popular numbers during the seventh-inning stretch, including "White Christmas."
Ever the showman, Crosby loosened up the crowd by suggesting that
the Senators might use the extra time between innings during his program to take extra batting practice since they had not yet scored a run.
Crosby then concluded with a few statements regarding the worthi-
ness of America's war effort before the game resumed.

In addition to Crosby's musical talents, famed baseball clown Al
Schacht charmed the crowd with his usual antics and imitations of
famous players. During his routine, Schacht replayed the famous
"called shot" home run struck by Babe Ruth in the 1932 World Series.
After the "Clown Prince" had belted the imaginary ball into the stands,

the legendary Ruth himself, a "surprise" promised by Povich, jogged onto the field to the "deafening roar of the crowd." Ruth circled the bases alongside Schacht and then spoke briefly about the role of war bonds in America's fight against fascism.

The success of the 1942 All-Star gala and the 1943 exhibition game between Norfolk and the Senators proved to be an inspiration for even grander undertakings, at least from a financial perspective. In the spring of 1943, the owners of the three New York Major League teams decided to coordinate their war bond sales campaign and player auction with an exhibition game pitting a talented Army team against select players from the Yankees, Dodgers, and Giants. The Army squad was composed primarily of soldiers from Camp Cumberland (Pennsylvania) and supplemented with Major League stars Hank Greenberg, Birdie Tebbetts, and Enos Slaughter, along with several others with big league experience.

In late August, after several months of promotion, the teams squared off before nearly forty thousand fans at the Polo Grounds with the New York all-stars emerging victorious, 5–2. Although the service all-stars accumulated fourteen hits to the nine by the Major League squad, the service players failed to capitalize on numerous scoring opportunities and their most dangerous hitter, Greenberg, was held hitless.

Possibly even more exciting than the game itself for many fans were the legendary stars of the past who entertained the crowd before the game. Babe Ruth, Walter Johnson, Tris Speaker, Honus Wagner, and Eddie Collins were among a group of retired players who participated in a pregame glorified batting-practice session. Hall of Famers Speaker and Collins showed their age by mishandling fly balls before a more adept Ruth deposited a Johnson offering into the right-field stands.

Although attendance for the game was substantial, the most impressive aspect of the exhibition was the amount of war bond pledges secured as a result—$800 million at the time of the game and nearly an additional $200,000 by the end of the season. Executives for the New York teams were determined to eclipse previous records for war bond sales in the area and succeeded resoundingly. In the promotional campaign in the weeks before the game players from the New York squads blanketed the local community and implored businesses and individuals to support Uncle Sam's soldiers and sailors by purchasing bonds. Because of the intense effort, the game proved to be the most financially successful baseball endeavor of the war.[38]

Major League teams were not the only ones to contribute to the numerous war-related charities by staging exhibitions with service teams. Many minor league organizations also joined in the fray. Although the affairs sponsored by minor league teams were understandably lower profile with smaller contributions, most were nonetheless financially successful, especially when they competed against service teams that fielded Major League stars. As we saw in chapter 1, for example, in August 1943 a team comprised of servicemen stationed on the West Coast, all with professional baseball experience, played a pair of Pacific Coast League (PCL) organizations, the Los Angeles Angels and Hollywood Stars. The service squad, which claimed, most notably, the recently inducted Joe DiMaggio and Hall of Fame pitcher Red Ruffing, competed for the first four and a half innings against the Angels and then finished the contest against the Stars. As one might expect, DiMaggio was the focal point of the game. He connected for two home runs among his four-hit total to pace the service team to an 8–2 victory in one of the most financially successful productions involving minor league squads. The exhibition drew a record 20,000 fans and produced nearly $25,000 in donations to provide athletic equipment for servicemen stationed overseas.[39]

The presence of DiMaggio in the Southern California contest unquestionably impacted the amount of money the game was able to generate, drawing fans who might otherwise have stayed away. This becomes clear when one analyzes a similar event held a month earlier just to the north in San Francisco. A talented contingent of service all-stars, all with professional experience (though none with the name recognition of the "Yankee Clipper"), trounced a squad of players from the San Francisco Seals and Oakland Oaks, both of the PCL. The attendance was a modest 6,395, and the financial tally—almost $4,000 —was not nearly as impressive as the affair attended by DiMaggio. Still, it provided a much welcome boost to the soldiers and sailors for whom the money purchased athletic gear.[40]

Elsewhere, other minor league teams helped to make substantial contributions through exhibition games even against service teams lacking big-name players. In 1944 the Chattanooga Lookouts scheduled a contest with the talented but relatively unknown Twentieth Armored Division Armoraiders out of Camp Campbell, Kentucky. The Armoraiders, loaded with players from various levels of the minor leagues, defeated the Lookouts in one of their thirty-one consecutive victories that year. Most notably, the two squads raised over $3 million in war bonds through the exhibition.[41]

Even the Negro Leagues became involved in contests with military teams to benefit war-related charities. While integrated baseball had yet to be achieved at the highest levels of the professional game, it was not at all uncommon both before and during the war for white and black all-star teams to compete against one another in exhibitions. In the early stages of the conflict, at a time when African Americans were still treated as second-class citizens across most of the United States, many black players readily accepted invitations to compete against white teams to bolster the war effort financially. The most prominent of these exhibitions, benefiting the Navy Relief Fund, occurred in spring 1942 at Wrigley Field, home of the Chicago Cubs. Organizers staged a contest between the Kansas City Monarchs, headed by the greatest African-American player of his era, "Satchel" Paige, and a squad of Major Leaguers in the armed forces captained by Hall of Fame pitcher "Dizzy" Dean. The former Cardinal great had received permission from the War Department to borrow several big leaguers then in the service, such as Bob Feller, Zeke Bonura, and Cecil Travis, for the charity game. Many years removed from his dominant years with the storied St. Louis Cardinals "Gas House Gang" and the victim of a perpetually sore arm, Dean started the game but pitched only one scoreless inning before relinquishing the mound to former Cardinal Johnny Grodzicki. Following Dean's departure, the service stars struggled against the masterful hurling of Paige, who surrendered only two hits in six innings. Eventually, the Monarchs emerged victorious by a 3–1 count before a crowd of thirty thousand—the largest of the year for any Wrigley Field contest.[42]

As more and more professional players began to swap their baseball flannels for military togs in the final months of the war, fundraising contests matching military teams against each another, either in single-game contests or extended series, began to predominate. Many proved financially lucrative. War-charities games involving service squads abounded, first on the domestic front and then overseas, though some of them were relatively small and uneventful. In July

1942, for example, the Camp Shelby (Mississippi) squad, headed by former Major League first baseman Zeke Bonura, competed against another service team in New Orleans before a relatively modest three thousand onlookers.[43] Organizers of the contest directed the game's proceeds to benefit the USO and the Army Emergency Fund.[44] Likewise, in San Francisco two military squads, the Naval Reserve Base Sailors and the Chico Flyers, locked up in a game to benefit the Army and Navy relief funds. The Navy representatives, led by former Brooklyn Dodger "Cookie" Lavagetto, dismantled their opponents 9–0, raising just over $1,600.[45]

Other fund-raising contests between military teams were better attended and so more financially successful. In June 1942, rookie Navy recruit Bob Feller and Army corporal Hugh Mulcahy, the former Phillies hurler, opposed one another in a service all-star game at the Polo Grounds that drew fifteen thousand fans despite terrible weather. Both rosters were composed almost entirely of Major League talent, yet Feller dominated the contest, a scheduled five-inning affair, by fanning seven and holding the Army squad to only three hits and no runs. In contrast, the Navy lineup tapped Mulcahy for six hits in the 4–0 victory. Mulcahy's relatively poor showing was not completely unexpected. He had pitched a complete game for his regular division team in Massachusetts the previous day and then immediately boarded a train for New York. Recognizing the difficulty of pitching on consecutive days, the former Phillies star had requested that he be allowed to skip the all-star game and remain with his regular service team. But the War Department ordered him to participate, and Mulcahy, showing obvious weariness, paid the price.[46]

The final full year of the war saw another relatively successful venture involving military teams. In the summer of 1944 representatives from Camp Campbell (Kentucky) and Camp Sibert (Georgia) staged a two-game series that produced approximately $50,000 in war bond sales. Camp Campbell was, in fact, known for its fund-raising abilities, even inspiring *The Sporting News* to declare that the athletes there had "few peers" in generating financial contributions to the war effort.[47]

Although most charity-motivated baseball contests between military teams were held domestically, there were several notable exceptions. One of the most important international games occurred in Panama toward the end of 1942, when service players, most with professional experience, formed two teams—the Atlantic Side All-Stars and the Pacific Side All-Stars—for a one-game Caribbean Series. A record crowd of four thousand crammed into a makeshift stadium in Balboa to witness Cardinal Terry Moore, a key figure in the team's World Series victory earlier that fall and a recent Army inductee, pace the Atlantic squad to a 4–3 victory. Before leaving the game with a slight shoulder injury in the sixth inning, supported his own effort with a run-scoring triple, later scoring on a teammate's single. Moore also excelled off the field during the Caribbean Series. Army officials assigned him the task of devoting two weeks to promoting the game, and Moore even helped to organize a very profitable war bond dance in conjunction with the game that raised over $300,000 in pledges.[48]

It was across the Atlantic in Great Britain, however, that military teams staged the most numerous fund-raising games on foreign soil. Only weeks after American soldiers and sailors began arriving en masse, organizers began scheduling games to support a variety of war-related causes. Most of the exhibitions involved various combinations of American service teams squaring off against each another, although there were exceptions. The first major fund-raising contest in Great Britain actually involved an American contingent playing a Canadian squad. In August 1942, just two years after the infamous Battle of Britain ravaged the British countryside, the opposing teams traded blows in Wembley Stadium before sixty-five hundred spectators. Among them were Mrs. Winston Churchill and several other Britons enduring their first encounter with America's national pastime. Though members of the Canadian team attempted to explain baseball's rules to the novices in the crowd, most seemed unable to completely grasp the game's intricacies. Perhaps the most disconcerting feature of the contest to the unschooled in the crowd were the jeers and insults the American and Canadian spectators hurled at the umpires and players. Such boorish behavior was strictly taboo in the traditional sporting culture of Britain's upper class. One British observer commented that such interaction between onlookers and participants "seem[ed] hardly sporting," and would never have been tolerated in a proper cricket match. These cultural gaps notwithstanding, the Canadian team upset the favored American squad 5–3 in a contest that raised $3,800 for the Red Cross.[49]

The following year baseball again "encroached on the sanctity of one of England's most famous soccer grounds" when officials scheduled a highly publicized doubleheader at Wembley Stadium for military personnel and civilians. After a game between amateur American and Canadian teams, select teams from the U.S. Army Ground Forces and the Army Air Corps competed against one another in the main event. In promoting the contest to an audience largely ignorant of the sport, organizers distributed thousands of flyers that identified the names of each position in the field on a diagram depicting the dimensions of the diamond. The games were attended by twenty-one thousand spectators, "including high-ranking British and American military leaders" such as the American commander in the European theater of operations, Lt. Gen. Jacob Devers. More importantly, the contests generated nearly $9,000 for the Duke of Gloucester's Red Cross and St. John Fund.

The second game of the doubleheader provided the most excitement for fans, as it was the first all-professional baseball game in Great Britain since a tour by the New York Giants and Chicago White Sox in 1924. A total of eight Major League players filled the two teams' rosters, with the remaining slots filled by minor league talent, including an unaffiliated pitcher for the Army Air Force named William Brech. Although both offenses struggled, Brech dazzled the crowd by hurling a no-hitter against a quality lineup. Brech was also responsible for his squad's only run of the game when he struck a slow roller that the opposing team mishandled, allowing the only run of the game to score. The game so impressed Lt. Gen. Ira Eaker, head of the Eighth Air Force, that he rewarded the victorious team with a thirty-day tour of British camps, during which they played twenty-nine games and lost only once.[50]

The following summer organizers staged an almost identical event at Wembley Stadium, which was advertised as including "many first class professionals" and produced almost identical financial results. Again, the star of the exhibition was a minor league pitcher, this time Chuck Eisenmann, a veteran of the Pacific Coast League in the prewar years. Eisenmann led the Ground Forces squad to a runaway 9–0 victory over the Ninth Army Air Force team with "mastery and showmanship" that included fifteen strikeouts and only three hits allowed.[51]

Elsewhere in Great Britain, smaller exhibitions involving service teams became the norm throughout the war. In northern England during spring 1944, for example, the Newcastle United Football Club sponsored a baseball game between U.S. Army and Navy clubs that drew ten thousand spectators, most of whom were "completely baffled" Britons. The exciting contest, won by the Army crew 13–12 in the final moments, elicited approximately $2,000 in donations for the British Red Cross among other recipients.[52] Liverpool's Goodison Park, home of the Everton Soccer Club, was the site of a similar contest involving two Army Air Force nines. That game piqued the interest of the eight thousand spectators and raised more than $3,000 for the St. John's Ambulance Fund and the British Red Cross.[53]

Thus, fund-raising was a major reason why baseball and the American military were inexorably intertwined in locales around the globe throughout World War II. On the domestic front, Major League Baseball operated under the pretext that it existed in large part to provide ample support for the war effort. Professional baseball officials sponsored numerous games and exhibitions designed specifically to solicit financial donations for the American military. Likewise, Major League Baseball's massive equipment donations also provided grateful servicemen with baseball gear that would otherwise have been unavailable. For their part, military officials utilized both Americans' fascination with the game at home and the novelty of the national pastime abroad to generate the financial resources to battle fascism. The mutual benefits that baseball and the American military realized through their cooperation fostered bonds that grew stronger as the war wore on.

Chapter 3 The Game's the Thing

Organizing Military Baseball

Organizing baseball teams and leagues for servicemen became a defining characteristic of military athletics both at home and abroad during World War II. Because many American leaders viewed baseball as an important supplement to the war effort, in almost every location that American soldiers and sailors congregated on a large scale, baseball established a foothold and prospered. The catalysts for this phenomenal growth were individuals who, through ingenuity and creativity, managed to organize players and teams and promote the game, often amid chaotic conditions.

Certainly the most successful of the wartime baseball organizers was former Major League first baseman and Army master sergeant Zeke Bonura, who eventually became known as the "czar of North African baseball."[1] After a brief stint in the Army before the U.S officially entered World War II, Bonura received his recall notice shortly after Pearl Harbor. Immediately, he seemed resigned to the fact that the escalating conflict had dealt a fatal blow to his successful professional career. He had divided an unspectacular 1941 season between the service and floundering in the minor leagues hoping to catch on with a Major League club. After December 7, however, the former American League star stated that "Uncle Sam needs me more than baseball" and vowed that his return to the highest level of baseball would have to be postponed.[2]

At the time of his induction, Bonura's professional prospects were not completely dim despite the fact that he spent the 1941 season toiling in the minor leagues. Bonura was only a few years removed from campaigns with the Chicago White Sox and Washington Senators that had placed him in the upper echelon of American League first basemen. From 1934 to 1939, in fact, Bonura had averaged 19 home runs, 107 RBIs, and a .315 batting average. Moreover, though most of his contemporaries considered him a defensive liability, he even led American League first basemen in fielding during the 1934, 1936, and 1938 seasons.[3]

During his initial stint in the Army, Bonura honed the organizational skills on which he would capitalize in later years. While stationed at Camp Shelby (Mississippi) before the war, Bonura was the player-coach of the camp baseball team while also supervising an intramural softball league.[4] Upon Bonura's recall to service the following year, military authorities again assigned the former Major Leaguer to Camp Shelby, where his genius began to flourish. Reclaiming the helm of the programs there, Bonura procured equipment for the camp's baseball squad through a variety of means, including contacting representatives of the Major League's Ball and Bat Fund, petitioning minor league teams for donations, and soliciting aid from former Major League teammates and opponents. Bonura was also instrumental in accelerating the construction of a new baseball diamond at Camp Shelby, although the field was not exactly without flaws. A huge ridge in left field which "angle[d] upward . . . then slope[d] steadily down to a spot below the horizon" intersected the playing surface. Bonura, a right-handed hitter who predominantly hit to the left side, had learned to use that unusual topography to his advantage.[5]

By the middle of 1942, Bonura had apparently developed the Camp Shelby squad into a fairly formidable team. After poor early-season performances, such as a 22–3 defeat at the hands of the Southern Association's New Orleans Pelicans in April, Bonura rallied his squad to a 10–2 victory in early August over a group of Navy all-stars stationed in the southern Gulf. Bonura was so confident in his team's abilities that he requested, unsuccessfully, that the War Department allow the Camp Shelby nine to schedule a contest with the Great Lakes Bluejackets, one of the most talented military squads and managed by former Detroit Tiger catcher Mickey Cochrane.[6]

Although the proposed exhibition with Great Lakes never materialized, in the following year Bonura continued on to bigger and better achievements overseas. In the spring of 1943, Bonura left Camp Shelby for Oran in Algeria where officers assigned him the task of organizing a variety of athletic programs, including baseball teams and leagues. His endeavor was complicated by the unstable and fluid military situation in the area. Although momentum had begun to shift in favor of the Allies following the Operation Torch offensives late in 1942, German forces continued to launch successful counterattacks until May 1943. Despite the distractions, Bonura was extremely productive in his new surroundings, initiating the expansion of military baseball in North Africa. In addition to simply encouraging soldiers to participate on teams, Bonura located adequate equipment, supervised the construction of fields, and coordinated schedules involving hundreds of teams. At one point, Bonura even offered a baseball school for soldiers and sailors who wished to learn the intricacies of the game or improve their skills.[7]

In a letter to his parents in spring 1943, Bonura mentioned that the military situation was "well in hand in Africa"—the Germans were finally been expelled from the area that May—and the men had found time to get "a league going" and engage in "some spirited games."[8] Bonura was so determined to provide fellow soldiers with adequate diversion and recreation that he often braved harrowing conditions. The former Major Leaguer even endured direct fire from the German air force in North Africa on several occasions, including once during a visit by the "Clown Prince of Baseball," Al Schacht. Schacht recalled visiting troops within Bonura's jurisdiction in North Africa to perform his usual routine when "many times [I had] to dive for cover as enemy planes roared overhead." Bonura, apparently unfazed by the imminent danger, "would laugh every time it happened." Throughout the war he continued tirelessly to promote military baseball down to the company level despite operating in these less than ideal conditions.[9]

With the defeat of the Axis forces in North Africa complete by the summer of 1943, military baseball there mushroomed in an amazing fashion under Bonura's direction. The former Major League first baseman supervised the coordination of over 150 teams in six leagues comprising well over one thousand players—approximately a quarter of the total number of organized participants in that region. Soldiers in the area justifiably dubbed Bonura the "Judge Landis of North Africa" for his triumphant endeavors to promote and expand military baseball.[10] One soldier even commented that Bonura was so important to the athletic programs in North Africa that he could not be "give[n] enough credit" for his efforts. The individual concluded by stating that without Bonura, soldiers might have still played baseball in North Africa, but because of his expertise and handling of details in a "big league manner" servicemen were "that much more proud to play ball."[11] The former Major Leaguer presided over the game in the southern Mediterranean region with such unusual skill and was so successful, in fact, that in 1943 General Dwight Eisenhower personally presented him with a Legion of Merit award for his contribution to military athletics.[12] Bonura's citation read partly as follows: "By his resourcefulness, enthusiasm and leadership he [Bonura] was able to overcome many shortages in needed assistance and construction materials, and he established twenty baseball fields in the area through the use of volunteer assistants and salvaged materials."[13]

Following the impressive Legion of Merit award, Bonura continued to promote athletic activities for servicemen, including a well-publicized North African World Series late in 1943. The former American League star orchestrated a number of games between military squads from various locales in North Africa, with the top two, the Casablanca Yankees and the Algiers Streetwalkers, squaring off in the final. Bonura arranged for the game to be a "big-time" affair, which was reflected in the wide exposure and radio coverage the game received from military media outlets. Bonura also secured baseballs signed by General Eisenhower, which he presented to the Casablanca team, the ultimate victors, as a reward for their stellar play.[14]

The former first baseman not only organized games and various other athletic affairs during his first few months in Africa; he also utilized his unique position to scout talent for the minor league Minneapolis Millers, the last professional team for which Bonura played before the war. Mike Kelley, the owner of the Millers, sent his former player several blank contracts, which Bonura then used to sign promising young prospects competing in North Africa. In the summer of 1944 Bonura reported that he had bound a number of men to professional deals, although ultimately things did not quite proceed as planned. Two of his prospects sustained debilitating injuries—one had his pitching hand blown off in combat and another suffered severe shrapnel wounds to his abdomen—that precluded both of them from ever again playing baseball.[15] Later that same year, Bonura also attempted to launch a war bond tour of the United States with many of the best players in the region, many of whom he surely would have attempted to sign. The tour, however, never advanced beyond the planning stages, and Bonura remained in the area to fulfill other obligations.[16]

While Bonura was relentlessly promoting the national pastime among his fellow countrymen, the former Major League star was also instrumental in attempting to popularize the game among other nationalities in North Africa. Bonura schooled local Arabs on the American sport, but apparently few were able to become proficient under his tutelage. In one notable instance, an oblivious Arab strolled across the diamond during a game and grabbing the valuable and scarce piece of timber being used for second base, walked off with it. Sensitive to the humor in the incident, *The Sporting News* reported that the miscreant was the "first Arab to steal a base in Africa."[17] Although not all of the indigenous people embraced or even comprehended the game, in exchange for Bonura's patient efforts to teach them, some of the novice Arab baseball players provided him with the use of full-blooded Arabian horses. On the other hand, many French citizens in the area did gravitate toward baseball to a much greater degree than the Muslim majority. Bonura insisted that the French had "taken to the game" immediately upon its introduction and attended American contests in large numbers.[18]

In another notable undertaking during the summer of 1943, Bonura attempted to instruct British soldiers in North Africa on the finer points of squarely striking a round ball with a round bat. Bonura's instruction proved fruitless despite hours of intensive practice until he advised the pitcher to begin delivering the ball around ankle level at which point the British, with their cricket swings, began to rip the "offerings all over the lot."[19] By the following spring, British soldiers in the Mediterranean apparently had become so enthralled with the game that one division issued one hundred bats and two thousand balls for use by its organized teams.[20]

Soon after the Allied offensives that wrested Sicily and eventually Italy from fascist control, Bonura followed the advancing forces into southern Europe. Although Bonura successfully orchestrated several small-scale athletic affairs in Italy, the fierce fighting and the tenuous situation that existed there into 1944 precluded any baseball programs like ones he had created in North Africa. Allied leaders vastly underestimated the ability of the remnant German divisions in Italy to repel their advances, and as a result, some of the bloodiest battles in the European theater erupted on the Italian peninsula in 1943 and 1944. This led to major disruptions in troop and supply movements and caused even ordinary services, let alone nonvital activities such as baseball, to be inconsistent or completely absent. Thus, as one might expect, organized athletic programs were the exception and not the rule in Italy until late in the war when Allied forces had secured the area to a greater extent.

Bonura, however, did not idle in Italy long, but rather took his talents to the recently liberated southern portion of France in 1944 and began to organize baseball teams and leagues there with great success. Bonura scheduled the first game on French soil during World War II, which matched a squad of MPs against an infantry nine and drew over ten thousand spectators. Many French locals attended the contest "ask[ing] a million questions" but not quite grasping the particulars of the sport, until Bonura offered personal instruction.[21] The former big league first baseman even began expanding his athletic horizons in France by organizing prominent sporting events beyond baseball. Although Bonura had been involved in many facets of athletic promotion in addition to baseball from the beginning of his military stint, he increased his involvement in other sports as the war progressed. For example, by early 1944, Bonura had begun editing a Special Service publication entitled *Sports Lights*, which highlighted important military and civilian sporting events, athletes, and other relevant athletic news.[22]

Most importantly, the former Major League first baseman was instrumental in orchestrating two important gridiron spectacles—the Arab Bowl and the Mustard Bowl, played in Oran, Algeria, and Dijon, France, respectively, early in 1945. Organizing parades, bands, traditional game-day food, and even bowl queens recruited from the ranks of the Women's Army Corps, Bonura capitalized on his previous organizational experience to "create huge interest" in the games and solidify his position as the preeminent promoter of military athletics during World War II.[23] By the middle of 1945, with the war concluded, Bonura returned to the United States and briefly resumed his career in professional baseball by appearing in a handful of games for the minor league Minneapolis Millers in 1945. Although one might expect that the skills Bonura had acquired in the service would lend themselves perfectly to managing at the professional level, the several minor league teams Bonura piloted before abandoning baseball in the 1950s met with little success.

Another of the great military baseball organizers who thrived during World War II was Maj. Roscoe "Torchy" Torrance of the United States Marine Corps. In civilian life, Torrance was part owner and vice president of the Pacific Coast League's Seattle Rainiers. He had orchestrated an amazing change of fortune for the Rainiers when majority owner Emil Slick appointed him to supervise an overhaul of the team beginning in 1937. By the time of Pearl Harbor, the Rainiers were a perennial first-division team, capturing league titles from 1940 to 1942, at which point Torrance departed for military duty. During the war Torrance utilized his vast baseball expertise to become the South Pacific's equivalent of Zeke Bonura. In April 1944, on an unidentified Pacific island, Torrance established three leagues of ten teams each and comprising a total of more than six hundred Marines. Enlisting the aid of Navy Seabees armed with bulldozers and tractors, Torrance plowed under the existing jungle to construct twenty-one "first-rate diamonds," which had to be hand-manicured due to the absence of lawn-mowing equipment. The opening game of the Marines' baseball season that year had "the éclat of a World Series" contest, with all the "hoots and howls" you could find in Ebbets Field.[24] By the beginning of the 1945 baseball season, Torrance had expanded his operation in the South Pacific to include forty teams. This allowed Marines there to enjoy the national pastime while they took "time out from their more arduous task of moving against the land of the setting sun."[25]

Because he had access to many young players, the Marine major, like Zeke Bonura, utilized his unique position to scout for potential professionals. After spending two months at a Marine hospital recuperating from a fever he contracted during the invasion of Guam in late summer 1944, Torrance signed at least a dozen promising players to professional contracts. He told *The Sporting News* that there were at least two dozen prospects under his domain who had the talent and ability to begin playing professionally as soon as the war ended. When queried whether the harsh battle conditions of the South Pacific hindered the development of baseball talent, Torrance asserted that "[y]ou'd be surprised how quickly a man snaps out of it after going through an invasion." The minor league executive then illustrated his point by identifying several players, including Cardinal minor leaguer George Sifft, who "played a lot of ball between island-hopping, and [had] real ability."[26]

Not only did Torrance scout and sign players while in the South Pacific, but he also attempted to trade them with another prominent baseball executive based in his theater of operations—Bill Veeck. Although Veeck had little impact as an organizer of military baseball, his postwar contributions and his stint in the Marines deserve mention. As a young man in his twenties, Veeck capitalized on his family connections (his father was the general manager of the Chicago Cubs) to establish a foothold in professional baseball, eventually owning three American League teams at various points after the war. Veeck is best known for his attention-getting stunts during the 1950s, 1960s, and 1970s. As owner of the St. Louis Browns he once hired midget Eddie Gaedel (sporting the number "1/8" on his back) for one plate appearance, and he occasionally allowed fans to make managerial decisions by holding up "decision cards." However, his significant impact on professional baseball actually began even before the war. Early in his career, Veeck became a footnote in big league history when he planted the ivy on Wrigley Field's outfield walls, creating a fixture in baseball lore and a trademark that still defines the Chicago Cubs franchise. Veeck also made a futile attempt to integrate Major League Baseball years before Jackie Robinson graced the diamond for the Brooklyn Dodgers in 1947. In 1943, the Philadelphia Phillies declared bankruptcy, and the future Hall of Fame executive hustled to secure financial backing that would have allowed him to control the team. Some insiders incorrectly believed that Veeck planned to fill the Phillies roster with a number of Negro League stars since there was no official policy banning African-American players from the major leagues. However, even if this were true, Commissioner Kenesaw Mountain Landis almost certainly would not have allowed Veeck's plan to materialize since the former judge was not particularly enlightened in the arena of racial politics.

Veeck did, however, become general manager and owner of the minor league Milwaukee Brewers shortly before his induction into the Marine Corps. During his brief stint with the Brewers, Veeck became a close friend of Roscoe Torrance as a result of their constant interaction on player trades and similar business interests. By 1944, Torrance and Veeck were both in the Marine Corps and stationed in the South Pacific. Although military officials never assigned Veeck the task of organizing baseball teams and leagues on the same scale as Torrance, Veeck did monitor his Brewer team as closely as possible while attending to his military duties. Veeck occasionally dealt with Torrance when they swapped players to fill out their rosters back in the States, and, like Torrance, Veeck scouted potential talent whenever possible. Veeck eventually lost a leg in combat and returned home to complete a truly remarkable career in professional baseball.[27]

Although the achievements of prominent military baseball organizers such as Zeke Bonura and Roscoe Torrance were vitally important to the popularity of the game in the service, baseball also flourished in areas where charismatic leadership was absent. This was particularly true in domestic locales. Across the country, organized teams, leagues, and tournaments prospered on military installations, often before servicemen left to fight overseas. The editors of *The Sporting News* declared early in the war that the armed forces had within its ranks the foundation for a stellar network of organized military baseball. Because of the vast number of professional players and the even larger number of avid sandlot enthusiasts who had been or would be inducted into service, the baseball weekly suggested that this "wealth of material" would make "all-embracing program[s]" the norm.[28]

On most bases and camps, comprehensive baseball programs involving as many servicemen as possible constituted the ideal though not the universal situation. In a study conducted during the war, the Special Services division of the U.S. Army discovered that less than one-quarter of servicemen felt that the military provided GIs with ample opportunity to join organized teams.[29] At least one Marine, upon finishing his basic training in San Diego, recalled competing in a number of baseball games, although most were "not really organized."[30] Similarly, a member of the Eighth Infantry Division, which eventually served in Europe, asserted that he "never had [the] luxury" of competing on the diamond in any coordinated contests following his induction.[31]

Other servicemen, however, recalled their military baseball experience differently, including another soldier from the Eighth Infantry, Herbert Bell, who remembered competing "all day and up in the night" on occasion.[32] Likewise, a number of other GIs recalled that baseball was an integral part of their military training, particularly after they had completed basic training and were awaiting embarkation overseas. Sam Sambasile, a member of the Army Air Force and eventual POW, insisted that he played a fair amount of baseball in the months before traveling across the Atlantic.[33] Two other soldiers, Joseph Donnelly and Art Primer, also revealed in interviews after the war that organized military baseball was common on the home front. Primer, in fact, competed so much in 1944 while stationed in Texas that, though it was only March, he became sunburned from his time on the diamond.[34]

On military installations that featured organized baseball, it often became an extremely popular form of recreation for servicemen. At Camp Grant (Illinois) in 1942, for example, over 150 hopefuls attended open tryouts for the select team that was to represent the camp's soldiers against other service squads.[35] Moreover, at one of the larger Army compounds in the United States, Jefferson Barracks (Missouri), baseball was given a "leading role in the athletic program" during the war. As early as the spring following Pearl Harbor, military officials there had organized nearly twenty-five teams and chosen an all-star team composed of the camp's best players to "seek additional recognition" in the St. Louis area.[36] By 1943, proponents of the installation's baseball program, apparently convinced that some soldiers were "not participating fully," suggested that malingerers should "get in there and get [their] share of the fun and training."[37]

Despite the fact that many military officials were extremely supportive of athletic programs in general and baseball specifically, circumstances occasionally tested the limits of this support. At Cochrane Field (Georgia), for example, the baseball team enjoyed access to a "good diamond, new portable bleachers, fine baseball weather, but so little free time for its players and soldier fans" that servicemen there were rarely able to compete.[38] Also, the constant relocation of GIs that was common throughout the war threatened the existence of some teams. In Michigan, Fort Custer's "shifting personnel" nearly caused the installation's commander, Lt. Col. E. M. Stenjem, to disband the squad. However, Stenjem adjusted to the fact that he did not "know from day to day if [they would] be able to put a full team on the field" by alerting other teams on Fort Custer's schedule that they might find it necessary to cancel contests on short notice.[39]

Although logistical reasons prevented some servicemen from competing on the diamond as often as they might have liked, others found that race limited their playing opportunities. In 1941, President Roosevelt signed Executive Order 8802, which forbade businesses with federal contracts to discriminate on the basis of race. The executive order, however, did not apply to the armed forces, and it was not until an official edict by President Truman in 1948 that all branches of the armed forces became integrated. As a result, only on the largest domestic military installations, such as the Great Lakes Naval Training Station, did military commanders afford African Americans even segregated baseball programs, let alone integrated ones. The most prominent example of an African-American serviceman being denied the right to compete on the military diamond was the man who would later break Major League Baseball's color barrier—Jackie Robinson. While stationed at Fort Riley (Kansas), Robinson attempted to join the baseball team but was denied even a tryout because of his race. Robinson's future Brooklyn Dodger teammate, Pete Reiser, was then a member of the installation's squad and recalled an officer commenting to Robinson that he would have to join the "colored team." This was an obvious insult since no such team existed at Fort Riley. Robinson stewed over the incident and decided not to join the football team, which was integrated, despite repeated overtures and even demands from superior officers that he do so.[40]

Overseas, the situation for African Americans was markedly better, if not completely equitable. Removed from the racial hostilities that permeated domestic military installations, African-American baseball enthusiasts—at least the most talented of them—were allowed to compete in integrated contests in various locales around the world. One example was European Theater of Operations World Series mentioned in chapter 1. There, Negro League players Willard Brown and Leon Day competing on an integrated team against an all-white squad composed primarily of professional players.[41] Elsewhere, other African Americans participated in integrated contests throughout the war. In the South Pacific, Kansas City Monarchs' shortstop Jimmy

Clarkson and an amateur black player, Tom Jones, starred for an Army team that eventually won the New Caledonia World Series. Before his postwar trailblazing efforts as the first African American in the American League, Larry Doby also competed in integrated contests in the South Pacific, along with Major Leaguers Mickey Vernon and Billy Goodman.[42]

Not all African Americans, however, viewed the situation overseas as much of an improvement. Hall of Fame Negro Leaguer Buck O'Neil felt that the inconsistency in treatment black servicemen experienced away from the U.S. mainland actually led to more anxiety on and off the baseball field than in the States. O'Neil reasoned that at least back home one knew what to expect, whereas the rules, both official and unofficial, regarding the treatment of African Americans overseas varied by location, attitudes of officers, and the number of black servicemen in a particular location.[43]

In addition to the blatant racism evident throughout the armed forces, military baseball grappled with other difficult issues, including recruiting the vast number of umpires needed to operate extensive baseball programs on the various bases, camps, and forts at home and abroad. All of the services attempted to locate within their ranks experienced umpires or those willing to learn the trade, a fact reflected in the number of officiating schools the military sponsored throughout the war.[44] Because of their desperate need for umpires, military officials often employed whoever was willing to embrace the assignment. In a contest featuring two Army teams in North Africa, for example, a general accepted the duties behind the plate. Commenting on the arrangement, the armed forces publication *Stars and Stripes* half-joked that "one of the very principles of democracy is the right to shout" at an umpire. "[W]hat can you do when a general is making decisions [but] shut your trap"?[45] In another game, the situation was actually reversed, when a general was called out on strikes by a corporal serving as umpire, which prompted *Stars and Stripes* to declare that "there's still some justice left."[46] Another unique umpiring situation involved Army private Londe Humble, stationed in Massachusetts. Though standing only five feet tall, "no one [took] any liberty" with the diminutive umpire because, aside from the traditional chest protector and mask, Humble sported a .45-caliber service pistol on his hip, apparently to dissuade argumentative players.[47]

Once military officials had organized the key elements of baseball programs on military installations, the next issue was scheduling competition between teams from different bases, camps, and forts. This was especially true on the home front, where the relatively stable environment and concentrations of impressive diamond talent at several large Army and Navy outposts was conducive to organizing high-profile leagues, tournaments, and single-game affairs. However, early in the war Secretary of War Henry Stimson ruled that, except in rare instances, servicemen would not be allowed to engage in extended absences for athletic purposes. This effectively dashed the plans of baseball supporters who may have envisioned military baseball mimicking the structure of the professional game.[48]

Proponents of military baseball responded by creating dozens of service leagues composed of teams with varying levels of competency located near each other. At about the time of Stimson's declaration, for example, organizers in Louisiana coordinated a league of teams from several installations that completed a sixty-game schedule, a postseason tournament, and an all-star contest.[49] In a similar fashion, California naval and Coast Guard officers created a six-team loop in the southern part of the state. Squads from both branches of the service competed against one another for bragging rights, and a trophy and gold-plated baseballs were presented to each member of the victorious team.[50] Outside of organized leagues, there were also many tournaments involving military teams throughout the war. In Maxwell, Alabama, in 1944, for example, more than twenty-five teams, primarily from Alabama and Georgia, competed over two months for recognition as the best service squad in the region.

Arguably the most important domestic military baseball tournaments were those that allowed both civilian and service squads to compete. Not only did these tournaments reinforce the positive aspects of athletic programs for GIs, such as morale, teamwork, and maintaining fitness, but they also "served as a mechanism for relieving civilian concerns [regarding the large numbers of servicemen] in their midst."[51] Soothing civilian apprehension became particularly relevant as the number of American servicemen swelled to more than ten million by war's end.

In some instances, combined military and civilian tournaments nearly foundered because of the travel restrictions placed upon service squads. The prestigious state tournaments sponsored by the National Semi-Pro Congress, for example, forced teams to play the numerous district qualifying games in their home state even if a neighboring state's tournament was closer, and they banned professional players outright. These restrictions made it difficult or impossible for many military nines to compete in the various semipro state championships organized around the country. At the beginning of the 1942 season, Special Services captain Leroy Mounday of Fort Riley (Kansas), proprietor of one of the better military squads in the Midwest, suggested amending the rules for the state semipro tournaments to better accommodate service teams. Mounday's recommendations to the National Semi-Pro Congress included exempting them from district qualifying, allowing professionals to participate, permitting them to compete at the site of the closest state tournaments, and authorizing flexibility in the scheduling of games.[52] By May 1942, the Congress had acceded to Mounday's recommendations and welcomed service teams into their sanctioned events.[53]

Without question, then, on the domestic front military baseball flourished to a remarkable extent, encompassing hundreds of thousands of soldiers and sailors. Once servicemen arrived overseas, however, logistical concerns, enemy movements, and climatic factors, among other considerations, hampered the feasibility of organizing wide-scale athletic programs. Marine corporal George Paulson, for example, insisted that while he was stationed on the home front there were "very few [Marines] that didn't play baseball," but that in the South Pacific combat conditions limited their ability to compete on the diamond as much as they would have liked.[54] Another veteran of the Marines, Chuck Maier, similarly recalled that he also played baseball while stationed on the West Coast for basic training and afterward while awaiting shipment overseas. However, like Corporal Paulson, when Maier arrived in Pacific combat zones concerns for safety and military schedules often prohibited Marines from regularly participating in athletics.[55]

Army veterans of World War II experienced similar situations in their participatory athletic programs. Army colonel Earl Peak recalled that, while on the domestic front, soldiers participated widely in baseball programs to increase morale and instill unit cohesiveness. Overseas, however, combat conditions and the lack of adequate equipment rarely gave soldiers the luxury of spending time on the diamond.[56] Colonel Peak noted in his personal diary that official orders instructing officers to "participate in athletics at least two hours a day, rain or shine" were occasionally ignored because less than ideal circumstances for recreation prevailed.[57] In response to a query regarding the nature of his recreational activities, Army sergeant William Faust clarified the point: "Come on—what did one do in Africa or Sicily? Nothing 'til the campaign was over."[58]

Even in locales where soldiers and sailors had ample time and opportunity to participate in the national pastime, they occasionally chose not to do so—for various reasons. In southern Italy, Army Special Services director Leon David observed that it was "difficult to whip up any interest in athletics" because of the heat and dust, although he did witness sporadic softball games.[59] Although most servicemen in the South Pacific had access to substantial amounts of athletic equipment the stifling heat and humidity of the tropical climate forced many to turn to other recreations. One group of servicemen there predictably voted swimming their favorite off-duty activity, and many responded that they "just did not feel like" competing on the diamond after completing the "heavy work load" required in the South Pacific theater. Despite the reluctance of some to engage in the national pastime, baseball did finish second behind water sports among those surveyed.[60]

In spite of imperfect conditions for baseball overseas, the game amazingly blossomed in unexpected regions. In the tropical South American country of Suriname, for example, teams reportedly traversed one hundred miles on foot through the jungle to compete with rival units in league contests.[61] Also, on one island of the South Pacific's Marianas chain, servicemen launched ten baseball leagues and constructed an astonishing sixty-five diamonds, four of them fitted with lights by the ambitious soldiers.[62] Navy recruit Guido Biancalana recalled that during the island hopping that characterized war in the Pacific, he and his fellow shipmates formed a team and scheduled games whenever they reached dry land. After the Americans recaptured the Philippines, Biancalana also remembered competing against an Army Air Force squad at Rizal Stadium in Manila. Interestingly, the structure's walls bore engravings indicating that the stadium had hosted an American Major League tour featuring Lou Gehrig nearly ten years earlier.[63]

Elsewhere in the South Pacific, one Navy Seabee revealed that the men he served with had a keen interest in baseball and had organized "the hottest league he ever played in"—one that never canceled games because of rain.[64] Similarly, baseball flourished on the island of Tarawa just five months after American forces had wrested the atoll from the Japanese. Enemy soldiers entrenched on the island killed or wounded thousands of American Marines over several days late in 1943 in some of the fiercest fighting of the war. Once the Marines gained control of the strategically located island, they constructed a fabulously maintained diamond that hosted games between various local garrisons through the duration of the war.[65]

Also in the South Pacific, military officials organized magnificent diamond spectacles in New Hebrides and New Caledonia during the final year of the war. In New Hebrides, now known as the Republic of Vanuatu, Army and Navy squads competed in a variety of games and tournaments, including a best-of-five series before "several thousand servicemen—plus a few popeyed Melanesian natives." The Navy narrowly defeated the Army representatives in the final game amid a "scene [that] was typical of a World's Series," including photographers and professional broadcasters.[66] Several months later, on New Caledonia, an Army team defeated another Navy squad in an even grander spectacle, in which numerous professional ballplayers competed. The three- game series attracted nearly twenty-five thousand spectators in total, reflecting the enthusiasm of the servicemen stationed there. The "moderate temperatures and slight rainfall permit[ted] the diamond sport 12 months in the year" and thus fostered an ideal situation for the proliferation of baseball.[67]

Soldiers in Hawaii organized a unique competition between Army enlisted men and noncommissioned officers. On one occasion, many of the enlistees had apparently exhausted their supply of beer and so devised a method involving baseball to acquire more. They orchestrated a contest with amended rules that stipulated that players had to consume one beer—supplied by the officers—for each base they advanced. Reportedly, "when the game was finally over nobody knew who won. They lost track of the score long before the fourteenth inning when the game was called on account of extreme darkness. The time was only 1730, but the players were blind by then, anyway."[68]

Baseball also developed in other unexpected areas around the globe, often in spectacular fashion. By 1943 Army teams were competing against one another in India and, given the British residents and diverse native Indian population, were attracting an international array of spectators. Although Japanese forces threatened India early in the war by overrunning British-controlled Burma, Allied forces were able to prevent an enemy invasion of the subcontinent and subsequently established some stability there. Once India became relatively secure, American military officials organized a large number of games, leagues, and tournaments. In one instance, approximately three thousand onlookers, half of them British and Indian, enjoyed a contest between two American squads. A former sports editor for the *Los Angeles Times*, Paul Zimmerman, attempted to narrate the proceedings in order to clarify the intricacies of the game to the spectators, apparently with some success.[69]

Likewise, in the northern Russian port of Murmansk, determined and innovative soldiers gained another foothold for baseball in another unlikely location. Once the United States entered the war in late 1941, Murmansk became a key hub for delivering vital supplies to a depleted Soviet Union. Thus, throughout the conflict a number of Americans passed through the city, some remaining there for logistical purposes. By 1944, servicemen had organized the White Sea Baseball League with a bare minimum of baseball equipment. When no bats could be located, resolute GIs "whittled Russian pine logs" into the appropriate instruments and hand-wound and sewed makeshift baseballs.[70]

The American pastime also often flourished in much more trying and dangerous conditions, including areas close to the front lines. In one particular instance in August 1944, American soldiers in France narrowly escaped injury when, in the middle of the first inning, an Allied plane on maneuvers hurtled to the ground and exploded just beyond center field. Although certainly distracted, the players decided to continue the game, which proceeded until British minesweepers next appeared to disrupt play. Unbeknownst to the competitors, the demolition crews had earlier ignored the playing surface since it had recently been used as a transit area and, therefore, presumed safe.

Only two hours before, however, two men had been killed and four others wounded by mines near left field. The demolition crew, rather than alarm the players by announcing their intentions, slowly stalked the perimeter of the playing field until, satisfied it was secure, they began to encroach upon the diamond itself. Initially believing the British soldiers were just curious onlookers, the American servicemen realized soon enough that the men surrounding the field were concerned with more than just taking in a baseball game. Freezing in their tracks once they learned the truth, the members of both teams remained stationary until their British counterparts signaled they could safely resume playing ball.[71]

Members of the American armed forces were even able to introduce baseball in the most extreme of combat situations—POW camps. Captured Navy nurse Dorothy Danner recalled American soldiers and sailors competing in contests while imprisoned by the Japanese in the Philippines. The Japanese were known for their brutal treatment of enemy detainees, especially in the Philippines, where thousands of Allied soldiers were tortured and killed. Once the Japanese captured enemy servicemen, they usually confined them in internment camps where food was often scarce, torture was common, and prisoners were rarely afforded the luxury of leisure activities such as baseball. Nurse Danner, however, referred to the camp in which she was held, Los Banos, as a "country club" partly because the Japanese caretakers allowed prisoners to exercise and play baseball.[72]

Although baseball was a rarity in Japanese POW camps, it was much more common in German internment facilities. Adhering to Geneva Convention regulations regarding the treatment of enemy combatants, German military officials generally allowed POWs a great deal of freedom in their everyday activities. POW Jack Kreicji, a member of the Army Air Force and not a particularly avid fan of baseball, recalled that during his time spent as a "guest of the enemy," they allowed him and his fellow prisoners to "play a little."[73]

Likewise, in an evaluation of Germany's Milag Nord prison camp shortly after the war, American military officials noted that Allied prisoners were permitted to play a substantial amount of baseball. The Red Cross provided, along with valuable food rations, a "great deal of equipment" for these athletic contests.[74] One British airman downed over German-held territory even revealed that he and his fellow prisoners at the Stulag Luft III POW camp (made famous in the movie *The Great Escape*) competed on prisoner-constructed diamonds. Games involving an international array of participants, naturally including many Americans, continued into 1944 until German officials, desiring more space to house incoming prisoners, erected barracks on the playing area.[75]

Although baseball flourished in unexpected and precarious sites during World War II, it blossomed to an even greater extent in more secure overseas locales where large numbers of American fighting men convened. In New Zealand, for example, dozens of leagues and hundreds of teams allowed servicemen an avenue for recreation and relaxation. When Americans competed, they often "brought more than the game, they brought the atmosphere" of a traditional American contest. On one occasion in Wellington, New Zealand, two Marine teams battled each other in a game that drew an impressive twenty-five thousand spectators. The squads entertained the largely ignorant crowd with the play on the field, but what especially transfixed them were the heated arguments between the players and the umpires—a unique experience for the traditionally less raucous Kiwis.[76]

Likewise, American representatives in Australia also organized games. Before the hostilities were yet a year old, servicemen were re-introducing the Australian populace to the national pastime while competing for the MacArthur Cup, bestowed on the best team in the region. Reportedly, seminal figures in professional baseball history, such as Albert Spalding and Cap Anson, had toured Australia with a cadre of other talented players during the late nineteenth century. This tour had sparked enough interest in the island nation to result in the formation of several baseball leagues (the descendants of which are still in operation today). When American servicemen arrived in World War II, therefore, they had little trouble locating playing fields, equipment, and, most importantly, local teams to play against. In April 1942, for example, promoters arranged an "International Baseball Day" between a Navy squad and a Victoria team with the purpose of ensuring "Allied good will."[77]

The American game also firmly established itself throughout Great Britain and eventually the European continent during the waning months of the war thanks to the large numbers of American servicemen there. By 1944 approximately 1.5 million American fighting men had gathered in the British Isles in preparation for the Normandy invasion, and their sheer numbers ensured that they made a significant impression on the local populace. The running joke regarding the inundation of "Yanks" was that they were "overpaid, oversexed, and over here." American servicemen fanned out all over Britain, introducing the natives to many American tendencies and habits, including baseball. Soldiers stationed in Northern Ireland, for example, participated in a vigorous baseball program that began early in the war despite the local weather, which took the "form of continuous drizzle to torrential downpour" and threatened nearly every contest.[78] Games between armed forces teams there often played out to the bewilderment of Irish spectators, ignorant of the game. During one heated competition, two American squads battled to the end without stopping for tea, a fact that puzzled an Irish writer in attendance. Unlike British cricket or other more familiar modes of recreation, he noted, in American baseball there was no half-time or break. Instead, "the game's the thing."[79]

Although baseball proliferated throughout the British Isles, the area in and around London became thick with American teams. Competition between rival squads was already substantial by the summer of 1942, when servicemen began to occupy parks and other open venues on hastily constructed diamonds.[80] In one notable instance, baseball even graced the lawn of Windsor Castle when two talented Army teams competed before the venerable Queen Mary. Following the game, the winning pitcher, Leo Toye, approached the Queen and requested she autograph the game ball. The officer guarding the Queen was "horrified" at the breach in etiquette, but Mary nonetheless agreed to the appeal and penned her name.[81]

By 1943, over one hundred thousand GIs were competing in organized leagues and countless others in various pickup games across Great Britain. In that same year, military officials organized the "highly competitive" London International Baseball League, which included, most notably, the talented Central Base Section Clowns, one of the most outstanding service teams during the war. Also in 1943, athletic promoters in England initiated the beginning of the European Theater of Operations (ETO) World Series, which became an annual event through the end of the war.[82]

After the success of the D-Day invasion and the relocation of many American soldiers and sailors to the continent, baseball again followed the military's massive flow of humanity. As the Allied position became more secure after the winter of 1944–1945, the volume of organized diamond competition increased. By the spring and summer of 1945, teams from across northwestern Europe were competing regularly. In July, for example, a service squad based in Paris flew in a team from Belgium to stage a spirited contest.[83] Later that month, military officials in France formed the strong xvi League, which was extremely competitive and included a number of professional players.[84] Also in July, the 472d Air Service squad, operating in a league in the recently occupied German city of Nuremberg, flew into Paris to compete against a local rival.[85] Most importantly, in the late summer of 1945, the over two hundred thousand servicemen on organized teams competed for the right to declare themselves ETO champions. The third annual contest, won by an Army squad, was staged at Soldier Field in Nuremberg, site of many Nazis rallies.[86]

Once American military authorities had established organized baseball programs, maintaining the various teams and leagues despite personnel movements and supply disruptions became a prime concern. Even in the worst circumstances, officers often provided incentives such as trophies or plaques to encourage both participation and success on the playing field. But the continuation of the military game primarily depended on the procurement of adequate amounts of athletic equipment. The previously mentioned Ball and Bat Fund provided massive amounts of baseball gear for many regions, which were supplemented by outright equipment purchases by the military itself. From the outset of the war, hundreds and eventually thousands of "A" and "B" kits containing bats, balls, gloves, and protective gear circulated around the globe. By summer 1942, nearly one thousand kits had been sent to various military installations, primarily on the home front.[87] By the beginning of 1943, a report asserted that the military had made available to servicemen in the Mediterranean approximately one hundred thousand baseballs, forty thousand bats, thirty thousand gloves, thirty-seven hundred body protectors, eleven hundred sets of uniforms, and seven hundred bases. In all, over three hundred teams operated in the theater, excluding numerous other informal games.[88] The following year another report claimed that the

Army supplied enough baseball gear to equip fifty thousand teams, while the Navy retained the potential to furnish eleven thousand squads with adequate supplies.[89] In the days and weeks immediately after v-e Day, the military furnished American servicemen in Europe alone with over 130,000 bats, 72,000 baseballs, and 85,000 gloves.[90]

Despite the overwhelming volume of athletic supplies provided for servicemen, many teams didn't have enough baseball gear. Early in the war, the newspaper for Jefferson Barracks in Missouri highlighted this predicament with a cartoon depicting a catcher wearing a gas mask. The caption read: "It's the only mask I could find."[91] Nevertheless, most domestic military installations were able to secure enough equipment to satisfy service players. Overseas, however, problems often emerged that were usually attributable to the uncertainties of combat situations. The rapid relocation of fighting men, disruptions of supply lines, inadequate organization, or a combination of all three often deprived servicemen of opportunities to participate in athletic programs.

In foreign locations, more than 40 percent of servicemen felt that they were "not given enough opportunity to participate in sports and athletics," primarily because of a lack of equipment.[92] The branch of the Army responsible for soldiers' recreational activities, the Special Services, often did not have the "flexibility needed to operate under varying conditions, especially in combat areas."[93] Because of enemy troop movements, air strikes, and ordinary military maneuvers, Special Service officers were often unable to supervise the delivery of sports equipment "designed for automatic issue at embarkation points."[94] During a tour of Italy shortly after the Allied invasion there, Maj. Leon T. David remarked that there was a noticeable shortage of bats and balls, which had a substantial negative impact on GI's morale.[95] Likewise, in the South Pacific, Major League outfielder and Navy enlistee Gene Woodling recalled that while he supervised recreational leagues for fellow sailors on the island of Saipan he constantly encountered a scarcity of baseball equipment.

Even in areas where Special Service representatives distributed adequate amounts of athletic equipment, the deliveries were often several months late and thus uncoordinated with the "seasonableness of sports" such as baseball. In a postwar study, the War Department decided that, in future military engagements, "supply procedures should be standardized" in combat areas to make delivery of sports equipment more efficient and more reliable.[96]

Another obstacle to sustaining organized military teams and leagues was constructing and maintaining enough playing fields to accommodate, in some cases, thousands of soldiers and sailors. Several domestic military installations boasted superior athletic programs where baseball diamonds were numerous and often a source of pride. For example, the commanding officer at Great Lakes Naval Training Station in Illinois, Capt. Robert Emmet, ordered that the primary playing field for the outstanding 1944 squad be entirely reconditioned and resodded before the heart of the season. Emmet also directed that the stands be remodeled to maximize the stadium's seating capacity and the viewing pleasure of the thousands of sailors who attended games.[97] Likewise, the diamonds at Jefferson Barracks (Missouri) consisted of six-inch deep cinder below two inches of clay—fields that many Major League teams would have envied. Such a surface was ideal for drainage and, by eliminating inconsistent hops, ideal for playability.[98] Camp Roberts (California) also possessed an impressive field constructed "almost single-handedly" by former minor leaguer Otto Meyers, then serving in the Army. He equipped the diamond with a sodded infield, a sprinkler system, and an efficient drainage system, creating one of the best-conditioned service playing surfaces on the West Coast.[99]

Other military installations attempted to improve their facilities by adding lights to lengthen the time available for games and practices. Although the War Department placed many restrictions on professional baseball teams regarding the scheduling of night games, military installations generally had more freedom to stage lighted nighttime events. However, lighting systems were usually not incorporated within typical military athletic budgets and thus had to be acquired through other means. By the 1943 season, a number of minor leagues had closed down for the duration of the war, and military officials seized on this opportunity to acquire unused lights for their own athletic programs. Service representatives around the country petitioned disbanded professional franchises for the temporary use of lighting equipment that may have otherwise lain dormant. In a typical transaction, two Illinois outposts, Camp Grant and Fort Sheridan, secured unused lighting systems from local disbanded professional teams that allowed them to greatly expand their baseball programs.[100]

One of the most interesting developments involving night baseball, however, materialized overseas in an area far removed from generous minor league organizations. During the summer of 1944 on a New Guinea artillery field still encountering isolated Japanese resistance, one could reportedly find the "best lighted" diamond in the world. American soldiers "installed floodlights for night games in the jungle league" by employing coconut trees as makeshift poles and surrounded the field with twelve 800-million-candlepower lights fastened to their tops. Servicemen even positioned four floodlights around home plate to prevent any distortion from the shadows created by such luminous conditions. According to *The Sporting News*, no Major League stadium at the time could "boast even one-twelfth of the candlepower" of this highly charged New Guinea outfit.[101]

Fighting men in other areas overseas undertook similar extraordinary measures to simply construct playing surfaces on which to compete. In an unidentified location in the South Pacific, Marines "enlisted the aid of Navy Seabees [who] went to work with tractors and bulldozers" to carve out over twenty baseball diamonds from the jungle. To exacerbate matters, once the Seabees had completed their construction the sole lawn mower on the island broke. Undeterred, inspired Marines "went to work on the infield with grass machetes."[102] Likewise, Hall of Fame outfielder Enos Slaughter recalled that in the South Pacific, the Army also utilized bulldozers to chisel fields from the tropical surroundings, including one in Saipan that Slaughter rated as a "nice ball park."[103] Another big league player, Hugh "Losing Pitcher" Mulcahy, revealed that while he was stationed at Leyte in the Philippines, Army officials ordered "big coconut trees knocked down" and tons of earth moved so the lush area surrounding his camp could be transformed into an adequate diamond.[104]

Elsewhere, American servicemen often confiscated baseball fields and other arenas abandoned by the enemy. Several months before the Japanese surrender, *Washington Post* writer Shirley Povich reported from the Marianas that soldiers and sailors had taken over several diamonds constructed by Japanese fighting men. According to Povich, the abandoned fields "must all have been [built by] hitters" because they all had cozy outfield dimensions.[105]

In the European Theater, American troops also confiscated enemy athletic arenas and transformed them into baseball facilities as Allied forces crushed German resistance. Soldier Field in Nuremberg, Germany—the location of the previously mentioned 1945 ETO World Series—was but one example. There, military officials authorized the construction of a superior field where, just months before, the "SS strutted for Der Fuehrer."

Once playing fields had been constructed, appropriated, or otherwise acquired, military officials gave careful consideration to naming them. At Foster Field (Texas), for example, Army Air Force leaders, after lengthy deliberation, decided to name their diamond in tribute to New York Yankee legend Lou Gehrig.[106] Usually, however, ballparks were named after servicemen who had been integral figures in military baseball and/or had perished in combat. At Camp Lee (Virginia) during the final year of World War II, authorities identified former minor league hurler Henry Nowak as worthy of such an honor. Immediately preceding his induction into the Army, Nowak had been tantalizingly close to reaching the Major Leagues. The St. Louis Cardinals had even listed him on their roster before the 1941 season before optioning him to the New Orleans Pelicans after spring training. Before the 1942 season opened, Nowak answered the call of his country and was soon stationed at Camp Lee where he was a stellar performer on the baseball team before relocating overseas. On New Year's Day 1945, Nowak was killed during the intense fighting of the Battle of the Bulge. The dedication of Nowak Field several months later was attended by National League president Ford Frick, along with other "outstanding military, congressional and baseball dignitaries."[107]

Another professional player who lost his life in battle, James Trimble, received a similar honor on the island of Guam. Only nineteen at the time of his death, Trimble had so impressed Washington Senator owner Clark Griffith that Griffith signed the young pitcher at the close of his high school career. Trimble, however, enlisted in the Marine Corps before he could have an impact on professional baseball and eventually traveled to the Pacific theater. After a tremendous few months competing for his division team on Guam, during which he pitched his squad to the regional championship, Trimble was one of the over five thousand Marines killed in the intense fighting on Iwo Jima in 1945. The combat was so intense, in fact, that Marines ultimately captured only 213 of the approximately 20,000 Japanese soldiers entrenched on Iwo Jima before the invasion. Just a few months after his death, Marine officials renamed the main field on Guam in James Trimble's honor.[108]

A fellow minor league pitcher, Jack Patterson, also received the honor of having a baseball complex posthumously named for him. Patterson was among the relatively small number of Marines who paid the ultimate price in wresting the island of Guadalcanal from Japanese forces early in the war. By 1945, Marines on Guadalcanal had constructed an impressive athletic compound that included a collection of three baseball diamonds, which they subsequently christened in Patterson's memory.[109]

Because of the efforts of men like Zeke Bonura and Roscoe Torrance, baseball in the American military had expanded and flourished around the world. Other groups and individuals also contributed in many ways to the massive increase in military baseball programs despite threats of enemy attacks, equipment shortages, and inadequate playing fields in some areas. These undertakings allowed servicemen in most locales to participate in a sport that both helped them recuperate mentally and find a needed break from military routines. Without the individual catalysts, military organizations, and other groups who supplied much of the necessary baseball equipment, soldiers and sailors would unquestionably have had far fewer opportunities to enjoy baseball. The resulting negative impact on morale would doubtless have made military life less bearable and thus perhaps victory more difficult to achieve.

Chapter 4 **Finest Team Assembled**

Exceptional Military Teams

In addition to organizing participatory baseball programs to include as many soldiers and sailors around the world as possible, all of the armed forces attempted to assemble elite squads for reasons of morale, pride, and interbranch rivalry. Many commanding officers of military installations shared the philosophy of Navy rear admiral A. E. Montgomery of the Naval Air Training Center in Corpus Christi, Texas: "representative athletic teams are . . . a potent factor in helping maintain the high morale of all hands. The teams belong solely to the Bluejackets and play competitively for their entertainment."[1] Similarly, other military leaders were seemingly driven, in the words of one author, by the "screwy idea that the excellence of [their] ball team[s] reflected on the excellence" of their commands. Thus, efforts by military authorities to obtain the services of professional stars such as Joe DiMaggio, Ted Williams, Bob Feller, and numerous others increased as the war progressed.

Occasionally, the military authorities' efforts to amass baseball talent was extraordinary and borderline unethical.[2] Authorities at Great Lakes Naval Training Station in Chicago, for example, regularly contacted professional athletes who were eligible or likely to become eligible for the draft and encouraged them to enlist in the Navy. Great Lakes officials then promised the athletes they would make every effort to have them assigned to the naval installation and accorded special privileges for participating in the Great Lakes athletic programs. One of the athletes contacted, Frank Baumholtz, who played in the

Major Leagues and the fledgling National Basketball Association, re-called being sent "many letters" early in the war by Great Lakes officers urging him to enlist in the Navy. Officials assured him he would be given a choice assignment that would allow him to join the rosters of the training station's basketball and baseball teams and devote the substantial time required for each.[3] Another example of questionable behavior involved George "Birdie" Tebbetts, a catcher for the Detroit Tigers before his induction into the Army. As the key organizer for the Waco Army Air Field's baseball team, Tebbetts frequently convinced generals and other high-ranking Army officials to divert various professional athletes to Waco to bolster the baseball program there.[4]

Even without substantial personnel manipulation, military officials did not have much difficulty assembling talented teams. During World War II, the armed forces had in their employ some of the greatest players in the history of the game along with hundreds of others blessed with big league talent. Not even two months after the United States declared war on the Axis powers, the roster of an all-star military team could have included names such as Hank Greenberg, Bob Feller, and Cecil Travis. By the following season names such as Joe DiMaggio, Ted Williams, and Phil Rizzuto could have been added. As the months progressed, the number of elite players in the service increased proportionately until it eventually included over 90 percent of all the Major League players active at the outset of hostilities.

Military athletic promoters naturally attempted to capitalize on this continual torrent of professional players and, in many cases, compiled impressive pools of talent at several of the larger installations around the world. This was especially true for many military teams operating within the continental United States because of the stability and consistent training regimens inherent in stateside locales. Throughout the war, several military squads fielded numerous all-stars, future Hall of Famers, and other skilled professionals, which led to a quite impressive consolidation of talent on several teams.[5]

This was particularly true in the Navy where journalist Jack Troy of the *Atlanta Constitution* noted that they took their "baseball seriously" throughout the war.[6] Although the U.S. Navy possessed several truly outstanding baseball squads, collectively the greatest of all World War II military baseball teams were the ones representing the Great Lakes Naval Training Station (Illinois) during the 1942–1944 campaigns.

Boasting an ever-changing but always strong lineup, the Bluejackets had access to a continual supply of minor and Major League talent partly because of the massive number of sailors who completed their naval training at Great Lakes—approximately 35 percent of all U.S. Naval trainees.[7] As noted earlier, Great Lakes officials also actively recruited talent to strengthen the station's athletic programs.

With such an influx of skilled players, the Bluejackets destroyed virtually every other military team they competed against and often outclassed Major League competition as well. The Great Lakes squad set the standard for military baseball during World War II despite the fact that reassignment of their players to other naval outposts obligated it to annually replace the majority of its roster.

Examining the rosters of the Bluejacket squads from 1942 through 1944 shows the striking preponderance of talented players, particularly in 1944. Although individually more accomplished players competed for other military teams, when considered as a group the talent of the Bluejackets exceeded that of any other military team. A common joke among Navy personnel was that "you could throw a baseball anywhere on the station and at least two big leaguers will try to catch it."[8] No fewer than forty-three Major Leaguers, six All-Stars, and two future Hall of Famers represented the Bluejackets during those three years.

Furthermore, one of the greatest catchers in the history of professional baseball, Gordon "Mickey" Cochrane, directed the team from the bench. The former Philadelphia Athletic and Detroit Tiger star enjoyed a distinguished career throughout the 1920s and 1930s before a beaning in 1937 nearly killed him and abruptly ended his playing career. Cochrane was also a player-manager for the Tigers from the 1934 season until his injury and continued at the helm of the franchise strictly as manager until the 1938 campaign. He twice led the Tigers to the pennant, including a victorious trip to the World Series in 1935, and boasted a very respectable career winning percentage of .582. Tiger management, however, decided to replace him during the 1938 season—a move that left Cochrane bitter and disillusioned with professional baseball. Cochrane, in fact, never again managed in the Major Leagues and was involved in private business outside of baseball when the war began. After Pearl Harbor, the thirty-eight-year-old former catcher, who was exempt from the draft because of his age,

Table 1. Great Lakes Team Rosters, 1942–1944

(Records in parentheses. Major Leaguers denoted by bold type.)

POSITION	1942 (63-14)	1943 (52-10-1)	1944 (48-2)
1B	**Chester Hajduk**	**Johnny Mize**	**Johnny McCarthy**
2B	**Benny McCoy**	**Chester Hajduk**	**Billy Herman**
3B	**Ernie Andres**	Carl Fiore	**Merrill May**
SS	**John Lucadello**	**Eddie Pellagrini**	**Al Glossop**
LF	**Don Padgett**	**Glenn McQuillen**	**Mizell Platt**
CF	Earl Bolyard	**Barney McCosky**	**Gene Woodling**
RF	**Joe Grace**	**Joe Grace** **Leo Nonnenkamp**	**Dick West**
C	**Frankie Pytlak** **Sam Harshaney**	**George Dickey** Warren Robinson **Marv Felderman**	**Walt Millies** **Bill Baker** **Clyde McCullough**
P	**Russ Meers** **Johnny Rigney** **Jim Reninger** Frank Marino Cliff Clay Don Dunker Fred Shaffer	**Vern Olsen** **Bob Harris** **Johnny Schmitz** **Tom Ferrick** **Jack Hallett** **Frank Biscan** Pete Hader	**Virgil Trucks** **Jim Trexler** **Bob Klinger** **Schoolboy Rowe** **Si Johnson** **Bill Brandt** **Ed Weiland**

Rosters obtained from "No Sparring on 1944 Tars! Mickey Says They're Best," *The Sporting News*, 17 August 1944, 12. Final record of 1944 team obtained from "Hoisted Greatest Record for Great Lakes Team," *The Sporting News*, 14 September 1944, 12. The team rosters listed in table 1 are not entirely complete, as the names of players who competed only for a few games or did not finish the season were not available. Due to personnel losses resulting from reassignment, the 1945 team, despite the addition of Bob Feller, was not as strong as in previous years and was therefore excluded.

offered his services to the Navy. Military officials decided to capitalize on his athletic expertise by providing Cochrane with full rein over the Great Lakes Naval Training Station's select baseball team. The Great Lakes team proved to be a jewel in the crown of the U.S. Navy's athletic program and dominated military baseball from 1942 to 1944.

The 1942 team was the weakest of the three yet was still blessed with many individuals of superior ability. Finishing the season with a winning percentage of over .800, the Bluejackets won an impressive seventeen straight games at one point and did not lose to another military team during the campaign despite being handicapped early in the spring with cold weather. The Great Lakes contingent also finished the year with four wins and six losses against Major League competition and was named by a panel of sportswriters as the top service squad in the nation.[9]

The infield of the 1942 Navy squad was composed entirely of future or former Major Leaguers, although Chester Hadjuk and Ernie Andres could only be considered technically so since they had spent only a combined sixteen career games in the big leagues. Johnny Lucadello and Benny McCoy, however, were solid players whose batting averages hovered at a respectable .265 during their Major League stints. The two outfielders with Major League experience—Don Padgett and Joe Grace—also were serviceable performers during their big league careers, both compiling averages well over .280.

The two catchers for the 1942 squad had substantial Major League experience, including Frankie Pytlak, who was not particularly strong defensively but did hit over .300 four times in his twelve-year career, spent primarily with Cleveland. The other backstop, Sam Harshaney, enjoyed a four-year Major League tenure with the St. Louis Browns. The pitchers of the 1942 Great Lakes squad included Russ Meers, Jim Reninger, and, most notably, Johnny Rigney, who usually took the mound against most formidable opponents. Rigney was the Bluejackets' most consistent hurler during the 1942 campaign and enjoyed several stellar seasons with the White Sox both before and after the war, winning as many as fifteen games a year.

The 1943 Great Lakes representatives improved slightly over the previous year's team, winning nearly 84 percent of their games, including five of the first ten against Major League competition. They also claimed fifteen former or future big league professionals on their

1. The ever graceful Joe DiMaggio at the plate for his Santa Ana Army Air Force squad in 1943. Note the packed stands and the camera in the background recording the Yankee legend. *The Sporting News*

2. Hall of Fame pitcher Bob Feller toes the mound for the Great Lakes Naval Training Station team during warmups in 1945. *The Sporting News*

3. Red Sox great Ted Williams poses in his diamond flannels while playing for an unidentified Navy team. *The Sporting News*

4. Zeke Bonura (far right, with bat in hand) poses proudly with an unidentified Army team in North Africa early in the war. *The Sporting News*

5. The "Yankee Clipper" lashes at a pitch during an exhibition contest in April 1943 between his Santa Ana Army Air Force squad and the Pacific Coast League's Los Angeles Angels. Despite his best efforts, DiMaggio's team lost the game 6–5. *The Sporting News*

roster, including four who rotated in the outfield. Cochrane identified his 1943 fly chasers—Glenn McQuillen, Barney McCosky, Joe Grace, and Leo Nonnenkamp—as the most capable outfield of any of the three strong Bluejacket teams.[10] Of the four, McCosky was unquestionably the most talented. He posted a .312 lifetime average over eleven Major League seasons, and even tallied a .340 mark only three years before his tenure at Great Lakes. The other three outfielders enjoyed less success in their chosen profession but all garnered at least four years on big league rosters, not including the time spent in the Navy.

The addition of Hall of Fame first baseman Johnny Mize, a lifetime .312 hitter in fifteen Major League seasons, significantly improved the infield of the 1943 contingent. Mize was not only an exceptional hitter, but was nicknamed the "Big Cat" because of his remarkable agility and quickness for a man who was well over six feet tall and 200 pounds. Another new face for the 1943 season, shortstop Eddie Pellagrini, a light hitting but strong fielding veteran of eight Major League campaigns also bolstered the infield. The catchers included only one with Major League experience, George Dickey (the brother of the Hall of Fame Yankee backstop, Bill Dickey), who barely compiled a .200 career average. The pitching staff, however, was composed almost entirely of Major League moundsmen. Cochrane relied primarily on Tom Ferrick, who tallied a 3.47 lifetime ERA with five American League teams, and Vern Olsen, who boasted a 3.40 career ERA.

By the following season, Cochrane had assembled his most talented squad, which was certainly one of the best military teams ever to have competed during the war. Boasting a lineup overflowing with Major League ability, the 1944 Bluejackets compiled a .960 winning percentage. This included a thirty-three-game winning streak and a final tally of forty-eight wins against only two losses. More impressively, they claimed seven out of eight games against big league opponents, with victories over the Philadelphia Phillies, Boston Red Sox, and the St. Louis Browns, the 1944 American League representatives in the World Series. Great Lakes' only defeat against a professional squad occurred in August during a contest with the Brooklyn Dodgers, a first-division National League team, although the Bluejackets rebounded shortly thereafter with a "thumping" 17–4 victory over the Cleveland Indians.[11] Great Lakes' stellar record against Major League competition is tempered somewhat by the fact that professional rosters had been depleted by that point in the war, and teams usually traveled to exhibition games with fewer players than normal. Thus, players occasionally occupied positions with which they were not familiar, and teams often rested starting players to prepare them for regular-season contests. However, many of the individuals involved insisted "that the major leaguers were trying" to win the contests to avoid embarrassment and made every effort to defeat service teams.[12]

With "better pitching and a tighter defense" compared to previous seasons' squads, the 1944 contingent breezed through service competition; neither of their two losses came against military teams. Although skipper Cochrane declared the 1943 outfield superior to the 1944 fly-chasers, he did acquiesce that "as a whole [the 1944 team was] stronger than either" of the two previous year's representatives.[13] The 1944 Great Lakes squad, which included five All-Stars and one future Hall of Famer, was enough to make any Major League manager envious. With more than forty World Series appearances between them, the Bluejacket players had the talent and experience to overwhelm nearly every team they encountered. Led by former or future All-Stars Billy Herman, Virgil Trucks, Merrill May, Gene Woodling, Clyde McCullough, and Tiger great "Schoolboy" Rowe, the 1944 Great Lakes squad was truly remarkable.[14] Brooklyn Dodger second baseman Billy Herman, the Hall of Famer on the roster, was just coming off arguably his best campaign as a professional in 1943, when he hit .330 and drove in 100 runs before joining the Bluejackets. Herman added not only immense physical talent but also exceptional leadership skills and keen baseball savvy. Future American League star and fellow Bluejacket Gene Woodling asserted that Herman had the "best baseball mind [I] was ever around"—a profound statement given that Woodling enjoyed a seventeen-year big league career and played on the great Yankee teams of the early 1950s.[15]

Virgil "Fire" Trucks, a fixture in the Detroit Tiger rotation before and after the war, emerged as the Bluejackets' pitching ace in 1944. One of only four pitchers to ever toss two no-hitters in the same year, Trucks was manager Cochrane's choice for mound honors in most of the team's important contests, including exhibition games against Major League competition. Trucks' most impressive outings in 1944 came against the Philadelphia Phillies, Boston Red Sox, and the St.

Louis Browns, holding them to zero, one, and two runs, respectively.[16] Against the Phillies, the season's first Major League foe, the former Tiger hurler held the opposition hitless for his four innings of work before relinquishing the mound to Bill Brandt. In an outing a few weeks later, Trucks showcased his talents against the Red Sox, striking out twelve and allowing only two hits en route to a complete-game 3–1 victory.[17]

Trucks was not the only competent Bluejackets pitcher, however; all the remaining members of the staff had at least some Major League experience. In fact, the pitching corps was so laden with talent that Cochrane felt comfortable naming former Tiger star and 1943 Great Lakes mound ace "Schoolboy" Rowe as his starting right fielder when the team suffered a shortage of capable outfielders.[18] A winner of 158 games—including an amazing sixteen in a row in 1934—and the proprietor of a very respectable 3.87 ERA during his thirteen-year Major League career, Rowe also excelled at the plate, especially for a pitcher. The Tiger hurler compiled a .263 batting average during his big league stint and exhibited exceptional offensive skills for the Bluejackets, batting over .350 in 1943 and winning an exhibition game against the Phillies with a timely round-tripper.[19] Rowe even exceeded the offensive production of Major League position players such as Gene Woodling. A .284 career hitter for six big league teams, Woodling's .342 average for the 1944 season was the lowest among the Great Lakes starting nine.[20]

Other prominent members of the 1944 Bluejackets include Merrill "Pinky" May, an outstanding defensive third baseman and All-Star whose Major League career was abruptly ended by the war. Moreover, two-time All-Star and fifteen-year veteran Clyde McCullough together with two other catchers with Major League experience—Walt Millies and Bill Baker—gave Cochrane arguably the best backstop combination of any military team. Several factors, however, made the 1944 squad the last truly exceptional military team at Great Lakes. First, by 1945 the war was well in hand on all fronts, so Navy officials decided to disperse their talent more widely to entertain a greater number of sailors around the globe. Second, by 1944 the draft had exhausted most of the exceptional players from professional rosters so the pool of talent from which Great Lakes had access was not as deep as in previous years. To be sure, pitching great Bob Feller, after a long stint in the

South Pacific, did join the Bluejackets for the 1945 season as player-manager, but Navy officials removed such exceptional players as former teammate Ken Keltner and Detroit Tiger stalwart "Pinky" Higgins early in the season for overseas duty.[21]

Although no other military baseball teams surpassed the 1942–1944 Great Lakes squads in overall talent, the teams that represented the Norfolk Naval Training Station (Virginia) in 1942 and 1943 ran a close second. The Norfolk baseball program had the good fortune to fall under the command of Capt. Harry Adrian McClure, an ardent supporter of the game. Because of Gene Tunney's physical fitness program based out of Norfolk, many of whose students included professional athletes, McClure had access to a plethora of exceptional players.[22] Once talented sailors had been assigned to Norfolk, Captain McClure also had slightly better luck than Great Lakes officials keeping them from being reassigned so frequently, primarily because of the close relationship McClure maintained with the chief of naval personnel, Adm. Randall Jacobs.

McClure's concern for the success of his diamond crew often went beyond typical loyalty for the home team. He often sat in the dugout with the players during games yet was completely ignorant about the complexities of baseball. In one notable instance, McClure was tardy for the opening pitch of one contest but sent ahead an assistant to declare that the game could begin without him, though McClure wanted the Sailors to "withhold their scoring until he arrived." Occasionally, McClure solicited opinions from those knowledgeable about the game to determine which players he should pursue. During a lull in the action of one contest, McClure asked a surprised Shirley Povich of the *Washington Post* if he had "ever [heard] of a pitcher named Johnny Vander Meer"—the talented left-hander who remains to this day the only pitcher ever to have fashioned consecutive no-hitters in the Major Leagues.[23]

With McClure's backing and an impressive assemblage of talent, the 1942 Norfolk Sailors compiled a stunning 92–8 record, including victories in their final twenty-seven games. However, unlike the Great Lakes squad, this record is diminished by the fact that Norfolk scheduled no contests against Major League competition and very few against upper-level minor league opponents. Nevertheless, the 1942 contingent did employ a spectacular pitching staff that included Hall of Famer Bob Feller, ten-year Tiger veteran Fred Hutchinson, and Maxie Wilson, who enjoyed a brief stint in the big leagues. The three stars won nineteen, twenty-two, and twenty-three games, respectively, for the dominant Norfolk team.

The remainder of the team was predominantly composed of minor league athletes except for a select few with former or future Major League experience. A pair of two-year big league veterans performed admirably: Vinnie Smith, a catcher with the Pirates, and Ace Parker, an infielder for the Philadelphia Athletics in the late thirties whose later gridiron career earned him enshrinement in pro football's hall of fame. Jimmy Brown, a forward with the Boston Celtics as well as a minor league baseball player, patrolled left field for the extremely successful 1942 squad. The Sailors even claimed a professional trainer, Jimmy Ewell, who before the war had "eased the aches and pains of the local Norfolk minor league team.[24]

By 1943, although Feller had been reassigned away from the team, Norfolk's squad reached its pinnacle when its roster was enhanced by Major Leaguers Don Padgett, Benny McCoy, Jim Carlin, Tom Early, Charlie Wagner; All-Stars Dom DiMaggio, Johnny Pesky, and Walt Masterson; and future Hall of Famers Harold "Pee Wee" Reese and Phil Rizzuto. Holdovers from the previous year's team, including Fred Hutchinson and Vinnie Smith, completed a squad with enormous potential. Its solid pitching staff would now center primarily on Hutchinson, Masterson, Early, and Wagner.[25] A solid starter in eleven seasons with the Detroit Tigers, Hutchinson won nearly one hundred games in his career and participated in one World Series. Walt Masterson never competed in the postseason during his fourteen years in the big leagues, but he nevertheless earned births in two All-Star games while pitching effectively for the Senators and Braves. Tom Early and Charlie Wagner, although less successful than their two fellow pitchers, won a combined fifty games in stints with the Braves and Red Sox, respectively.

Although pitching certainly was a strength of the 1943 squad, the talent of the Sailors' position players was truly exceptional, especially when considering the defensive capabilities of the squad's infield. Manager Gary Bodie had the enviable task of choosing between two future Hall of Fame shortstops, Brooklyn Dodger "Pee Wee" Reese and New York Yankee Phil Rizzuto. After trying Reese and Rizzuto at short and third, Norfolk officials decided to "farm out" the Dodger shortstop to the Naval Air Station team—a squad that was created primarily to offer the Sailors adequate competition.[26]

The other starting infielders for Norfolk who had Major League experience included second baseman Johnny Pesky, a magician with the glove, and thirteen-year veteran and four-time All-Star first baseman Eddie Robinson. In the outfield, Dom DiMaggio, a .298 lifetime hitter, seven-time All-Star, and the youngest brother of the immortal Joe DiMaggio was the most talented of the Norfolk fly chasers and added offensive punch to a team rife with defensive stars. Don Padgett, after competing the previous year for Great Lakes, transferred to the Virginia military installation and proved to be a valuable utility man, logging time at catcher, first base, and the outfield.[27]

Even with this grand collection of talent, at least one anonymous Norfolk Naval trainee remained unimpressed. Upon attending several Sailors' contests, the sailor remarked that "Dom DiMaggio [was] far below par," Don Padgett was "awfully slow," and Johnny Pesky was "sleeping" during games. The trainee did concede that Tom Early and Charlie Wagner did "all right" and the "Scooter," Phil Rizzuto, was "marvelous."[28]

Such opinionated observations notwithstanding, by the end of the 1943 season, a debate raged within naval circles regarding the supremacy of the two dominant military baseball programs, the Great Lakes and Norfolk Naval Training Stations. Great Lakes advocates noted that they scheduled many more minor and Major League teams than did their East Coast rivals. During the 1943 season, Norfolk competed against only one Major League opponent, the Washington Senators, in the fund-raising spectacle orchestrated by Shirley Povich discussed in chapter 2. But Norfolk proponents countered that though they lacked a plethora of Major League victims and their more than twenty-five losses was not as impressive as in 1942, they had played the extremely strong Norfolk Air Station more than fifty times. The Air Station squad was composed almost entirely of professional players, including stalwarts such as "Pee Wee" Reese and fellow Dodger Hugh Casey. As such, they obviously were a more formidable opponent than many of the less talented semipro, college, and military teams that dotted the Bluejackets' schedule. Although members of each station expressed interest in settling the issue on the field, naval regulations prohibited teams from leaving base for more than forty-eight hours.[29]

Thus, it became impossible to completely resolve the issue before the conclusion of the 1943 season. By the following year, Gene Tunney's athletic program had been relocated to Bainbridge in Maryland, thus stifling the flow of professional athletes to Norfolk and effectively ending Norfolk's baseball dominance.

A third exceptional team sponsored by the U.S. Navy was located at the Sampson Naval Training Center (New York), the second-largest American naval installation after Great Lakes. Sporting a nifty 70–7 combined record from 1943 through 1945, the Sampson Bluejackets claimed nearly a dozen Major Leaguers on its rosters during those three years, including All-Star catcher Mickey Owen and the talented pitcher Johnny Vander Meer. The Bluejackets also fielded, most notably, eighteen-year Major League veteran Eddie Yost along with pitchers Hal White and Jim Konstanty, who spent twelve and eleven years in the big leagues, respectively.[30] Apparently unable to locate adequate opposition since they only averaged about twenty-five games per year, the Sampson squad temporarily split into two teams in 1944 (one headed by Vander Meer and the other by White) to "provide more entertainment for Navy personnel."[31] The Bluejackets did occasionally tangle with Major League opposition, for example, destroying the Boston Red Sox (a .500 team) 20–7 on twenty-four hits in a 1944 affair.[32]

Another exceptional Navy baseball program thrived at the Bainbridge Naval Training Center (Maryland), which regularly battled Norfolk for naval baseball supremacy on the East Coast. The 1944 contingent was particularly talented, with three All-Stars and seven other Major Leaguers on its roster and claiming victories over four big league teams during a stellar 56-15-1 season. Bainbridge even surpassed Norfolk as the top service team in the area by splitting the ten games they played together and earning a superior record against common foes. The only real weakness for the 1944 squad was on the mound: none of the hurlers had any substantial big league experience.[33]

Several other domestic naval outposts also claimed talented teams during World War II, including Bronson Field (Florida) where Red Sox slugger Ted Williams led a strong club in 1944. Joining Williams in the lineup were three others with Major League experience: Nick Tremark, Ray Stoviak, and sixteen-year veteran outfielder Bob Kennedy.[34] Likewise, sailors at Lambert Field (Missouri) were able to support a squad that performed spectacularly, especially against Major

League competition. The 1943 version of the Wings boasted seven former or future big leaguers and managed to defeat the Cincinnati Reds, who finished the year in second place; the St. Louis Browns; the Brooklyn Dodgers; and the Cleveland Indians. Lambert Field's only loss against Major League opposition came during a rematch against the St. Louis Browns. The Wings even felt confident enough to schedule a three-game series with the strong Great Lakes squad, though they won only one of those contests.[35]

The United States Army also sponsored many strong diamond contingents. None, however, were as talented as the top Navy teams primarily because the Army lacked an installation of comparable size to the large Naval training stations so its professional talent was much more dispersed. One Army squad, however, the McClellan Field (California) Commanders, did accumulate a significant number of professional players and could possibly have rivaled some of the elite Navy representatives. The 1943 team was particularly skilled, with virtually every position occupied by a player with Major League experience. Cincinnati Red stalwart Mike McCormick and St. Louis Brown regular Walter Judnich patrolled the outfield, while fellow professionals Dario Lodigiani and Bob Dillinger solidified the infield. Early in the season, both four-time American League All-Star and two-time batting champion Ferris Fain and future Hall of Fame second baseman Joe Gordon joined the Commanders' very impressive array of position players. On the mound, Rugger Ardizoia, a Yankee for a brief time after the war, and Bill Schmidt, a stellar Pacific Coast League performer, threw to future Yankee backup catcher Charlie Silvera. With such a gathering of talent in 1943, McClellan Field generally outclassed most military opponents, except several other West Coast teams that had acquired Major League talent of their own. By the beginning of 1944 season, the Army had ordered the transfer of many of the notable players from the previous year's team to Hawaii where they formed the nucleus of another exceptional contingent.[36]

The state of Texas also harbored several outstanding Army teams, including two in the San Antonio area alone, at Randolph Field and the San Antonio Aviation Cadet Center. Before the war, the Randolph Rambler baseball program was legendary, having won the very competitive local service league title each year since 1932. They won so regularly, in fact, that other military officials dubbed them the "Yankees of Army Baseball." By 1943, however, their reign as the dominant team in Texas began to slip with the induction and assignment of Major League players to other installations in the state. Without the aid of high-level professionals and despite the fact that much of their opposition boasted big league talent in 1943, the Ramblers did manage to maintain a tenuous hold on diamond supremacy in the area.

By 1944, however, the San Antonio Aviation Cadet Center Warhawks, which had employed St. Louis Cardinal star Enos Slaughter the previous year, formed a formidable squad by added two of his Cardinal teammates, pitcher Howard Pollett and catcher Del Wilber. Slaughter, who had torched service pitching for a .498 average in 1943 and again hit over .400 the following year, was the driving force behind the Warhawks' title drive. The Cadet Center finished the season with a 21–3 record and disposed of the Ramblers in a tightly contested series.[37]

Detroit Tiger catcher Birdie Tebbetts and Washington Senator pitcher Sid Hudson, veterans of four and two All-Star Games, respectively, headed another successful Army team in Texas at Waco Air Field. Under the direction of Tebbetts, the Wolves won prestigious semipro tournaments in Houston in 1943 and 1944 against teams that fielded Major League talent, including pitchers Tex Hughson, a Dodger All-Star, and former Cardinal regular Howard Pollett.[38] Another Army squad in Texas merits mentioned, though not exclusively for their ability on the field. The Sheppard Field Mechanics did employ eleven minor leaguers during a successful 1942 season, but it was the following season's club that was truly extraordinary. At one point in that campaign, every member of the Mechanics, including the manager and the batboy, was left-handed. The strange occurrence inspired one writer for the *Stars and Stripes*'s African Edition to opine that "those 6-4-3 double plays [would be] killers to see."[39]

Elsewhere around the country, the Army had another proficient squad at the New Cumberland Reception Center (Pennsylvania), which listed six Major League players in its regular lineup during the 1943 season. Hank Greenberg had spent some time there early in the war, but by the 1943 season he had departed for other assignments. Nevertheless, the Army contingent remained strong, with pitcher Tommy Hughes, a solid performer for a dismal Phillies team, and one other hurler, Fred Caligiuri, who had completed a modest Major League career the previous season. Four position players also played at the big league level, although none had any extended success in professional baseball either before or after the war.[40]

Similarly, the Army stockpiled an abundance of talent, including several former or future Major Leaguers, at the Jefferson Barracks Reception Center (Missouri). The 1942 nine employed three big league players, George Archie, Johnny Sturm, and the player with the most professional experience, Phillie second baseman Emmett Mueller.[41] The following season, the Reception Center squad added Dick Sisler, future Philadelphia Phillie All-Star and son of Hall of Famer George Sisler to bolster the remaining crew.[42] In Virginia, Army officials assembled a comparable pool of talent at Camp Pickett for the 1944 season. After a solid 1943 season with little professional assistance, the Army squad added two exceptional catchers, ten-year Major League veteran Mickey Livingston and Jake Early, who spent most of his nine-year career with the Senators. On the mound, Camp Pickett offered Ernie White, an outstanding pitcher who compiled a lifetime 2.78 ERA in seven campaigns with the Cardinals and Braves.[43]

Another notable Army contingent operated out of Camp McCoy (Wisconsin) where two talented soldiers, "Bama" Rowell and Cecil Travis, displayed their diamond skills during the 1944 season. Rowell was a six-year utility player for the Braves and Phillies, and Travis was a truly gifted athlete who seemed destined for the Hall of Fame until an unfortunate combat incident late in the war. Together, they led the Camp McCoy squad against the finest semipro and military teams in the area, including the stellar Great Lakes organization. They were victorious in twenty-five of their first twenty-seven games and even captured the Wisconsin state championship crown.[44]

Perhaps the most remarkable, if not the most talented, Army squad during the war were the Camp Campbell Armoraiders (Kentucky) who in 1944 established themselves as the best service team in the southern region. With seventeen former professionals (though no Major Leaguers), the Armoraiders defeated numerous other military teams that boasted big league talent and by July had amassed a thirty-one-game winning streak. Many of their wins came at the expense of Major League pitchers assigned to military installations in surrounding states, including nine-year American League veteran Steve Sundra and six-year National Leaguer Tommy Hughes. Camp Campbell also destroyed the competition in the Tennessee semipro tournament.

Emerging as the state champions they solidified their position as one of the most proficient service teams of the war years.[45]

The United States Marine Corps also claimed several of the top wartime military squads, including a pair on the West Coast. The San Diego Devildogs were arguably the most talented of the two teams, finishing with a 46–6 in 1942, their most successful campaign. During the year they defeated the Pacific Coast League's San Diego Padres and a number of other local minor league organizations on their way to finishing as the champions of the Eleventh Naval District. Over half a dozen Devildog players on the roster had previously competed in the minor leagues. Only pitcher Calvin Dorsett had big league experience (three seasons with Cleveland), and he was transferred midway through the summer.[46]

Just to the north, the other prominent California Marine baseball squad, the Mare Island Leathernecks, operated successfully against local competition, especially during the 1942 campaign. The commander of the Marine installation was Col. M. E. Shearer, "the teams' most enthusiastic fan" who "attend[ed] almost every game." Shearer ensured that the athletic facilities were superb and adequate equipment could be located to supply the Leathernecks with everything needed to dismantle the opposition. With a handful of minor league players, the Mare Island squad also added Calvin Dorsett from the San Diego nine to round out a team that finished 50–14 in 1942, including a tremendous stretch in which they won forty-two of forty-five contests. The Leathernecks' record is even more impressive when considering that they competed against teams from Camp Roberts, Mather Field, and McClellan Field, all of which employed many professionals and, in some cases, Major League players.[47]

Likewise, the Coast Guard retained two exceptional teams during World War II, one on each coast. In 1943, the West Coast representative, the Long Beach Army Ferrying Command squad, sported a future Hall of Famer in Red Ruffing, two All-Stars in Harry Danning and Max West, and another talented Major Leaguer in Nanny Fernandez.[48] Arguably an even more talented Coast Guard team operated out of Curtis Bay, Maryland. In 1945 the Cutters assembled a lineup laden with Major League experience, including its offensive leader, Sid Gordon, a thirteen-year National Leaguer with a .283 average and over 200 home runs lifetime. Other stars included Hank Majeski, a big leaguer for thirteen seasons despite missing four years in the service, and two-time All-Star and fifteen-year veteran Hank Sauer. By the end of the year, however, reassignment and discharges related to the end of the war had leeched the majority of talent from the roster.[49]

Outside of the continental United States, a number of other strong service teams also flourished, particularly later in the war when overseas areas became more secure. By 1945, teams in the Panama Canal Zone, for example, had access to Major League All-Stars such as Cardinal outfielder Terry Moore and Red Sox hurler Mickey Harris and often held games between the numerous talented outposts there.[50] The best military teams outside of the United States, however, resided in Hawaii where the competition between military leaders to exercise diamond supremacy was overwhelming. By the end of 1943, as the threat of Japanese forces in the Pacific subsided, the Army transferred a number of its top players from West Coast military installations to the Hawaiian islands. Many took up residence at Hickham Field in Honolulu where officials of the Seventh Army Air Force were ready to absorb many of the McClellan Field regulars from California, including big league veterans like Walter Judnich, Ferris Fain, Dario Lodigiani, Bob Dillinger, Mike McCormick, Joe Gordon, and Charlie Silvera, along with several minor league stars. Later, the team added the great Joe DiMaggio and Red Ruffing for a devastating lineup.

Perhaps the strangest event involving the acquisition of talent at Hickham Field centered on pitcher Eddie Funk, a talented minor league hurler, though never fortunate enough to wear a big league uniform. Funk was stationed at another Army installation in Hawaii where he had performed admirably for his base's team. The commanding officer at Hickham, Gen. William Flood, coveted the young pitcher but could not pry Funk away from the commander of the rival base. Destiny intervened when two dogs owned by Funk's commanding officer took ill and the only veterinary care available was at Hickham Field. Flood offered to care for the dogs in exchange for the pitcher, a deal accepted by Funk's CO. Apparently unfazed at being "traded" for the medical care of two dogs, Funk proceeded to "pitch excellent ball" for the Seventh Army Air Force squad in the following months.

While the Army was stockpiling a staggering amount of talent on their Hawaiian teams through the end of 1943, the Navy still kept most of their best players stateside until the latter half of 1944. With little opposition from rival service teams, Hickham Field, in particular, dominated local nines with ease, even those with former big league players. In the summer of 1944, for example, the Fliers punished the previous year's service league champion, a Navy contingent, who started the very capable Walt Masterson on the mound. The Army team knocked Masterson out of the game in the first inning and completed their rout 21–1. Later, the Fliers also decimated another talented military team by a score of 10–2, resoundingly displaying their preeminence in Hawaii.

The success of the Hickham Field team, along with a scattering of other professionals stationed in the Army's Hawaii base, certainly convinced Army brass that they had at their disposal the best collection of players in the region. This confidence inspired Lt. Gen. Robert Richardson Jr., the head of Army forces in Hawaii after 1943, to initiate discussions with Adm. Chester Nimitz regarding the "Servicemen's World Series," briefly discussed in chapter 1. As commander of the Pacific Fleet, Nimitz is probably best known for the brilliant "island hopping" strategy he promoted to win the war against Japan. However, Nimitz also proved to be a master strategist in the athletic arena by discreetly accumulating talent for the much-hyped Servicemen's Series. As we saw, the Navy mobilized quickly to relocate talented players for the affair, humiliating the Army contingent before disbanding and dispersing the team throughout the South Pacific.[51]

The embarrassment inflicted on the Army actually inspired the accumulation of more talent in the Pacific theater and subsequently the creation of several other exceptional military teams. Enos Slaughter recalled that the Army's humbling performance irritated many high-ranking officials, including former Dodger executive Larry MacPhail, then an officer in the Army Air Force: "it turned out that the Navy was beating the [Army] pretty badly over in Honolulu. That didn't sit well with Larry MacPhail, who had gotten himself a commission in the Air Force. So he had a hand in getting us shipped out to Honolulu. About forty-five ballplayers, mostly major leaguers and Triple-A players, were assembled in Kerns, Utah, and then sent up to Seattle where they put us aboard a ship and we all wound up in Honolulu."[52]

Slaughter and the other players, however, were delayed slightly because of logistical complications and didn't arrive in Hawaii until late 1944. During the delay the Navy had dispersed most of its talent throughout the Pacific to entertain sailors in island locales and thus the expected diamond battles between the two services never really materialized. When the massive delivery of baseball talent finally arrived, Army officials stationed Slaughter and other soldiers such as Howard Pollett, Birdie Tebbetts, American League infielder Billy Hitchcock, and National League outfielder Joe Marty at Hickham Field. However, the Army, like the Navy, had already sent most of the players they had previously collected there, thus erasing the possibility of forming potentially one of the best military teams of the war.

Even scattered throughout the Pacific, many of the great players in both branches of the armed forces combined to form very talented squads. All-Star relief pitcher Mace Brown, a ten-year Major League veteran and Navy man during World War II, later revealed that military officials formed teams that operated on several Pacific islands and competed in a number of leagues. The rosters included Johnny Mize, "Pee Wee" Reese, Billy Goodman, Barney McCosky, and Mickey Vernon, along with dozens of others with Major League experience. Vernon recalled that Larry Doby, the first African-American player in the American League and an eventual Hall of Famer, even competed for one of the squads. Likewise, the Army divided its talent primarily into two factions and stationed them on many of the same islands occupied by the Navy contingents. Virtually all of the Army's players stationed in Hawaii—Slaughter, Tebbetts, Hitchcock, and Fain, among others— relocated to locales such as Tinian, Guam, and Saipan to compete in leagues and other individual contests.[53]

Halfway across the globe on the diamonds of Europe, an abundance of military teams competed during the war. One notable team in England in 1943 gained recognition not necessarily for the talent of its squad, but for the charismatic first baseman of a bomber squadron who "handled himself like a veteran" in several games. Screen legend Clark Gable "had a clean swing at the plate and connected for some good wallops" while holding down the first sack for his base team.[54]

Other teams, however, were more renowned for their extraordinary play on the field than their celebrity status off of the diamond. The first of the exceptional military teams in Europe naturally operated in England until Allied offensives secured an ever-increasing foothold on the continent. Early in the war, several contingents compiled impressive arrays of talent and racked up tremendous records against American and Canadian military teams. An Army Air Force squad organized in 1943, for example, won twenty-eight of twenty-nine games and was arguably the "finest team assembled in England" early in the war. Among their ranks were a number of minor leaguers, former Red Sox first baseman Paul Campbell, and future White Sox pitcher Ross Grimsley. After a particularly exciting victory, one general referred to the squad as the "best baseball team I have ever seen in action."

Another extremely talented Army team that operated in England before moving to France was the Central Base Section (CBS) Clowns. Formed by former Pacific Coast League pitcher Chuck Eisenmann and fortified with other minor league talent, the Clowns compiled a 43–3 record during the 1943 campaign. Eisenmann decided upon his squad's unique moniker because he reasoned "he had a bunch of characters for ball players." Early on, however, the Clowns were hindered by the lack of baseball fields in England. In response, Eisenmann created a portable mound pieced together with wood and artificial turf that could transform the abundant soccer fields scattered about the English countryside into ready-made diamonds. With Eisenmann pitching the majority of the time, the Clowns continued competing against service teams after they relocated to France following the D-Day invasion. Although the Clowns were still a formidable opponent during the last two years of the war, their claim to being one of the dominant military squads in Europe was arguable because of the influx of Major League talent fortifying other rosters.[55]

One of those teams represented the Seventy-first Infantry Division and included in its 1945 lineup Major League outfielders Harry Walker, Johnny Wrotsek, and Maurice Van Robays, along with big league pitchers Ewell Blackwell, a six-time All-Star, and Ken Heintzelman. Moreover, Cincinnati Red infielder Benny Zientara, along with a number of minor leaguers, anchored a strong infield. Walker, who military officials had assigned to manage the team, recalled that the contingent was extremely talented, but often had difficulty traveling to games because much of the infrastructure in France and Germany had been destroyed during the Allied invasion. Walker requested a plane from his commander to facilitate movement and, after some debate, the Cardinal outfielder received his request.

With a B-25 as well as immense baseball talent at their disposal, the

Seventy-first Infantry team breezed through most competition during the 1945 season before reaching the European Theater of Operations championship series in Nuremberg (see chapter 1). There they faced a solid but less skilled contingent composed primarily of semipro and minor leaguers as well as Negro League stars Leon Day and Willard Brown. The Overseas Invasion Service Expedition (OISE) squad edged out the Seventy-first in a five-game series, even beating Ewell Blackwell in the deciding contest 5–1, to reign as diamond kings in Europe.[56]

By the end of World War II, military baseball had witnessed an explosion, not only in the numbers of teams, but also in the quality of many of these squads. Many military leaders viewed a winning athletic team as a direct reflection on their command and attempted by means bordering on the unethical to secure desired athletes. Due in large part to the influx of Major League talent through the war, Navy teams at the Great Lakes, Norfolk, and Sampson Naval Training Stations all boasted tremendously successful baseball programs. Although the Navy sponsored the best service teams, primarily because of the size of its installations, the other branches of the armed forces also claimed exceptional squads. With all of the branches competing for superiority on and off the battlefield, World War II truly ushered in a golden age for military baseball with a quality of play unsurpassed before or since.

Chapter 5 Qualified to Serve

Major League Stars' Military Experiences
during World War II

By the conclusion of World War II, millions of Americans had served the Allied cause of halting fascism on the battlefields, in the skies, and on the seas. Among these multitudes of gallant servicemen were carpenters, mechanics, farmers, and engineers—as well as the vast majority of the nation's professional baseball players. Before the war was yet a year old, the armed forces had claimed such diamond legends as Bob Feller and Hank Greenberg in addition to dozens of lesser-known players. Early in the war, *The Sporting News* adorned the front page of a May 1942 issue with a huge *V* (for victory) formed out of caricatures of the players then in the service. Feller, Greenberg, Hugh Mulcahy, and Cecil Travis were all depicted, a clear reflection that baseball was contributing mightily to the struggle for freedom. By the end of the war, the ranks of America's fighting men had expanded to include Ted Williams, Joe DiMaggio, Stan Musial, and Warren Spahn along with virtually ever other talented Major Leaguer, not to mention most minor leaguers. By the time the last shots were fired, approximately fifty-four hundred to fifty-eight hundred professional baseball players in the United Sates had served in the armed forces in some capacity.[1]

These players, though a small fraction of the men who served, received a disproportionate amount of publicity and, at times, criticism during their military lives. It seemed to be an unwritten rule during World War II that Major League stars and other celebrities were to be exempted from exposure to dangerous situations. Although the death rate for American military personnel approximated 3 percent, no active Major League player lost his life in combat, and only a handful were injured. Moreover, many of these injuries were either training mishaps or noncombat-related accidents. This obviously preferential treatment evolved partly because, according to one author, Americans historically have "demand[ed] that our sports heroes serve and . . . foam at the mouth in our columns and statehouse chambers when they balk [yet are] not all that eager to put them in harm's way."[2] For America's professional baseball players more specifically, it was the decision makers who did not want to place these "sports heroes" in danger. Who wanted to be the general or admiral who authorized combat duty for Joe DiMaggio or Ted Williams only to see them perish on a South Pacific island or over the skies of Germany?

Despite the obvious favoritism granted to many Major League players, officials were determined to maintain at least a semblance of fairness and equitable treatment toward professional athletes. Former Major League pitcher George Earnshaw, the coach of the baseball team at the Jacksonville (Florida) Naval Air Station, noted that athletes there were granted "no favors."[3] At Great Lakes Naval Training Station, a hotbed for the accumulation of professional talent, officials revealed that conditions for its Major League players were a "distant cry from the luxurious big leagues." Officers expected athletes to "hit the deck at 5 A.M. like any other sailor and put in a full day's work before they report to baseball practice."[4] Likewise, a columnist for South Carolina's *Greenville News* insisted that athletes would not be allowed to skirt military duties for more pleasurable pursuits on the diamond.[5]

Such insistences must have seemed quite preposterous to one Phil Masi, an Army private from New York stationed at Fort Dix (New Jersey) in 1944. Already in camp for over three weeks, he had yet to be assigned K.P. duty. Masi assumed that he was just fortunate to have escaped a task routinely rationed out to other soldiers, though he was not exactly sure why. However, the root of his fortune became apparent when a sergeant presented Masi with a catcher's mitt and suggested he "get used to the feel of it." When Masi revealed that he was not the Boston Braves' catcher of the same name, and in fact was inept on the diamond, his luck soon changed—the following day he was assigned K.P. and within a week had been relocated to Colorado.[6]

The unwritten rules regarding the treatment of athletes throughout the war led some critics to suggest that they fostered resentment among other servicemen. Writing for *Yank*, Dan Polier dismissed such arguments and stated that the "not-so talented guys" were not complaining but rather ecstatic to have the opportunity to serve with many of their diamond heroes. Polier asserted that those who opposed allowing baseball players to fight the war away from the front lines had never had the opportunity to read the thousands of letters from fighting men "telling [their] folks with a great deal of pride that [they were] in a company commanded by" one of their favorite players.[7]

Such assertions could, of course, be dismissed as the effusions of a baseball fanatic rather than a real reflection of servicemen's opinion. However, several members of the armed forces who endured the worst of wartime conditions also insisted that professional players in the military, though almost certainly treated differently, were just following orders and fulfilling their assigned roles. Army Air Force POW Jack Kreicji, whose experiences certainly entitled him to resent the athletes' privileged positions, instead revealed that he approved of allowing athletes to occupy posts that kept them from harm.[8] Likewise, fellow POW Sam Sambasile contended that though he assumed baseball players were receiving special treatment he felt no ill will toward them.[9] Marine Chuck Maier, a veteran of fierce fighting in the Pacific, reasoned that military officials probably did coddle athletes during the war, but baseball players "were serving a purpose" best suited for their abilities.[10] Another Marine who also saw extensive combat action, George Paulson, clarified the issue: "Joe DiMaggio did a lot more good with a bat than he could have done with a rifle."[11]

Thus, with many military officials and servicemen at least tacitly approving the shielding of Major League players from potential death or disability, these players were free to shoulder the unique responsibilities their talents suited them for. With a few notable exceptions, many of baseball's greats fought the war "in cleated shoes" and "were sidetracked into safe berths where they wore a baseball uniform as often as they wore Army or Navy fatigues."[12] Because of their rare talents most well-known baseball players neither "sought [n]or participated in combat," but rather supervised athletic programs and competed in an array of exhibitions, all-star games, and service league contests.[13]

To be fair to the athletes who benefited from such benign treatment, there was virtually no action, short of insubordination, that a serviceman could take if a high-ranking military official decided to assign them certain tasks or responsibilities. For recognizable figures such as Joe DiMaggio, these responsibilities often mirrored his lofty standing in the eyes of most Americans. By the beginning of the 1942 season the New York Yankee icon had established himself as the nation's preeminent sporting figure. His fifty-six-game hitting streak in 1941 and general stellar play anchored a Yankee team that had dominated Major League Baseball since the age of Ruth. Imagine DiMaggio's surprise then when the chorus of cheers usually showered upon him were replaced with a smattering of boos, even within the friendly confines of Yankee Stadium. Throughout the 1942 campaign, cries of "draft dodger" followed DiMaggio around American League parks despite the fact that his marital status pushed him well down the draft list. By the end of the year, the "Yankee Clipper" was "morose" over fans' treatment by him, and in February 1943 he voluntarily joined the armed forces.[14]

After passing a physical examination that, interestingly enough, revealed DiMaggio's vision to be only average, the Yankee outfielder requested and was granted assignment to the Army Air Force.[15] If DiMaggio was concerned that his time in the service would be spent trudging through the jungles of the South Pacific eluding enemy fire, his fears were completely unfounded. Aside from exchanging his $42,000 contract for the Army's standard $21 monthly salary, DiMaggio's service experience in California, Hawaii, and the East Coast could arguably not have been more pleasurable. DiMaggio did have to deal with a difficult divorce during his stint, and he also suffered from a tremendously painful stomach condition, which led directly to his relocation from Hawaii to New Jersey. For the most part, however, commanding officers fawned over him and provided DiMaggio with benefits not available to other soldiers. For example, DiMaggio received, along with other professional players, a training table that included some of the best steaks money could buy. DiMaggio dined so well, in fact, that as a soldier he actually tipped the scales at about ten pounds over his playing weight of one hundred and ninety-eight. Reportedly, the Yankee star also had his uniforms altered by a tailor, received a pass whenever he requested one, and accepted gifts from generals eager to please the Yankee legend. Upon leaving for Hawaii to join other Major League talent, for example, Army officials presented DiMaggio with a case of Scotch to bolster the spirits of the individual they hoped would prove a tremendous attraction for soldiers in the Pacific. While in Hawaii, Brig. Gen. William Flood "spared his stars all the normal Army tedium," and DiMaggio, along with the other professionals under Flood's command, "loll[ed] in the sand and surf, [got] a tan," and drank beer to the point where their "main battle hazard was probably cirrhosis."[16]

The "Yankee Clipper" felt that he was extended so much special treatment that in 1943 he openly demanded combat duty from his superiors. Always conscious of his public image and concerned that he was perceived as being pampered while others died, DiMaggio requested he be thrust into the fray because he "didn't enlist to play baseball."[17] DiMaggio's superiors, however, rejected this plea, and most of DiMaggio's time in the military was spent competing in exhibition games and on base teams.

To DiMaggio, many of the games he played in the military must have had the appearance of Major League contests. Competing with and against such big league stalwarts as Ferris Fain and Johnny Pesky as well as fellow Yankees Joe Gordon and "Red" Ruffing among others, DiMaggio adjusted to military life quite well. Although some of the games "could get sloppy," particularly those involving minor league or semipro teams, the great DiMaggio performed admirably on the field.[18] In an exhibition contest during the summer of 1943, for example, DiMaggio paced a contingent of former Major Leaguers with four hits and two home runs to beat a group of Pacific Coast League players.[19] A few months later in a similar contest, DiMaggio again homered to provide the decisive blow in a 4–1 victory over a minor league all-star team.[20] Upon arriving in Hawaii, DiMaggio made his presence felt by blasting a 453-foot home run in his debut appearance at Honolulu Stadium to the delight of the soldiers in attendance.[21]

After leading the Hawaiian service league in 1944 with a .401 batting average over ninety games, DiMaggio was sidelined by a painful ulcer that forced him into a hospital and later back to the mainland. Some newspapers speculated that DiMaggio might be discharged late in 1944 because of his illness. However, Army officials instead relocated him to Atlantic City, New Jersey, where he was primarily responsible for coordinating physical fitness programs for fellow soldiers. Although he rarely graced the diamond while in New Jersey, DiMaggio did make one appearance at an indoor softball game that made a lasting impression on a young soldier named Sam Elkins. Elkins recalled that DiMaggio would wander around Convention Hall in Atlantic City, which the Army had appropriated for use as a recreational facility. If prodded or if one team happened to be short a player, DiMaggio occasionally competed in pickup softball games, which were normally slow-pitch affairs. On this particular evening, however, soldiers had organized a fast-pitch game with one of the "fastest softball pitchers [Elkins] had ever seen." During DiMaggio's first two plate appearances, he struck out swinging because of his unfamiliarity with the unique speed and trajectory of the underhanded pitcher's motion. With the great Yankee Clipper easily humbled twice, the possibility for success a third time did not seem promising. During his next at bat, Elkins watched as DiMaggio took the first two strikes, closely eyeing the velocity and location of each pitch, then unleashed his picturesque swing and deposited the next pitch into the balcony of Convention Hall.[22]

While stationed in New Jersey during the winter of 1944–1945, DiMaggio often made sojourns into New York City, which led some to speculate that he might attempt to rejoin the Yankees for the 1945 season. This proved to be only wishful thinking on the part of the Yankee faithful, however, since DiMaggio did not gain his release from the Army until September 1945. Even though a few weeks remained in the 1945 campaign, DiMaggio insisted that it would take him at least that long to return to playing shape and decided to postpone his postwar debut until the following season.[23]

Another notable Major Leaguer who served an extended period in the armed forces without seeing combat was Philadelphia Phillies' pitcher Hugh Mulcahy, the first big league player drafted into the service. The Army Air Force summoned Mulcahy to duty during the peacetime draft before the 1941 season, and he did not return to the big leagues until 1945. Before his induction, the talented Mulcahy toiled in relative obscurity for an absolutely horrid Phillies squad. In the four years before his military service, Mulcahy lost seventy-six games, which prompted sportswriters to dub him "Losing Pitcher" because of the frequency with which that term and his name were paired in daily box scores. Upon joining the Air Force, Mulcahy insisted that his "losing streak was over" and he had become part of a winning team.

For the duration of his Air Corps stint, Mulcahy avoided combat and was responsible primarily for supervising athletic programs and pitching for various military teams.[24] Mulcahy later insisted, however, that he was not treated any differently because of his status as a professional athlete. As proof, he offered the fact that he "took [his] turns at K. P. just like everyone else."[25] Despite his insistence, before the war was yet a year old, the former Phillie hurler had already been commissioned a lieutenant—a relatively rapid ascent—and assigned the unperilous task of creating a baseball program at Camp Edwards (Massachusetts). Before his shipment overseas, Mulcahy undertook similar ventures at Fort Jackson (South Carolina) and in Memphis. Mulcahy's duties were typical for an athlete—organizing teams and leagues and coordinating schedules and various other related tasks.[26] Within weeks of Mulcahy beginning his new assignment at Camp Edwards, several retired big league players in the area offered to aid him in his endeavors. Jack Ryan, a former catcher who broke into the big leagues in 1889, as well as "Jumpin'" Joe Dugan and Joe Gilmore all joined Mulcahy to form certainly one of the most experienced coaching staff in all of service baseball.[27]

Although by his own admission Mulcahy "didn't play a great deal of baseball" while in the Army, published reports suggest that he did toe the mound for a number of different military teams.[28] Early in his military career while stationed in Massachusetts, Mulcahy pitched regularly for his division team, and he was usually quite successful. It was during his time in the Northeast that military officials ordered the former Philadelphia star to participate in a fund-raising exhibition between Army and Navy all-stars at the Polo Grounds, where he was to face the recently inducted Bob Feller. Mulcahy asked to be excused from the game because he was listed to pitch for his division squad the day before the exhibition and did not want to disappoint his teammates. The War Department, however, denied his request, forcing Mulcahy to travel to New York. Instead of abandoning his division squad, Mulcahy decided to pitch in his regular game anyway and then quickly board a train for New York. Pitching valiantly on consecutive days, Mulcahy was not as sharp as Feller who defeated the Army contingent 5–0.[29]

Mulcahy also competed briefly on Army teams in South Carolina and, most importantly, in Memphis, where the former Phillie hurler propelled the Second Army club to the "unofficial Southern Service championship." In the final contest against Fort Ogelthorpe (Georgia), Mulcahy outclassed former St. Louis Cardinal mound ace Johnny Beazley to earn the Second Army squad diamond supremacy in the Southeast.[30] After his Memphis assignment, Mulcahy then traveled overseas to the Pacific Theater where he remained for the rest of the war, all the while responsible for many of the same duties he had concerned himself with in the States. Mulcahy organized baseball teams and leagues for soldiers in the South Pacific, at one point "knocking down big coconut trees" in the Philippines to construct playing fields, while also participating several games himself.[31]

Throughout the summer of 1945, Mulcahy bolstered the pitching staff of the Eighth Army Chicks, performing well enough to qualify his squad for the Philippine World Series at Manila's Rizal Stadium. Mulcahy was reportedly ecstatic to have an opportunity to pitch during such an event, even though just days before play was to begin there Army experts had to clear the stadium of over eight hundred booby traps and a dead Japanese soldier. In fact, Mulcahy was so eager to compete in the series that he even delayed his discharge for a week so he would not have to depart for the States before the opening of the festivities. Unfortunately, a deluge flooded Rizal Stadium, postponing the series until after Mulcahy bid his farewell.[32] Upon his return home, the Phillies star rejoined the big league team for the remainder of the 1945 season and pitched, largely ineffectively, until the 1947 campaign.

New York Yankee great Phil Rizzuto was another notable Major Leaguer who logged significant time in the armed forces without deployment to the front lines. With two years in the big leagues and two World Series appearances before Pearl Harbor, the timing of the war for the "Scooter" could not have been worse from a professional perspective. Following the 1942 season, Rizzuto decided that the Navy needed him more than did the Yankees and enlisted for the duration. Upon his induction, Rizzuto was treated "like any other gob" when he reported sporting a pair of "beautiful sideburns." Barbers promptly removed in accordance with the Navy's strict grooming requirements.[33] Rizzuto, however, was one of the few professional players to confess that his status as a Major Leaguer did confer certain privileges, most notably the opportunity to play probably as much or more baseball than any other Major Leaguer who served. When asked whether his

commanding officers and fellow sailors treated him differently and re-
served special assignments for him because of his Major League talents
and experience, Rizzuto replied, "definitely." Rizzuto also conceded
that such inequitable treatment probably led to some resentment
among fellow fighting men and their parents since professional athletes were "playing ball while [other servicemen] were overseas fighting for their lives." Rizzuto, however, added that although he enjoyed preferential treatment, he felt the Navy received everything they
gave him and more in return through his fund-raising and recruiting
efforts.[34]

Navy officials first assigned Rizzuto to Norfolk, where his military
service got off to an ominous beginning when a fellow sailor stole two
valuable autographed World Series baseballs from Rizzuto's locker.[35]
The situation improved quickly for the Yankee shortstop, however, as
he joined the 1943 Norfolk team—one of the best in the history of
the armed forces. While at Norfolk, Rizzuto also became an expert war
bond salesman, disposing of $50,000 of the investments on one occa-
sion and over $60,000 worth on another.[36]

Following the 1943 campaign, Rizzuto relocated to Australia where
he began to manage service teams and compete in a variety of all-star
games and exhibitions. One of the most interesting Australian teams
for which Rizzuto was responsible was the "Stumpy" club, composed
entirely of men who had lost limbs in battle. The former Yankee shortstop set about adjusting the game to suit their abilities. The rules required every competitor to use crutches throughout the contest, so,
instead of having these men run the bases, Rizzuto designated certain areas of the field where the ball landed as an out, single, double,
triple, or home run. Rizzuto admitted that at first the games were "not
a pleasant sight" because the horrific nature of many of the participant's injuries were a constant reminder of the tragedies of war. However, the Yankee great claimed that "nobody could stop them" from
playing, and therefore he took it upon himself to organize games and
amend rules for the "Stumpy" club. It was surely experiences such as
this that inspired Rizzuto to comment that he "was one of the lucky
ones to get back in one piece."

When not supervising various baseball programs in Australia, Rizzuto competed in a number of all-star contests for the Navy. During
many of these games Rizzuto arguably played some of the best base-

ball of his life, dazzling onlookers with spectacular defense. Although never known for his offensive skills while in the Major Leagues, during this all-star games Rizzuto compiled staggering statistics against stiff competition. One of Rizzuto's most memorable moments on the field transpired during the famed "Servicemen's World Series," staged in Hawaii in fall 1944. Rizzuto, ordered to Honolulu for several weeks to ensure his participation, outshone all of the other big league stars there by garnering twelve hits in the series, which his Navy contingent dominated. Rizzuto also proved spectacular in the field, committing not a single error despite often playing out of position at second and third. Later that fall, Rizzuto also proved instrumental in destroying another all-star Army team, this time back in Australia. Returned to Brisbane after the Honolulu series, the former Yankee shortstop again displayed his brilliance by collecting three hits and spearing a line-drive shot with his bare hand. The Army squad, obviously outmatched and with little professional talent in its ranks, succumbed to Rizzuto and company 17–0.[37]

Another of the diamond elites who logged significant time in the service and was involved primarily in baseball-related activities was St. Louis Cardinal outfielder Enos Slaughter. By the end of the 1942 season, Slaughter had just completed a magnificent campaign in which he led the National League in hits and triples and was a driving force in the Cardinals' conclusive World Series victory over the Yankees. Before the season was over, however, Slaughter had enlisted in the Army Air Force, entering the service in January 1943. As the baseball season was approaching, several officers at Texas military installations requested that Slaughter be transferred to their command to strengthen their military teams. Eventually, officials decided on Fort Worth's Sheppard Field as Slaughter's assignment despite the fact that it had no baseball team. That situation remedied itself within weeks, however, as Slaughter was transferred to the San Antonio Aviation Cadet Center, which boasted a superior diamond program. In San Antonio, Slaughter became irked when his request to become a pilot was denied, and he received orders to become a bombardier. He had little interest in simply "pushing a button" and appealed for amended orders. Army officials responded by preparing the Cardinal Hall of Famer for transfer to an unknown location before an influential colonel intervened. According to Slaughter, the colonel notified the proper authorities that "they wouldn't have much of a team" if they removed the out-fielder, and thus it was another two years before Slaughter relocated.[38]

While in San Antonio Slaughter's primary duty was playing baseball and, more importantly, playing it well. During his first season in a very competitive service league of military teams in and around San Antonio, Slaughter hit at a spectacular .498 clip. By the following season, Slaughter had been joined at the San Antonio Aviation Cadet Center by former Cardinal teammates Howard Pollett and Del Wilber, forming an imposing lineup that easily defeated area squads. Slaughter dipped to a .420 average in 1944 but only because the "pitching started getting better" with the arrival of hurlers who had big league experience.[39]

At the end of the 1944 campaign, Slaughter received orders for immediate departure overseas. The assignment was not related to traditional military obligation, however, but instead concerned the embarrassing defeat the Navy had levied on the Army in the "Servicemen's World Series" in Honolulu. The former Cardinal outfielder was one of nearly four dozen professional players the Army gathered for transfer to Hawaii to challenge Navy teams. As discussed earlier, however, by the time of Slaughter's arrival the Navy had already shipped the majority of its star players to various islands in the South Pacific to bolster servicemen's morale. After Slaughter's brief stay in Hawaii, the Army decided to embark on a similar venture and sent Slaughter and several other Major League players to a variety of locales to entertain fellow soldiers. The future Hall of Famer recalled competing in exhibition games before thousands of troops and claimed their contests drew "better crowds on Saipan" than the Philadelphia Phillies did at home (not as outlandish as it sounds given that the Phillies' perennial last-place teams historically suffered miserable attendance). Slaughter remained in the South Pacific for the duration of the war, but returned to the Major Leagues "in pretty good shape" shortly after the cessation of hostilities to eagerly resume his career.

Cincinnati Red pitcher Johnny Vander Meer must also be included among the great players of the World War II era who served his country primarily on the diamond. Known mostly for his amazing record of consecutive no-hitters, Vander Meer also displayed his talents for the U.S. Navy during the war. Departing from the Reds after the 1943 season, the ace left-hander took up residence at Sampson Naval Training

Station (New York) before its 1944 baseball campaign began. Sampson, fielding one of the strongest military teams on the East Coast, started Vander Meer against most of its toughest opponents. He pitched extremely well throughout the 1944 season, defeating teams such as the Boston Red Sox and four other upper-level minor league organizations while averaging well over one strikeout per inning. The left-hander was not only pitching well, but he took the mound so frequently that he declared the extensive practice he gained in the Navy actually improved his skills. Vander Meer claimed that his control vastly improved once he became a sailor, for example, and he lost the "wildness that bothered [him] for so long."[40] A brief glance at his postwar statistics verifies this statement to some extent. While pitching for the Cincinnati Reds until 1949 his walks dropped dramatically, although so too did his strikeouts.

Before the end of the 1944 season, Vander Meer was one of the many sailors assigned to Hawaii to compete in the previously mentioned "Servicemen's World Series" against the Army. The talented pitcher proved instrumental in the Navy's victory, and his "tight hurling" in the second contest sealed an 8–2 decision.[41] After the series, Vander Meer followed many of his fellow baseball-playing sailors on a yearlong Pacific tour, during which he competed on the diamond almost every day. Vander Meer's military service seemed to agree with him physically. Extremely healthy, he weighed in at more than fifteen pounds over his prewar playing weight when he rejoined the Reds in 1946.[42]

An American League pitcher who served in the Navy, Virgil Trucks, enjoyed a similar military experience. Playing with the Detroit Tigers through the 1943 season, Trucks was a late arrival to the armed forces but nevertheless competed in a substantial number of games until his release in 1945. Upon his induction into the Navy, Trucks immediately joined the stellar Great Lakes squad headed by Mickey Cochrane. Anchoring a pitching staff that included several other Major Leaguers, Trucks performed splendidly during the 1944 season, averaging nearly one and a half strikeouts per inning and posting a stingy 0.88 ERA, including a minuscule 0.94 mark against Major League teams.[43] Although tough on big leaguers opponents, Trucks simply overwhelmed lesser competition, for example, amassing nineteen strikeouts in one impressive outing against a talented semipro team in July.[44]

After the 1944 campaign at Great Lakes, Trucks, like Vander Meer, was assigned to Honolulu to compete in the "Servicemen's World Series." Trucks was even more valuable than the Cincinnati Reds' pitcher, winning the opener with an impressive four-hit shutout. Trucks also took the mound several days later, after the series had been decided, and won the fifth game with some relief help.[45] At the conclusion of the exhibition games in Hawaii, Trucks joined many of his fellow sailors during the next year's tour of the Pacific and was released by the Navy in time to join the Detroit Tigers for the last weeks of the 1945 season.

New York Yankee second baseman Joe Gordon also managed to avoid combat in a military career primarily spent competing on the field. Gordon, a late arrival to the service in 1944, endured harsh criticism when a photograph of him appeared in 1943 showing him on a hunting excursion sporting a "necklace of wild ducks." The picture quickly prompted many Americans and baseball fans to label Gordon a draft dodger. He had apparently failed to adhere to an unofficial mandate by baseball owners that encouraged players never to be photographed in pleasurable pursuits or to be quoted complaining of wartime "hardships," such as having to carry one's own luggage.[46]

Nevertheless, in the spring of 1944, the former Yankee began his service stint in the Army Air Force at McClellan Field (California), where officials had assembled a number of Major Leaguers. With Gordon and veterans Ferris Fain and Walter Judnich, among others, the McClellan squad dominated military baseball on the West Coast. As did many of the great players then in the service, Gordon relocated to Hawaii for the "Servicemen's World Series" in the fall of 1944 and joined the losing Army team. The Army's devastating defeat could not be attributed to Gordon, however. He performed well, homering in the fourth game and even starting a triple play in the series opener.[47]

After the series, Gordon and the other soldiers in Hawaii received orders to tour the South Pacific to entertain soldiers worn down by months of fierce combat with the Japanese. Gordon thus competed in contests in the Marianas, Saipan, and Iwo Jima after Allied forces had secured those locations. The Yankee second baseman even anonymously graced a softball game between novice Army and Navy teams on Guam, when the Army's manager inserted Gordon, identified as "Joe Hollister," as a pinch hitter. After one swing, the former Yankee great betrayed his big league identity by lashing the first pitch just foul but at an amazing distance. Suspecting chicanery the Navy squad immediately halted play. Finally, the Army players admitted their ruse, and Gordon was promptly ejected.[48] Gordon spent most of 1945 jumping between South Pacific islands before his release late in the year allowed him to return to the Yankees the following season.

Although Detroit Tigers' catcher "Birdie" Tebbetts enjoyed experiences in the Army similar to the other players chronicled in this chapter, he somewhat distinctively did not often venture far from his semipermanent assignment in Waco, Texas. Aside from brief excursions to Miami and Honolulu, Tebbetts served the majority of his tenure at Waco Army Air Field supervising a number of athletic programs. His induction late in the 1942 season interrupted an All-Star campaign with the Tigers, and Tebbetts immediately began his assignment in Texas. As player-manager of the Waco Wolves, Tebbetts "lined up a good array of baseball talent," including such Major Leaguers as Walt Masterson, Sid Hudson, and "Hoot" Evers.

At the end of 1942, Tebbetts relocated briefly to Miami for instruction in physical training but returned to Waco before the 1943 season. Leading superior teams—some of the strongest military squads in Texas—the next two seasons, Tebbetts was a member of the large contingent of players assigned to Hawaii after the "Servicemen's World Series." Unlike most other professional players, however, Tebbetts did not tour the South Pacific extensively during the waning months of the war, instead returning to Waco. During his final year in the Army, the former Tigers catcher again proceeded to acquire and retain Major League talent for his Waco Wolves, who in 1945 repeated their dominating performance of the previous seasons.[49]

Many older Major League veterans and retired big leaguers, whose flagging skills might have rendered them less valuable to military baseball, avoided combat by winning assignments related to their athletic experiences. Although the military draft exempted those over thirty-eight, future Hall of Famer Ted Lyons enlisted in the Marine Corps late in 1942 at a virile forty-one years old after a twenty-season career with the White Sox. Columnist Ed Burns of *The Sporting News*, noting that Lyons' fellow players generally recognized him as one the league's strongest and physically fit players of any age, questioned what training Lyons might possibly require. The only thing Lyons required before being turned "loose on the enemy," Burns insisted, was a "boat passage to a nest of chesty Nazis or measly Japs."[50]

Within weeks of his entry into the Marines, Lyons himself expressed hope that he would soon receive "a daily assignment in pitching against the Japs."[51] Instead, the Marines employed Lyons in various athletic duties, including one notable assignment in the Marshall Islands. To foster congenial relations with the islands' native peoples, who had been under Japanese control since early in the war, Lyons and other Marines organized a baseball camp to expose the locals to America's national pastime. Lyons worked with the islanders who "wore themselves out trying to throw curves, knucklers and fast balls."[52] Near the end of the war, Lyons, by now forty-five, remained optimistic about his chances of resuming his big league career, insisting that he could "pitch all right up there [the major leagues] in 1945" if hostilities ended in 1944.[53] Lyon's prediction barely proved accurate as he enjoyed only one unremarkable postwar season on the mound for the White Sox.

Another seasoned veteran who spent substantial time in the armed forces was New York Yankee catcher Bill Dickey, one of the best performers in history at his position. Dickey was so good, in fact, that he had been selected for ten of the previous eleven Major League All-Star games before his military service. Despite his relatively advanced age—thirty-seven—the Navy claimed Dickey in the draft and employed him immediately at various installations supervising athletic programs. Dickey's most important assignment revolved around Honolulu's "Servicemen's World Series" in 1944 (discussed in chapter 1), during which he managed the victorious Navy contingent. He was not the first choice for the honors—that distinction went to Mickey Cochrane—but Cochrane was unavailable and suggested Dickey for the job. Dickey utilized his influence as a professional athlete to secure the services of such talented individuals as Johnny Mize and Phil Rizzuto, among others, and even personally accompanied "Schoolboy" Rowe, Virgil Trucks, Walt Masterson, and Johnny Vander Meer from the States to Hawaii. With such a powerful collection of players, Dickey had at his disposal every tool he needed for victory and did not disappoint his superior officers.[54]

As we saw in chapter 4, Dickey's opponent during many Major League campaigns, Mickey Cochrane, was also involved extensively in military baseball. Having retired as an active player after the 1937 season because of the effects of a fastball that fractured his skull, Cochrane stayed on as manager of the Detroit Tigers until the 1938 season, when management decided to terminate his contract. Cochrane spent several years away from baseball until, shortly after the outbreak of hostilities, he enlisted in the Navy. Deeming Cochrane poorly "qualified to serve as a commander of a destroyer or to fly a bomber or fighter plane," Navy officials assigned the former catcher to Great Lakes Naval Training Station, where he supervised some of the greatest military teams of the war.

Cochrane at first relished his position and from 1942 through 1944 managed teams that won a combined 163 games and lost only 16. However, the future Hall of Famer became disenchanted with his assignment when several of his superiors questioned his judgment after a defeat at the hands of the Brooklyn Dodgers in 1944, one of only two defeats his team suffered that year. Cochrane subsequently requested sea duty and was stationed at Pearl Harbor, ready to depart, when organizers began planning the "Servicemen's World Series." Before beginning his assignment at sea Cochrane helped Dickey and other naval personnel locate and redirect desired players to Honolulu. The Navy discharged Cochrane at the end of 1945, but he never returned to professional baseball in a managerial position.[55]

Although the professional stars profiled in this chapter "slay[ed] the enemy with base hits," as one writer has put it, many others, including some of the most recognizable names in the game, did not spend the bulk of the war playing ball or any other sports, yet still avoided combat.[56] Red Sox left fielder Ted Williams—arguably the greatest hitter of the World War II era and Joe DiMaggio's chief offensive rival in the prewar years—spent several of the war years in the armed forces without competing extensively for any military team. Like DiMaggio, Williams often felt the sting of fans' criticism during the 1942 season for remaining a civilian, although he was certainly not evading the draft. Williams was the sole supporter of his mother and therefore classified as 3-A, placing well down on the list of eligible draftees. By the close of 1942, however, his draft status had been amended, and Williams entered the Navy before the beginning of the 1943 baseball season.[57]

Unlike DiMaggio, Williams did not have the opportunity or inclination to spend the majority of his service time on the diamond. Even when he did compete for military teams, he often disappointed himself, and certainly his commanding officers, by playing below his lofty standards. Williams admitted that "I didn't have my heart" in many of the service contests he appeared in because of his concern with the war and his military duties.[58] Toward the end of his military stint in 1945, for example, Williams competed for the Navy in the "Little World Series," in which American and National League players then in the Navy squared off in Hawaii. Williams batted a relatively dismal (for him) .272 in five games for the losing American League squad and set the tone for his performance in the ninth inning of the series opener by flying out with the tying and winning runs on base.[59]

Williams did enjoy somewhat more success on the diamond while in the service, especially when completing his military training on the East Coast. For two squads, the Navy Pre-Flight Cloudbusters (North Carolina) and the Bronson Field Fliers (Florida), Williams displayed his masterful skills, leading both teams to extremely successful campaigns in 1943 and 1944, respectively.[60] The Red Sox Hall of Famer proved to be particularly adept at his adopted vocation as a pilot, however, and spent most of his days involved in aviation-related activities. In fact, during his first few weeks of training, Williams, one of the greatest hitters to ever don a Major League uniform, declared that he liked flying "so much I would quit baseball for it."[61] So engrossed was Williams in his duties as a pilot that he was reluctant to travel to New York to accept the 1942 American League Most Valuable Player award from the Baseball Writer's Association. The association had tried contacting Williams several times to notify him of their choice and invite him to a special dinner and presentation in his honor. When Williams finally responded he declined the invitation, citing his military obligations. The baseball writers did not let the issue rest, however, and contacted Navy officials in Washington to secure an exception so the talented slugger could attend the festivities in New York. Navy officials notified the writers that no rules or regulations in fact prohibited Williams from attending the gala and that any refusal must have originated from Williams himself. When Williams revealed that it had been his decision to nix the ceremony because it would have disrupted, albeit only slightly, his training, the Navy, seeing a positive publicity opportunity, ordered Williams to personally accept the award and make up any missed training upon his return.[62]

Williams not only enjoyed flying, but was apparently bestowed with the gifts required of a skilled pilot—superior eyesight, lightning reflexes, and an "inquiring mind." One commanding officer labeled Williams a "flying enthusiast" with "splendid equipment for a flier." Likewise, during the Korean War, when Williams was recalled to active duty and saw extensive combat action, future NASA astronaut and fellow squadron member John Glenn identified the "Splendid Splinter" as one of the best pilots he had the good fortune to know. Such compliments were apparently not simply hollow gestures. At various naval installations during World War II, the Red Sox slugger set records for "hits, barrel rolls, zooms and shooting from wingovers" and eclipsed many gunnery standards established by other pilots.[63]

Williams's military career, however, was not without occasional obstacles and uncomfortable moments. While stationed in North Carolina in 1943, Navy officials recruited him for a brief public speaking appearance. Williams obliged and spoke primarily about baseball and the state of the professional game during his era. Williams asserted that the modern player was more skilled than the diamond greats of previous years. Taking exception, a Navy captain who happened to also be an avid baseball fan declared that he did not believe that the players of Williams's generation were "nearly as good as such old-timers as Tris Speaker and Ty Cobb." Williams, who was always known for his candor and lack of diplomacy with those who disagreed with him, found himself in the unsettling position of refuting a superior officer. Betraying his natural instincts to forcefully offer his position, Williams stated with unusual tact: "Beg pardon, sir. I'm sorry, I may be wrong, but I must disagree with you, sir."[64]

The Red Sox star also endured physical ailments while in the service, though nothing that required extensive care or threatened his military service. Just a few months after his induction, Williams underwent a precautionary hernia operation for a condition that had plagued him most of his adult life though never significantly affected his play.[65] Williams also narrowly escaped serious injury and possible death during a routine flying assignment early in 1944. A fellow flight instructor noticed that the wing flaps were down on Williams's plane during an attempted takeoff—a potentially dangerous oversight. The instructor notified Williams of the fault before the situation became perilous and disaster was averted.[66] By the end of 1945, the "Splendid Splinter" had been released from the Navy without experiencing combat. For Williams, however, this first service experience was but the beginning of a military career as Uncle Sam called on him again several years later during the Korean War, when he flew nearly forty combat missions.

Detroit Tiger great Hank Greenberg was another of the exceptional World War II–era players to serve significant military stints without either reaching the front lines or competing extensively on military baseball teams. Greenberg, who compiled stunning offensive numbers before the war—including a serious run at Babe Ruth's record of sixty home runs in 1938—was one of the first Americans to enlist after Pearl Harbor. He had already devoted most of 1941 to the Army Air Force after falling victim to the peacetime draft instituted in 1940. The future Hall of Famer had actually been released from the Army immediately before Pearl Harbor but felt an obligation to renew his military commitment when America entered the war. Greenberg, like Williams, competed sparingly on the diamond while in the service, concerning himself instead with his other military duties.

When he began his service career, Greenberg progressed as many other athletes would after him by organizing athletic programs and physical training curricula at various installations around the country. Greenberg began at Camp Custer (Michigan) and then relocated to MacDill Field (Florida), where he supervised athletics and occasionally competed on the diamond. By August 1942, Army officials assigned him the task of directing physical fitness programs nationally, for which he traveled from coast to coast for the better part of a year. During his inspections, Greenberg, often working with other former Major League players, was responsible for ensuring that programs implemented at Army installations developed a "physical soldier" who was better suited for combat.[67]

Although Greenberg was directly involved in athletics activities for the Army, he rarely engaged in his civilian occupation. The Tiger first baseman confessed that the travel and training associated with his military responsibilities made it difficult for him to find time for baseball.

In certain situations, however, Greenberg did display his diamond skills. Early in 1942, for example, while the Tiger star was stationed at MacDill Field, George Earnshaw, a former Major League pitcher and manager of the Naval Training Station in Jacksonville, wrote repeatedly to Greenberg at the neighboring Army installation about scheduling a game. When Greenberg failed to reply, Earnshaw wrote the future Hall of Famer as follows: "Listen you big lug, I hear you have a ball club down there. We want a game. I may not have much left, but I can strike you out 3 or 4 times." Not surprisingly, Greenberg responded to the challenge by promptly contacting Earnshaw, and the two agreed upon a date for a contest between their squads.[68]

In 1944, the Army relocated Greenberg from the United States to the Chin-Burma-India theater. Even before American involvement in the Pacific War, the Japanese had undertaken massive offensives in east and south Asia. By 1944, Allied forces, including the contingent Greenberg joined, had begun to expel the Japanese from strongholds in the area. The Tiger slugger even pleaded with his superior officers for a chance to participate in combat. However, "as hard as he tried . . . Greenberg never made it all the way to the front," settling instead for the command of a squadron in China many miles from combat activity.[69] Although never directly in the line of enemy fire, Greenberg did endure one frightening incident, when he nearly perished in an accident involving a "Superfortress" B-29 bomber. He happened to be standing near a runway as the plane attempted a takeoff, but a malfunction caused the plane's bomb load to detonate, knocking the former Tiger star to the ground. Remarkably, although the plane broke into pieces and scattered about the runway the blast did not injure Greenberg or any of the crew.[70] By the middle of 1945 with the war well in hand, Greenberg received his release from the Army and returned to the Tigers in time to help them clinch the American League pennant.

Although like Ted Williams, Joe DiMaggio, and Hank Greenberg, the majority of Major League players avoided combat, there were notable exceptions, including one of the greatest pitchers of the era, Bob Feller. Compiling an amazing 107 victories with the Cleveland Indians before he was twenty-three, Feller enlisted in the Navy the day after Pearl Harbor, even though as his mother's sole supporter he was in no danger of being drafted. Nevertheless, the future Hall of Famer "thought what I did was right" because even though "there's never been a good war . . . the worse ones are the kind you lose."[71]

Immediately assigned to Norfolk, Feller competed on the diamond extensively in 1942 before proceeding overseas. The former Indian pitcher was a vital component for a Norfolk squad that finished the season with ninety-two wins and only eight losses. During two of his best outings, Feller struck out twenty-one opponents on a low-level minor league team and fashioned a two-hit, fourteen-strikeout performance against a more advanced minor league squad.[72] Before the year was over, Feller boarded the USS *Alabama* as an antiaircraft gunner, which was his assignment through 1944. Until the summer of 1943, Feller traversed the treacherous North Atlantic, a haven for deadly German U-boats. The *Alabama*, however, survived its service there and then relocated to the South Pacific.

Once in the Pacific, the *Alabama* docked in Hawaii briefly where Feller enjoyed a moment's respite in the sunny paradise, which could have become a permanent assignment. Owing to Feller's status as a professional athlete, Navy officials catered to him, allowing him to compete in exhibitions and games in lieu of other military duties. According to the former Indians pitcher, he also spent a great deal of time "drinking beer" and relaxing, which began to weigh on his conscience. Feller eventually concluded that he could not continue this lifestyle while others were risking their lives and soon requested combat duty. Navy officials granted his request by reassigning him to the *Alabama*, which subsequently saw significant action in the South Pacific.[73]

During the summer of 1944 the *Alabama* engaged in heavy fighting at Kwajalein and the Marshall Islands and also participated in the famous "Marianas Turkey Shoot," which decimated much of what was left of the Japanese air force. Feller recalled that he was fortunate to emerge from the war unscathed since many of his fellow sailors died in battle and enemy shells often strafed his station. In one particular combat incident, he was even responsible for saving one of his own crew members when a huge swell swept a young sailor overboard, with only Feller as a witness. Amid the confusion of battle, Feller notified his superiors who mobilized a destroyer to rescue the sailor.[74] By the end of his Pacific tour of duty, which lasted until early 1945, Navy officials had awarded Feller eight battle stars for his participation in major enemy engagements.

Between his combat experiences, the future Hall of Famer tried to maintain his good physical condition by dusting off his strong right arm whenever possible. Feller admitted that he regularly performed "chin-ups . . . push-ups . . . [skipped] rope and [ran] around the ship" on a jogging track he had devised along the *Alabama*'s perimeter.[75] While at sea, Feller also recruited "hardy souls" who were brave enough to catch one of the hardest- throwing pitchers in history and competed in games when the battleship docked at various ports of call.[76] At one point in 1944, the Cleveland Indian great pitched forty-seven consecutive innings against a number of military teams without allowing a single run.[77]

In the early spring of 1945, Feller returned to the mainland and accepted an offer to replace Mickey Cochrane as the head of the baseball program at Great Lakes Naval Training Station. With his combat experience behind him, his health intact, and the end of the war apparently imminent, Feller focused primarily on baseball at Great Lakes before rejoining the Indians late in the season. Playing for Great Lakes turned out to be a "golden break" for Feller, who used the time there to "chip the rust" off of his powerful right arm.[78] Hitting his stride by July, Feller dominated the Philadelphia A's in an exhibition game, striking out twelve.[79] Feller's most impressive victory, however, came against the Ford All-Stars, one of only two teams to defeat the stellar 1944 Great Lakes squad. The ace right-hander fashioned a no-hitter against the talented semipro team and seemed close to his Major League form.[80] In August, the Navy released Feller, which allowed him to resume his Hall of Fame career with the Indians. In the waning weeks of the 1945 season, he compiled five wins and a tidy 2.50 ERA.

Another prominent Major Leaguer who served amid dangerous combat conditions was Buddy Lewis, primarily a third baseman and a perennial .300 hitter for the Washington Senators. Although drafted in the spring of 1941 by the Army, Lewis obtained a deferment until the close of the baseball season that year, after which he joined the Army Air Force and trained to become a pilot.[81] Shortly after his induction, Lewis revealed his eagerness to join the fighting by commenting that he did not believe the enemy could "be any harder to hit than some of the American League's southpaw chuckers."[82]

Lewis first drew an assignment at Fort Knox (Kentucky), where he founded his platoon's first baseball team, and then attended various pilot training programs throughout the southeastern United States.[83] Although the former Washington star did not compete on the diamond for any extended period during his military tenure, he was one of the players Mickey Cochrane chose for the 1942 service all-star game in Cleveland in which a select military team was matched against the winner of the big leagues' mid-summer classic. Preparing for the July game, Lewis attempted to play himself into shape but apparently his training schedule could not accommodate participating in games for any local military teams. Lewis did, however, secure a position in the lineup for a semipro softball team, competing under the name "Merle Johnson" to avoid publicity before embarking to Cleveland.[84]

Following the July spectacle, Lewis spent most of the remainder of his military career away from the diamond and in the skies. Until he was reassigned to the China-India-Burma theater, Lewis flew domestic missions transporting cargo and important individuals to specific locations throughout the United States. In one particular instance in 1943, shortly before Lewis was shipped overseas, the former Washington star drew the task of delivering several gentlemen to the DC area. While in town, Lewis briefly visited his old team, which happened to be playing a doubleheader that day, and reminisced with some of his friends at Griffith Stadium. Military obligations forced Lewis to leave the second contest before its conclusion, but he promised his former teammates a farewell they would not soon forget. Washington outfielder George Case recalled that Lewis, shortly after his departure from the stadium, directed his plane "at a ridiculously low altitude breaking God knows how many laws and regulations . . . .[then] wiggled his wings a little and went soaring over the center-field bleachers and off into the blue sky."[85]

Shortly thereafter, Lewis relocated overseas where he performed his military duties admirably under combat conditions. Flying over five hundred missions in and around China "cargoing everything from mules to rations," Lewis exhibited supreme bravery during a complicated and dangerous Allied foray two hundred miles into Japanese-held territory in Burma. In March 1944, Lewis helped the famed "Wingate's Raiders" and "Merrill's Marauders" recapture key Burmese locations by towing two gliders with his C-47 transport plane deep into enemy territory without the usual fighter escort. Army officials rewarded Lewis with the Distinguished Flying Cross for his heroism.[86]

During the heart of the 1945 baseball season, the Army returned Lewis to civilian life, which allowed him to rejoin the Senators for the second half of the campaign.

Certainly the most interesting case of a Major League player actively involved in the war effort was Moe Berg, a veteran of fifteen big league seasons before the outbreak of hostilities. Though not technically a member of the American armed forces, Berg's story belongs in this chapter because of his pivotal and unusual role in providing the Office of Strategic Services (OSS) with intelligence that was utilized by the American military. From his youth, Berg displayed an amazing intellectual prowess, eventually gaining admission to Princeton University. While there, Berg displayed an affinity for languages, studying seven while attending the Ivy League school, including Sanskrit. Berg also competed quite successfully for the school's baseball team, leading the squad to an eighteen-game winning streak his senior season. Following graduation, the intellectually gifted Berg surprised many, including his parents, by choosing professional baseball as a vocation, signing with the Brooklyn Robins (later Dodgers) in 1923.

Berg thereafter enjoyed an eclectic Major League career, first as infielder then as a catcher, but never playing more than 101 games in any season. Although he never compiled gaudy statistics for any of his five Major League clubs—Berg averaged just .243 and hit a total of only six home runs during his professional career—he was such a positive influence in the clubhouse that he was able to extend his big league career to fifteen years. At the end of each season, the Ivy League graduate also avidly pursued his educational pursuits, obtaining a law degree from Columbia University and even spending a semester at the Sorbonne in Paris in the off-season.

Aware of his keen intellect and mastery of the Japanese language, American intelligence officers recruited Berg to collect information during a 1934 all-star tour of Japan by a team of talented Major League players. The cerebral catcher, who was rarely even a starter in his big league career let alone an All-Star, seemed out of place on a squad that included Lou Gehrig, Babe Ruth, and Jimmie Foxx. But Berg's real purpose in joining the squad was not to display his diamond talents, but to film vital factories, shipyards, and military installations under the ruse of an itinerant tourist supposedly visiting and filming notable tourist locations. The baseball-playing spy made certain that important military sites were often in the background of his home movies so officials in Washington could analyze potential future targets. Since the Japanese government prohibited the filming of strategic locations, Berg's mission was very dangerous and almost certainly would have resulted in his execution if Japanese authorities had discovered his real purpose. Luckily for Berg and American officials, the novice reconnaissance agent left Japan without being found out and rejoined his Major League teammates.

Shortly after Pearl Harbor, with Berg's Major League career recently concluded, he offered his services to the OSS. One of his most important assignments involved Werner Heisenberg, Germany's leading physicist during the war. The OSS ordered Berg to pose as a Swiss physics student and establish a relationship with Heisenberg while the latter was delivering a lecture in Switzerland in order to ascertain the extent of the German atomic program. If he learned that the Germans had progressed to the point where an atomic bomb seemed imminent, Berg was to kill Heisenberg before he could return home. Because of Berg's unaccented fluency in German, Heisenberg never suspected Berg to be an American agent and spoke openly about German nuclear scientists' inability to match the pace of their Allied counterparts. Recognizing the threat as negligible, Berg allowed Heisenberg to live and relayed his findings to Washington. Berg accepted several other assignments from the OSS during World War II before continuing his mysterious and eventful life back in the United States.[87]

Aside from those Major League players who endured combat or were otherwise exposed to dangerous situations, a smaller number were actually wounded during hostilities. St. Louis Cardinals outfielder Harry Walker, for example, received a Purple Heart for injuries received while engaging the enemy. Walker, an All-Star before he joined the Army after the 1943 season, was initially assigned to Fort Riley (Kansas) before crossing the Atlantic as part of General Patton's Third Army. Much of Walker's military stint was spent, not in combat, but managing an Army team that contained several other Major League players. Walker admitted that, though a private, he "got a lot of things done" for his team because of his status as a Major League player, including securing a B-25 as a mode of travel for his squad. Walker's talented team even reached the finals of the 1945 ETO championship in Nuremberg before losing the final game.

However, Walker also participated in a significant number of engagements with the enemy. He earned a Purple Heart, for example, when a shell fragment lodged in his hip during one engagement, and he claimed the Bronze Star by killing or capturing nearly thirty German soldiers on consecutive days in Germany. By his own admission, Walker shot approximately fifteen Germans and captured dozens more through the end of the war. Following v-e Day, Walker enjoyed several months in German territory competing in games and hosting baseball clinics for local youths until his discharge late in 1945.[88]

Another exceptional Major League player who received injuries during combat was Cecil Travis, a potential Hall of Fame third baseman for the Washington Senators. Travis joined the Army after completing a stellar 1941 season for the Solons during which he led the American League with 218 hits and torched pitchers at nearly a .360 clip. Travis fulfilled the first several years of his military service by competing on several domestic military teams in Wisconsin and Georgia, but in December 1944 he traveled overseas and participated in the Battle of the Bulge. For several days during the intense fighting, amid bitterly cold temperatures and overcast skies that kept Allied air forces grounded, Travis stayed in a foxhole to protect himself from enemy fire. The frigid weather, however, took its toll on the former Senator star, and his feet succumbed to severe frostbite. Doctors worked diligently to avoid amputation and accomplished that goal, but by the time he returned to the Major Leagues Travis's mobility was substantially curtailed. With his age—thirty-two—also a factor, Travis never regained his prewar form and retired because of his ineffectiveness.[89]

Certainly the individual who received the most publicity for a combat-related injury during the war was Bert Shepard, a career minor league pitcher before being joining the Army Air Force. Shepard's plane, participating in the first daytime raids over Berlin, was downed by German guns in the spring of 1943. Scheduled for a sortie later than day, Shepard had instead volunteered for a morning mission because he hoped to return to base in time to join his military baseball team for practice. An enemy antiaircraft shell disrupted his plans, however, by exploding into the cockpit of his P-38 and nearly dismembering the lower portion of his right leg. After crashing to the ground, Shepard remained alive, though just barely, when local German residents rushed to take their frustrations out on the downed American pilot. A benevolent doctor protected Shepard from the angry mob and eventually secured him adequate medical care. Shepard's right leg could not be saved, however, and doctors amputated it below the knee, apparently ending Shepard's career in professional baseball.

After being housed at a German POW camp, Shepard quickly adapted to his circumstances by fashioning a crude lower limb out of materials at hand. Shepard was then fortunate enough to be included in an Allied-German prisoner exchange, and he returned to the United States, still with a glimmer of hope that he might pitch again. The Washington Senators signed Shepard as a pitching coach early in 1945, and he impressed the remainder of the staff with his batting-practice performances. The manager of the Senators, Ossie Bluege, finally inserted Shepard into an exhibition game against the Norfolk Naval Training Station and later in a regular-season contest against the Boston Red Sox, during which he pitched extraordinarily well. Against Boston, Shepard's only regular-season appearance, the one-legged pitcher gave up only three hits and one run in five innings. Later that season, Gen. Omar Bradley personally presented Shepard with the Distinguished Flying Cross and Air Medal for his courage in the face of adversity. Shepard never again pitched in the Major Leagues, but spent four more seasons toiling in the minor leagues before retiring to enjoy other pursuits.[90]

Other lesser-known Major Leaguers also suffered injuries while serving their country, though very few were debilitating. Cleveland Indians pitcher Lou Brissie, although not a big leaguer until 1947, probably suffered the most severe wounds, surviving and eventually recovering from the effects of an enemy attack that broke both feet, shattered one of his legs, and damaged both hands and shoulders.[91] Likewise, enemy shrapnel injured American League pitcher Bob Savage three times in southern Europe, though none of his wounds were particularly grave.[92] Brooklyn Dodger outfielder Dick Whitman also received injuries in Europe, suffering frostbite and shrapnel wounds, but he recovered fully and returned to complete a six-year big league career.[93]

Although no Major League players active at the outbreak of World War II died during the hostilities, two individuals who enjoyed brief appearances in the American League—Harry O'Neill and Elmer Gedeon—perished in combat. O'Neill qualifies as a Major Leaguer only technically since he appeared in just one game without an at bat for the Philadelphia Athletics in 1939 before spending the next few seasons in the minor leagues. During the war, O'Neill joined the Marine Corps and met his untimely fate in March 1945 on Iwo Jima.[94]

Similarly, Elmer Gedeon, a University of Michigan track star and son of Major League second baseman Joe Gedeon, died in combat over France shortly before the D-Day invasion. An outfielder in the Senators' organization, Gedeon enjoyed a "cup of coffee" in the Major Leagues during the summer of 1939 when he played in five games for the club. After spending the 1940 campaign in the minors, Gedeon joined the Army Air Force before the 1941 season began and eventually trained to become a pilot. While preparing for his military duties the former outfielder was involved in a heroic effort to rescue a fellow airman from a burning plane. Gedeon and seven others were aboard a bomber attempting a takeoff in North Carolina when it crashed in flames. Two of the crew died and another surely would have if not for Gedeon, who re-entered the burning plane to pull out a fellow airman immobilized by a broken leg and back. The former Senator suffered severe burns on his back, hands, right leg, and cheek along with three broken ribs during the rescue. Following a recuperation of several months, Gedeon returned to action, but not before receiving the Soldier's Medal for his bravery and a citation, which read in part: "After extricating himself, Lieut. Gedeon, regardless of the fact that he had suffered broken ribs and severe shock, re-entered the burning wreckage and removed Corp. John R. Barrat, a fellow crew member, who had been rendered helpless, due to having received a broken back and broken leg in the crash. Corp. Barrat would have been burned to death had it not been for the unselfish actions of Lieut. Gedeon . . . [which] reflects great credit upon himself and the military service."[95]

With his recovery complete, Gedeon eventually garnered an assignment in England, which consisted of bombing raids over enemy-held France to soften the German defenses before the massive D-Day invasion. On Gedeon's thirteenth mission, German antiaircraft fire struck his plane, sending him and all but one of the crew to a fiery death, ending the promising baseball career of a heroic young man.[96]

By the end of World War II the vast majority of professional baseball players had served their nation in the armed forces. No Major

Leaguers who were playing when America entered the war died in combat, but as we have seen a number received either battle injuries or endured extended combat assignments. For most players, however, their status as national icons earned them a fairly easy military life playing exhibition games and competing on service teams. Military leaders were seemingly reluctant to place many of America's most prominent sports heroes in perilous situations. Instead, Major League players aided the war effort to the best of their ability and followed orders over which they had little control.

Chapter 6 **What Might Have Been**

The Impact of World War II on the
Careers of Major Leaguers

In December 1941, the outbreak of World War II wrought drastic changes in nearly all sectors of American society as the nation mobilized toward global conflict. This was particularly true in the realm of Major League Baseball, where over 90 percent of all players active in 1941 eventually served. The majority of Major Leaguers in the American military lost between one and four years of their baseball careers, an interruption that often proved devastating for their abilities to perform on the diamond. Although a small number of players endured debilitating injuries or illnesses, the primary impact of the war on players was simply the abbreviation and curtailment of their careers. For most occupations, a hiatus of a few years is relatively insignificant. However, the brevity of the period during which the typical professional ball player's skills are at their physical and mental peak magnifies any career interruption. Inevitably, the years the war era's players missed because of the conflict have led to unending speculation about what "might have been" on the diamond if historical fate had not intervened.

Although a comprehensive anecdotal and statistical account of war-era players' performances after they returned home would be quite lengthy, a review of some of the most dominant offensive players' numbers is illustrative. Although it is impossible to precisely project career statistics for players who spent substantial time in the armed forces, one can reach general conclusions by analyzing trends in players' performances before the outbreak of World War II. Joe DiMaggio and

Hank Greenberg, for example, both probably would have exceeded five hundred home runs and two thousand RBIs if not for their time in the military. DiMaggio's situation is quite fascinating primarily because there was such a disparity between his pre- and postwar offensive numbers. In his seven seasons before his induction, for example, DiMaggio never accumulated less than 114 RBIs in any single campaign and regularly had a slugging percentage over .600. Following his return, the Yankee center fielder drove in more than one hundred runs only twice in the six seasons before his retirement and never again slugged over .600. Also, whereas virtually every one of his prewar seasons were truly exceptional, only DiMaggio's 1948 year can be compared favorably to any his seasons before his 1942 departure for military service.

Despite this relative decline after his military service, most students of the game nevertheless recognize Joe DiMaggio as one of the greatest players in history. In contrast, DiMaggio's contemporary and annual rival for batting superiority in the American League, Hank Greenberg has traditionally been denied such accolades. This is partially attributable to the fact that he played in relative obscurity in Detroit rather than enjoying the spotlight and media attention of DiMaggio's New York. In addition, Greenberg was also the first true Jewish baseball star at a time when anti-Semitism was not unfashionable, especially in Detroit where Henry Ford and Father Coughlin set the tone for such ugly sentiment. Although Greenberg was never one to complain about mistreatment, others noted that he endured merciless harassment from opposing players and fans throughout his career. This included intentional attempts to injure him and verbal barbs such as, "Throw him a pork chop, he'll never hit it." Despite the physical attacks and unsavory comments, Greenberg was arguably the most dominant offensive player in the game and certainly among the five best hitters in baseball during the four years before he began his stint in the Army. The Tiger star then spent nearly five complete seasons away from the diamond at a time when his offensive numbers were at their apex. With an average no lower than .312 in the four years before his military service, Greenberg led the league in home runs twice, RBIs twice, and slugging percentage once. In those same four years, he also won the American League's Most Valuable Player award once and finished third on two other occasions despite almost certainly being hindered by the anti-Semitism of a number of the writers who voted on the award. Once Greenberg returned from his nearly five-year absence, he did enjoy brief periods of stellar play, but he never fully regained his prewar brilliance and was out of professional baseball by 1947.[1]

Another of the great players of the era, Stan Musial, also lost time because of his military service. Although he was absent for only one season, it was critical, since some of his total career statistics fell just short of important milestones. By missing the 1945 campaign, Musial narrowly missed the magical number of five hundred home runs—a total reached by only seventeen other individuals in the history of the game. Less obvious to the casual observer are his career hits and RBI marks, which fell just shy of noteworthy plateaus. If Musial had not been absent in 1945, he almost certainly would have been the second player ever after Babe Ruth to pass two thousand career RBIs.[2] Regarding his career hit total, although he still ranks fourth all-time today, at the time of his retirement the only player with more safeties in baseball history was Ty Cobb. Assuming a typical Musical season in his service year, 1945, Musial would have been within about 350 hits of the great Tigers' outfielder. In such a circumstance, it is not inconceivable that Musial would have attempted to prolong his career an extra couple of seasons to chase Cobb's otherwise "unattainable" record.

Of all the elite players of the World War II era, it was Ted Williams was arguably the most affected by his military service. With nearly five years from the heart of his baseball career sacrificed to the military— three of them in World War II—Williams narrowly missed shattering some of baseball's most hallowed records. Although Williams displayed his usual brilliance at the plate after returning from his three-year absence during World War II, he had seemed poised to reach even greater heights. When Williams began his military obligation before the 1943 season, he was coming off his career's two finest back-to-back seasons, 1941 and 1942, during which he hit .406 (1941) and led the league in home runs, batting average, and RBIs (1942). The Triple Crown in 1942 was not his last—he won another in 1947—yet Williams never exhibited quite the offensive skill in consecutive seasons as he did those two prewar years. Reaching the prime of his career as he was at that time, it is impossible to determine exactly how impressive his career statistics might have been without the three-year interruption. However, the Red Sox slugger almost certainly would have approached, if not exceeded, Babe Ruth's career home run record of 714—the record at the time Williams retired. With less than five hundred RBIs separating Williams from the most prolific run producer in history, Hank Aaron, the Red Sox star also would probably still hold the career for record runs batted in had he played during World War II and the Korean War.

Although the war impacted many of the premier players of the 1940s, military absences arguably affected even more the careers of players who fell just short of this elite status. Whereas virtually all of the great players of the World War II era, such as Greenberg, DiMaggio, and Williams, have been enshrined in the baseball Hall of Fame, several talented professionals fell failed to reach Cooperstown quite possibly because they sacrificed their prime years to the war effort. Probably the most glaring example of this is Yankees and Indians second baseman Joe Gordon, a nine-time All-Star who played in the postseason six times during his stellar career. Gordon's statistics compare favorably to fellow second baseman and Hall of Famer Bobby Doerr, who was a close contemporary and also World War II veteran. Doerr has the slight edge over Gordon in career RBIs, although the two campaigns Gordon lost versus Doerr's one would account for most of that disparity. Doerr also holds a twenty-point advantage in career batting average, although this might be somewhat deceiving. Doerr played his entire career in Fenway Park, notorious for its cozy left-field dimensions, while Gordon played during his prime in the more spacious Yankee Stadium. This almost certainly kept his batting average lower than it could otherwise have been. Despite the deeper outfield dimensions of Yankee Stadium, however, Gordon struck thirty more home runs than did Doerr. Doerr does hold a minimal edge in career fielding percentage; however, Gordon was by no means a defensive liability with a .970 career fielding average. Gordon also had greater range than most, if not all, of his contemporaries at second base—including Doerr—as indicated by the fact that the Yankee star led the American League in assists four separate years. The one area where Gordon has a tremendous advantage is in the six championship teams of which he was a major contributor. Gordon was a catalyst for the great Yankee teams of the late 1930s and 1940s and also won a World Series title late in his career with the Cleveland Indians. In contrast,

Doerr played in only the 1946 World Series with Boston and, although he hit a sparkling .409 during the seven game set, he never again returned to play in the postseason.

Comparing Gordon to another Hall of Fame second baseman, Tony Lazzeri, whom Gordon replaced in the Yankees lineup in 1938, makes possible an even stronger case for including Gordon among the game's immortals. An analysis of both players' career statistics shows that Gordon leads or has nearly identical numbers in almost every category. The only two notable exceptions are Lazzeri's advantages in career batting average and RBIs, twenty-four points and 216, respectively. Again, the disparity in RBIs can be attributed to Gordon's two-year hiatus for military service, while the difference in batting average can be partly offset by Gordon's superior power numbers—Gordon's 253 home runs compared to Lazzeri's 178. In balancing team championships, Lazzeri's impressive five World Series titles are still one less than the six won by Gordon. Furthermore, when applying the comprehensive statistic known as "Total Player Rating" (TPR), developed by the editors of *Total Baseball* to determine a player's overall performance, Gordon has a substantial career edge over Lazzeri of 28.2 to 16.9, respectively.[3]

Aside from the overlooked Joe Gordon, many other lesser-known position players also had their potentially exceptional careers interrupted or ended by the outbreak of hostilities. Most of these individuals not only had years of their careers stripped away, but the hiatus also inflicted irreparable harm to their baseball abilities, often causing a premature close to their chosen vocation. Philadelphia Athletics second baseman Benny McCoy, for example, enjoyed a promising three-year career before the war and his skills, which included exceptional speed and occasional power, seemed to destine him for stardom. McCoy, however, was one of the first Major League players to enter the military, and he never again played in the big leagues after the war. First baseman Buddy Hassett, a solid player for three teams, also saw his big league career come to a screeching halt with the outbreak of World War II. A .292 career hitter, Hassett's career spanned the seven years leading up to the war and ended when he entered the armed forces.

Unlike McCoy and Hassett, Washington Senator shortstop Cecil Travis did return to the Major Leagues after his military stint but without much success. Travis had been an exceptional hitter in the eight years before he entered the Army, batting lower than .300 only once with occasional home run power and a low strikeout ratio. He was also a three-time All-Star participant and led the American League with 218 hits during the 1941 season, his last before joining the Army. The Senator's star, however, suffered severe frostbite to his lower extremities during the Battle of the Bulge, and he never regained the mobility needed to perform at the Major League level. Upon his return, the Senators moved Travis to third base to accommodate his limited range hoping that he might regain his potent prewar batting stroke. Travis spent a dismal three years after the war battling American League pitching and managed to hit only .252 in his best postwar season. By 1947 he had retired from baseball, and a promising career had been derailed for reasons beyond his control.

One of Travis's teammates, outfielder Buddy Lewis, was another of the lesser-known players affected by their military commitment. In the six years before Lewis entered the Army Air Force, he never hit below .291 and three times batted over .300. While exhibiting occasional power and an ability to steal bases, the Senators' outfielder represented the Solons in the 1938 All-Star game and also led the league in triples in 1939. Upon his return to the Major Leagues following a three-year absence, Lewis never again hit .300 and, though he did represent the Senators in the 1947 All-Star game, his statistics that year did not compare favorably to any of his prewar campaigns.

From an individual perspective, therefore, it is abundantly clear that the war affected many professional players to greater or lesser extents. However, the question then arises whether the interruptions in players' careers, when viewed collectively, caused substantial declines in their abilities and statistics or if the trials and tribulations of a few have skewed history's perception of all the athletes who served in the armed forces. Analyzing the most important offensive statistical data on the players who served seems to confirm that the extended absences led to an overall deterioration of batting skill. Comparing solely the mean batting average before the war of players who served with that statistic after they returned shows that some factor clearly diminished the abilities of those athletes.[4] A dip in batting average of nearly ten points (.263 down from .272 in 1941) during these players' first full postwar season (1946) is clear evidence that Major Leaguers who sacrificed up to four years of their careers experienced a dramatic offensive decline. The impact of this statistic is blunted somewhat by the fact that, as a whole, big league averages declined approximately seven points between those two seasons.

However, an examination of other vital offensive numbers solidifies the assertion that position players were less effective hitters after the war than before. Players who served hit fewer home runs (6.52 in 1946 versus 7.88 in 1941) and drove in fewer runs (44.53 versus 54.65) in their first full season back in the big leagues. Again, this is somewhat offset by the fact that the number of home runs and runs scored across the big leagues declined in 1946 compared to 1941, albeit to a lesser extent than for the players who served.

Nonetheless, a less subjective demonstration of veterans' offensive decline can be gained by comparing their pre- and postwar TPR numbers. In 1941, players who would soon join the American armed forces collectively compiled a very impressive TPR, but following their return home it slipped noticeably (.528 to .255), though it remained respectable. Such a decline might seem insignificant if were not for the fact that the returning players were, on average, at an age when they should have been reaching their athletic peak. Historically, hitters tend to reach their optimum performance around thirty and begin declining thereafter. Players who served left for the war when they were on average twenty-six and returned when they were nearly thirty, yet their postwar performance did not reflect their "peaking" age range. To provide some perspective, at the same approximate ages of twenty-six and thirty (corresponding with the 1939 and 1943 seasons), position players who did not serve during World War II dramatically improved their TPRs, from .176 to .706. Thus, it seems clear that the TPRs of players who served declined when it should have been improving, supporting the conclusion that the overall degradation of batting skill was not simply an illusion skewed by the subpar performances of a few.

The most obvious explanation for this falloff is that Major League hitters succeed in part because of their quick reaction times to pitches, which are measured in mere fractions of a second. Any dulling of these reflexes, however minimal, through inactivity could have substantially impacted these hitters' ability to hit big league pitching as successfully as they might have had their careers not been interrupted. Though it is true that many Major League players competed extensively on military teams during their tenure in the armed forces, the level of competition was often below what they had faced as professionals. Competing against lower-caliber pitching over several years could have ever so slightly eroded their coordination and reflexes, and quite possibly explaining their postwar offensive decline.

As with position players, World War II also adversely affected the careers of hundreds of Major League hurlers, Hall of Famers, successful veterans, and sporadic journeymen alike. One of the pitchers impacted most by his wartime absence was Bob Feller, who lost virtually all four seasons to his service with the navy. An especially precocious talent before the war who was signed by the Cleveland Indians while still in high school, Feller accomplished more before reaching full maturity than any Major Leaguer before or since. Feller first threw a pitch for the Indians at age seventeen, was a regular performer by eighteen, and had become an All-Star by nineteen when he led the American League in strikeouts. The Hall of Famer also accumulated 107 victories by the age twenty-two—still a record for his age—and seemed poised to shatter many existing pitching standards before his military induction in December 1941.

By his own calculations, Feller's forty-four months of service deprived him of at least one hundred victories and "other pitching records which would have stood for decades."[5] An examination of Feller's statistics reinforces many of his claims, especially since the startling and accelerating quality of his three prewar campaigns suggests that his peak years might well occurred during the period claimed by the war. During his last season before entering the Navy (1941) and his first full season back from the war (1946), Feller averaged nearly twenty-five wins and led the league in strikeouts, including a remarkable 348 KS in 1946. Furthermore, Feller compiled his best statistical season *after* the war, when in 1946 he amassed a 2.18 ERA and spun ten shutouts despite his absence from baseball for virtually all of four years.

Given the decline in effectiveness other returning veterans endured, Feller's magical 1946 season seems somewhat surprising, especially since one would have expected his skills to have eroded given how little he played during the war. A Major Leaguer who also served during World War II, St. Louis Cardinal star Walker Cooper, even noted in 1945 while Feller was pitching for Great Lakes Naval Training Station that he was not the same pitcher as before the war. Although Cooper predicted Feller would remain successful after returning to the Indians, and possibly even eclipse some of his previous achievements, he observed that "some of the hop seem[ed] to be missing from that terrific fastball [Feller] used to have."[6] Feller himself, without admitting to a decline in his physical abilities, did acknowledge that when he returned to the Indians he had to readjust "his mental attitude" towards baseball since the gravity of the war made it difficult for him to view the game as seriously at first.[7] These anecdotal revelations make Feller's 1946 campaign all the more remarkable.

With dominant seasons, 1941 and 1946, bookending Feller's military service, one can only speculate on the Hall of Famer's potential statistics if he had not missed the war years. Using even a conservative estimate, Feller almost certainly would have reached the magical 300-victory plateau and quite possibly could have vaulted into the top five all-time for career wins. Feller also would have added substantially to his already impressive strikeout total, finishing his career with approximately 3,800 instead of his actual total of 2,581. Such a figure would have made Feller the leader in career strikeouts until the latter part of the careers of Steve Carlton and Nolan Ryan in the late 1970s and early eighties.

Aside from Feller, another Hall of Famer who endured a considerable disruption in his career was Boston (and later Milwaukee) Brave Warren Spahn, the winningest left-hander in Major League history. Spahn enjoyed a brief four-game stint in the big leagues in 1942 before joining the Army and action in the European theater. Projecting Spahn's lifetime statistics is more difficult because his career interruption came early on, before he had established himself as a legitimate mound presence. However, it is very likely that Spahn's military service stunted his progress, if only slightly, and led to a belated beginning to his stellar career. In 1946, still considered Spahn's rookie year and his first since returning to civilian life, he compiled a tidy 2.94 ERA in twenty-four games. He then began a stretch of seventeen remarkable years during which he won twenty games thirteen times and participated in All-Star festivities on fourteen occasions.

Even if one speculates that only two of Spahn's three missed years would have been anywhere near his postwar campaigns, the Braves star would have exceeded four hundred wins—a number that still would be a National League record and eclipsed in the American League only by Walter Johnson and Cy Young. Furthermore, Johnson's career total of 417 victories would have, in all probability, been within Spahn's reach, making him the winningest pitcher in the modern era. Also, just sixteen more shutouts, an easily reachable figure for Spahn considering that he led the league in that category four times, would have placed him in a tie for third in that category behind only Walter Johnson and Grover Cleveland Alexander. Although never a dominant power pitcher in the vein of Bob Feller, Spahn did top the National League in strikeouts for four consecutive years beginning in 1949. Without his absence during the war he probably would have placed second on the career strikeout list at the time of his retirement.

Two other Hall of Fame performers who had their careers curtailed, Red Ruffing and Ted Lyons, were affected in similar ways by their wartime absence. Ruffing, a stalwart for the great New York Yankee squads of the late 1930s, enlisted in the Coast Guard after a 1942 season in which he participated in his sixth and final All-Star contest and registered the only win for the Yankees in that year's World Series. Therefore, despite his relatively advanced age—Ruffing turned thirty-nine in May 1943—he was by no means an aging star hanging on by reputation alone. With fourteen wins in his final season before entering the service, Ruffing was poised to complete his career in style before World War II claimed two potentially productive years. Ruffing still displayed excellent mound skills upon his return, tallying a 2.89 ERA and 1.77 ERA in 1945 and 1946, respectively. In all likelihood, however, the war thwarted Ruffing's bid for 300 wins, which, had he reached that milestone, might have encouraged voters to select him for Hall of Fame induction sooner than two decades after his last pitch.

An even more interesting case involves Chicago White Sox Hall of Famer Ted Lyons, who enlisted with the Marine Corps at age forty-one after completing his twentieth Major League season. Like Ruffing, Lyons was not an aging veteran refusing to accept retirement and struggling to recapture past glories. Lyons, in fact, led the American League with a minuscule 2.10 ERA in 1942, his last season before joining the war effort, and completed all twenty of his starts for a White Sox team that finished sixteen games under .500 that year. Furthermore, according to *Total Baseball*'s statistic total pitcher index (TPI), which determines the ultimate value of a pitcher to his team, Lyons was the most productive pitcher in the league in 1942.[8] After his extended military career, spent primarily in the Pacific theater, Lyons returned for an encore season in 1946 at the age of forty-five. In limited appearances he compiled a 2.32 ERA, a very impressive number at any age.

As with Ruffing, Lyons fell just shy of 300 wins, amassing 260 victories for a team that was extremely inept for most of Lyons's twenty-one-year career. During the heart of his career Lyons adjusted his pitching style to adapt to a natural decline in velocity and had become a master of deception and location by the mid 1930s. White Sox management also lengthened his career by limiting his appearances, never allowing him to pitch more than thirty games in any one season from 1934 on. Instead, White Sox officials utilized Lyons, the most popular player on the team at that time, as a "Sunday pitcher" to attract fans on the days when crowds tended to be large.[9] Thus, with his variety of pitches and adequate rest granted him by management, Lyons continued to baffle hitters into his thirties and beyond. Thus, without his three-year hiatus it is not unlikely that Lyons would have exceeded 300 victories and might possibly now be among the more recognizable figures in baseball history.

Another intriguing case of a player who had his career abbreviated by World War II was Larry French, a talented left-handed pitcher for three teams during his fourteen years in the National League. Arguably the best pitcher not in the Hall of Fame, French skills seemed to be peaking just as the war erupted. In his last year with the Brooklyn Dodgers, French won nearly 80 percent of his decisions and compiled a remarkable 1.83 ERA. French even ended his career with the best final performance ever for a Major League pitcher—a one-hitter in his last start. Following this triumphant conclusion, French enlisted in the Navy and apparently found the military lifestyle more desirable than being a Dodger. After the war's end, French never did return to baseball and remained a sailor for another twenty-five years, retiring in 1969 with the rank of captain.

Although French played the first six years of his career with a Pirates team that never advanced to the World Series, he nevertheless won 197 games before his change of vocation. If World War II had not interrupted French's Major League tenure, he would have assuredly surpassed 200 victories and most likely by a substantial margin. Though he never won twenty games in a season, with 200 plus wins the left-hander certainly would have at least garnered greater consideration for Hall of Fame honors than he did. To place French's accomplishments in some perspective, at age thirty-four, his final season, he had a virtually the same number of wins as Don Sutton, a recent inductee into Cooperstown who surpassed the 300-victory barrier late in his career. A comparison with one of French's contemporaries, "Lefty" Gomez of the New York Yankees, provides more conclusive evidence that French should merit at least some serious consideration for the Hall of Fame. Gomez, a 1972 inductee, had a vastly superior career winning percentage—.649 to French's .535—but this was largely the result of Gomez's good fortune in pitching for the dominant Yankee teams of the 1930s and early 1940s. Gomez benefited from the support of such offensive stars as Babe Ruth, Lou Gehrig, and Joe DiMaggio during an era when the Yankees fielded some of the most talented teams in baseball history and secured an unprecedented number of pennants and world championships. French, however, actually claimed eight more career victories than Gomez, and both compiled very similar career ERAs. Comparing their composite TPIs, both pitchers again amassed virtually identical statistics, indicating that they performed about the same relative to their league contemporaries over their Major League careers. Strengthening the argument in favor of French is that he left the game just as his talent was beginning to blossom. The left-hander would most likely have continued to perform well for at least another five years after his departure, thus solidifying his claim for enshrinement in Cooperstown.

Other Major League pitchers who compiled statistics a rung below French's also deserve mention for the adverse affect military service had on their careers. Detroit Tiger teammates Virgil "Fire" Trucks and Tommy Bridges both missed most of two potentially productive years to the war. By the time of Trucks's departure following the 1943 season, he had established himself as an extremely effective starter and reliever, winning fourteen and sixteen games during his first two campaigns. He also amassed ERAs of 2.74 and 2.84 during that time and was positioned to become one of the top pitchers in the American League. As with most of his contemporaries, however, Trucks eventually departed for military service, interrupting a promising career.

The absence itself apparently impacted Trucks's skills only slightly, if at all, for he returned almost immediately to his prewar form and pitched admirably well into the 1950s. Trucks returned so successfully most likely because he competed extensively for the Great Lakes Naval Training Station squad and was therefore able to maintain his skills. The war did have a detrimental impact, however, in that Trucks did not quite reach two hundred career victories, a figure he almost certainly would have surpassed without his stint in the Navy. Trucks could have also easily attained a career TPI of over 20.0, which would have placed him ahead of such Hall of Fame pitchers as Jim Bunning, "Chief" Bender, "Catfish" Hunter, Don Sutton, and Herb Pennock, among others, whose careers were not interrupted by military service.

Trucks's former teammate, Tommy Bridges, compiled similar numbers during his sixteen-year span with the Tigers, though his case for the Hall of Fame may arguably be even stronger. Bridges was a six-time All-Star who twice led the American League in strikeouts and once in shutouts. In his last season before his military sabbatical, Bridges crafted his way to a stellar 2.39 ERA and twelve victories. Following his return late in 1945, Bridges accomplished little else professionally, retiring shortly after a disappointing 1946 season. With his two missed seasons added to his composite statistics, however, Bridges would have easily eclipsed two hundred career wins and certainly would have added to his impressive 28.7 TPI rating—a figure higher than many other pitchers enshrined at Cooperstown.

Another solid performer who had precious years of his career stripped away by military service was diminutive right-hander Murry Dickson, known primarily for his performances with the St. Louis Cardinals during the 1940s. Dickson's military absence was book-ended by exceptional campaigns during the 1943 and 1946 seasons during which he tormented National League batters for a combined ERA of around 3.00 and even led the league in winning percentage in 1946. Dickson's service with the Army thus cost him two years of his prime and certainly prevented him from having the opportunity to exceed two hundred wins.

Achieving that milestone might have even initiated some interest in electing the left-hander to the Hall of Fame. Assuming that his two missed seasons were similar to his other performances at that point in his career, Dickson assuredly would have also exceeded the 20.0 TPI barrier for his career. As with Bridges, that figure would have placed Dickson ahead of several pitchers now enshrined in the Hall of Fame. One drawback to Dickson's legitimacy as a candidate for Cooperstown (admittedly an insurmountable one in the eyes of Hall of Fame voters) was his career losing record: 172 wins against 181 defeats. Dickson was unfortunate enough to toil for some of the worst teams in National League history while with the Pittsburgh Pirates following a very successful tenure with the Cardinals. Dickson finished his Cardinal career with a record well over .500 and therefore was certainly not incapable of winning on a regular basis. The Pirates, however, were so bad during Dickson's interlude with them that they finished last or near last every year from 1949 to 1953—the seasons coinciding with Dickson's Pittsburgh career. One of Dickson's most impressive achievements in baseball occurred during the 1951 season when he notched twenty wins for a team that lost 90 games. The following year's squad was even more horrid, losing 112 games in a 154-game schedule, in which Dickson collected exactly one-third of their victories. Dickson's talent and performance should not be overlooked just because he had the misfortune to play for such an inept organization and his military service deprived him of several important statistical benchmarks.

Several other lesser-known hurlers garnered distinction before the war but were unable to successfully continue their careers after their returns. In 1942, for example, New York Giant Bob Carpenter had just completed his second consecutive eleven-win season and was on the cusp of a productive career. World War II, however, robbed him of three years, and upon his return to the National League Carpenter enjoyed only one additional win in two miserable seasons before closing out his big league tenure. Likewise, in 1942 Red Sox southpaw Bill Butland baffled American League hitters with a 2.51 ERA and two shutouts in only ten starts and nearly fifteen relief appearances. As with Carpenter, Butland won only one game after his military stint and was out of the major leagues by 1947.

Another interesting case involved Chicago Cubs right-hander Hi Bithorn, who pitched in the big leagues for only two years before his induction. Bithorn's last season before entering the armed forces was his most impressive—eighteen victories and a National League best seven shutouts in 1943. Upon his induction, Bithorn added nearly forty pounds to his 6'1" frame, lost some of his velocity, and never exhibited the same skill after the war that had led to his magnificent early success. Although he returned from the military for one full season and part of another for the Cubs and White Sox, Bithorn was out of baseball by 1947.

Thus, as with position players, military absences clearly negatively impacted several pitchers' careers, either by diminishing career statistics or stunting their professional development. And as with Major League hitters, the question then arises whether military service imparted a significant impact on all or only a few big league pitchers and, if so, to what extent. A general review of the major statistical categories for war-era pitchers reveals a trend similar to that found among position players, although the negative impact of military service does not seem to have been as severe for big league hurlers. For example, Major League pitchers who spent time in the armed forces averaged about one less win in the 1946 season (7.13) than they had achieved on average in the 1941 campaign (6.05). This is not completely surprising given that pitchers who served appeared in slightly fewer games on average in 1946 than they had in 1941.

Likewise, the number of strikeouts and walks returning pitchers allowed declined roughly in accordance with the decreased number of innings they pitched in 1946 relative to 1941. Pitchers who served averaged 51.42 strikeouts in 1941 versus 48.43 in 1946, and their average walks dropped from 51.10 in 1941 to 42.22 in 1946. Investigating further, the earned run averages of pitchers who served remained virtually unchanged in 1946 (3.92) when compared to the 1941 campaign (3.98). This is somewhat deceiving, however, since the volume of runs scored in the first postwar season dropped significantly, and overall ERAs in both leagues dropped by nearly half a run per game. Analyzing the TPIs of the pitchers who served indicates that a decline in effectiveness does seem to have characterized pitchers who returned from service: the TPIs of pitchers who served fell from .351 in 1941 to .170 in 1946. When these numbers are compared to the TPIs of pitchers of similar age who did not serve, the decline among those who served is a bit more revealing.

Pitchers historically have reached their athletic peaks a few years later than position players, usually around the age of thirty-two or thirty-three. Those who served reached this approximate age in 1946, while those who did not serve were roughly thirty-two in 1941. To provide a basis of comparison, the pitchers who did not serve were approximately twenty-eight in 1937 while those who served were a similar age in 1941. The group who did not serve enjoyed a noticeable improvement in pitching ability between 1937 and 1941. Their TPIs actually increased from .463 to .584 in these years, whereas, as we saw, the big league pitchers who served suffered a startling decline of over 50 percent in their TPI numbers. Thus, it seems apparent that military service did impart a substantial negative impact on big league pitchers during World War II.

Nevertheless, despite the suggestiveness of these statistical analyses for both position players and pitchers the specific conclusions to be drawn can only finally be speculation. What can be surmised for certain is that World War II had a dramatic bearing on the course of Major League players' careers and that without the outbreak of the war the history of the national pastime would have unfolded in an entirely different way. Although the professional and personal sacrifices many big league players made were immense, few, if any, would argue that at a time when so much rested on Allied victory the cause was not worthy.

Conclusion

By the end of World War II, the United States had endured nearly four years of continual sacrifice and hardship to soundly defeat the Axis Powers. During those years, millions of Americans answered the call, fighting in every corner of the globe to preserve the institutions of the nation. With the armed forces swollen to an extent never seen before or since, American military officials had to adapt quickly to accommodate this mass of humanity and maximize its formidable fighting potential. An important aspect of the training and success of these servicemen was maintaining a high level of morale. On the battlefield, this was accomplished primarily through such time-tested techniques as propaganda and providing adequate clothing, food, equipment. Away from the front lines, sustaining morale became somewhat more vague and difficult to establish. During their extensive down times, men often engaged in such behavior as drinking, gambling, and soliciting prostitutes, all of which was difficult to regulate and, some felt, sowed the seeds of discontent. To redirect the energies of soldiers and sailors into more constructive activities military leaders turned above all to athletics.

Because of baseball's popularity among American fighting men, the national pastime was the logical centerpiece for the military's athletic programs. By organizing teams of servicemen, officers aimed to inspire loyalty, camaraderie, and a sense of teamwork—all characteristics of high morale. Furthermore, whenever overtraining became an issue, military commanders utilized the game to preserve soldiers' and sailors' physical fitness without subjecting them to the tedium of repeated exercises.

For these reasons, professional baseball during World War II entered into a high-profile partnership with the American military to supplement the war effort and promote the game within servicemen's ranks. Contributing money and equipment as well as sponsoring exhibition games and tours by Major League stars, professional baseball organizations contributed financially to America's military effort while simultaneously satisfying the baseball appetites of soldiers and sailors. Professional players themselves also emerged as a significant and highly visible aspect of the military war machine, and the majority competed on service teams or became symbols for their fellow Americans to follow. The absence of these players left a significant void in professional baseball for the duration of the conflict that was neither easily nor adequately filled by the athletes who replaced them. Indeed, the quality of the professional game dipped so dramatically during the war that owners often employed players deemed disabled by draft boards or those too old, too young, or too tall for military service. The situation was so dire, in fact, that the perennially incompetent St. Louis Browns won the American League pennant in 1944—the point at which the draft and enlistments had utterly depleted the rosters of big league teams. Upon their return, Major League players continued to feel the impact of their service through the decreased productivity they endured on the field. Although none had had to sacrifice his life, several players were injured in combat, and many more returned with four years of their playing prime gone and their physical skills commensurately reduced.

Although any examination of the war years clearly illustrates America's fascination with baseball, those years also marked the beginning of the end for baseball as the true national pastime. Within a decade of the war's end, football and other leisure activities had begun to erode baseball's preeminent position in American culture. However, during the months and years indelibly marked by World War II, baseball rose to the forefront to provide inspiration, financial resources, and leadership for servicemen and civilians who needed them. Could the United States have won the war without baseball? Certainly. But the national pastime was so integral to American life that, just as certainly, without baseball many soldiers, sailors, and civilians would have felt that a key part of the America they were sacrificing for had been removed and everyday existence immeasurably diminished.

Notes

INTRODUCTION

1. Richard Crepeau, *Baseball: America's Diamond Mind, 1919–1941* (Orlando: University of Florida Press, 1980), 203.

2. Benjamin Rader, *American Sports: From the Age of Folk Games to the Age of Televised Sports* (Upper Saddle River NJ: Prentice Hall, 1999), 153.

3. "It's Not the Same Game in Japan," *The Sporting News*, editorial, 18 December 1941, 4.

4. William Mead, *Baseball Goes to War: Stars Don Khaki, 4-Fs Vie for Pennant* (Washington DC: Farragut Books, 1985); Bill Gilbert, *They Also Served: Baseball and the Home Front, 1941–1945* (New York: Crown, 1992); Harrington Crissey Jr., *Teenagers, Graybeards and 4fs: Volume 1: The National League* (Philadelphia: self-published, 1982) and *Teenagers, Graybeards and 4fs: Volume 2: The American League* (Philadelphia: self-published, 1982); William Kashatus, *One Armed Wonder: Pete Gray, Wartime Baseball, and the American Dream* (Jefferson NC: MacFarland and Co., 1995); Harold Seymour, *Baseball*, 3 vols. (New York: Oxford University Press, 1960–1990); David Quentin Voigt, *American Baseball*, 3 vols. (Norman: University of Oklahoma Press and University Park PA: Penn State University Press, 1966–1983); Benjamin Rader, *Baseball: A History of America's Game* (Urbana: University of Illinois Press, 1992).

5. Robert Creamer, *Baseball in '41: A Celebration of the Best Baseball Season Ever* (New York: Viking, 1991); Frederick Turner, *When the Boys Came Back: Baseball and 1946* (New York: Henry Holt, 1996)

1. VITALIZING SPIRIT

1. Bill Underwood, "Baseball, Too, Served during World War II," *50 Plus Lifestyles*, September 1995, 3.

2. "Soldiers Are Sports Minded," *What the Soldier Thinks*, January 1944, 12. This was a quarterly report published by the Special Services. The branch of the army responsible for recreational activities and monitoring the moods, tendencies, and morale of soldiers.

3. United States Army, *Special Services Companies* (Bad Nauiheim, Germany:

General Board, 1945), 1. This was part of a larger study compiled by the U.S. Army immediately after the war to identify the successes and failures in each section of the army during the hostilities in order to improve efficiency in future conflicts. For the importance of morale to military success, see virtually any comprehensive work concerning successful military operations, including the classic by Carl von Clausewitz, *On War*, edited and translated by Michael Howard and Peter Paret (Princeton NJ: Princeton University Press, 1984), 184–86. See also Sun Tzu, *The Art of War*, trans. Ralph Sawyer (Boulder CO: Westview Press, 1994), 142–43, and Napoleon Bonaparte, *The Military Maxims of Napoleon*, trans. George C. D'Aguilar (New York: Macmillan, 1987), 74–75.

4. Although there are numerous references to morale in Patton's diary entries from World War II, one example amply shows Patton's concern with the emotional well-being of his troops in western France in the days after the D-Day invasion. In August 1944, he referred specifically to meeting with officers under his command so as to instill them with renewed energy and confidence, quoting both Gen. Ulysses S. Grant and Gen. Robert E. Lee for inspiration. Information found in George S. Patton Jr., *War As I Knew It*, annotated by Col. Paul D. Harkins (Boston: Houghton Mifflin, 1947), 134.

5. "Marine Veteran Tells about Ghost Baseball," *Stars and Stripes* (Mediterranean Edition), 11 March 1944, 10.

6. As quoted in William B. Mead, *Baseball Goes to War*, 9.

7. "Japs Needle Brooklyn Fans," *The Sporting News*, 26 October 1944, 12.

8. "Pacific Marines Plan Baseball Careers," *Marine Corps Chevron*, 10 February 1945, 8.

9. Sgt. Francis M. Barr, "Leathernecks Form 30 Teams in Three South Pacific Leagues," *The Sporting News*, 27 April 1944, 10.

10. Phil Rizzuto, completed questionnaire for author, 28 August 1998.

11. Interview with author, 9 September 1999, Omaha NE.

12. "Baseball Genuine Incentive Says Naval Training Chieftain," *The Sporting News*, 6 July 1944, 17.

13. Andrew Nelson Questionnaire, World War II surveys, Military History Institute Archives, Carlisle Barracks, Pennsylvania. Nelson revealed that, for him, the most difficult aspect of military life was leaving the familiar surroundings of home and being thrust into an alien environment.

14. Maj. Leon T. David, "Factors Indicating the Status of Morale in a Command," 20 January 1942. Major Leon T. David Papers, Military History Institute, Carlisle Barracks, Pennsylvania.

15. William Ruf, World War II surveys, Military History Institute, Carlisle Barracks, Pennsylvania.

16. Ernie Pyle, *Here Is Your War* (New York: Henry Holt, 1943), 36, 218.

17. Wanda Wakefield, *Playing to Win: Sports and the American Military, 1898–*

1945 (Albany: SUNY Press, 1997, 82. Also see Minutes of Faculty and Staff Conference, 16 April 1942. In "Faculty Minutes of Special Services Branch School March 3 to November 21, 1942," Major Leon T. David Papers.

18. "The Off-Duty Life of the Soldier," *What the Soldier Thinks*, August 1943, 65.

19. As quoted in Wakefield, *Playing to Win*, 85. For more in-depth discussion of this topic, see Geoffrey Perret, *There's a War to Be Won: The United States Army in World War II* (New York: Random House, 1991), 453–54.

20. Maj. Leon T. David, "Factors Indicating the Status of Morale in Command," 20 January 1942. In Major Leon T. David Papers.

21. For quote see "Sports Vital, Says Rickey," *The Sporting News*, 11 December 1941, 3. Also see, David, "Factors Indicating the Status of Morale in a Command," 20 January 1942.

22. Wakefield, *Playing to Win*, 87.

23. "Athletics Vital—Army Health," *The Real McCoy*, 30 October 1942, 5.

24. Capt. John Runyon Questionnaire, World War II surveys, Ninety-second Infantry Division, Military History Institute Archives, Carlisle Barracks, Pennsylvania.

25. Private Art Primer to his mother, 30 March 1944. Available at *http:// www.private-art.com/archive/1944/mar/033044.html*; Internet; accessed 9 August 2000.

26. Wakefield, *Playing to Win*, 80. David's quotation found in Minutes of Faculty and Staff Conference, "Faculty Minutes of Special Services Branch School March 3 to November 21, 1942," Major Leon T. David Papers.

27. "A Four Way Service in Wartime," *The Sporting News*, editorial, 12 November 1942, 4.

28. Quoted in Wakefield, *Playing to Win*, 61.

29. "Baseball Makes 16th Grenade Tossers Expert," *The Armodier*, 30 March 1944, 1.

30. "The Role of Teamwork in War," *The Sporting News*, editorial, 30 July 1942, 4.

31. Carl T. Felken, "Sports Skill Paying Off in the Pacific, Says Todd of Marines," *The Sporting News*, 16 November 1944, 11.

32. "A Four-Way Service in Wartime," 4.

33. Minutes of Faculty and Staff Conference. In "Faculty Minutes of Special Branch School March 3 to November 21, 1942," 16 April 1942, Major Leon T. David Papers.

34. "In the Service," *The Sporting News*, 6 August 1942, 6. "Carrying on the Best Traditions of the Marines," *The Sporting News*, 29 April 1943, 6.

35. Wakefield, *Playing to Win*, 66. For more in-depth discussion of the sometimes tenuous relationship between athletics and military training, see the file

"Conversations with Maj. General Earnest L. 'Iron Mike' Massad," 1985–1986, p. 39, Military History Institute Archives, Carlisle Barracks, Pennsylvania.

36. Eugene Woodling, interview by William Marshall, Medina OH, on 11 December 1992. Taped interview is part of A. B. Chandler Oral History Project and is available at the University of Kentucky Library, Special Collections, Lexington.

37. George Paulson, interview by author, 9 September 1999, Omaha NE.

38. Chuck Maier, interview by author, 5 September 1999, Omaha NE.

39. Richard Nowak, interview by author, 1 November 2001, Omaha NE.

40. Earl Peak Questionnaire, World War II surveys, Military History Institute Archives, Carlisle Barracks, Pennsylvania.

41. Earl Peak, "War Diary of Col. Earl W. Peak," p. 6, World War II Survey file of Earl Peak, Sixth Infantry Division, Military History Institute, Carlisle Barracks, Pennsylvania.

42. Maier, interview.

43. A copy of Roosevelt's "green light" letter is available at *The Sporting News* Archive, St. Louis MO.

44. Mead, *Baseball Goes to War*, 35–37.

45. "Take Game to Fighting Men Overseas," editorial, *The Sporting News*, 25 May 1943, 4. "Players' Task Force Faces Big Challenge," editorial, *The Sporting News*, 23 September 1943, 8.

46. "We are the People," editorial, *The Sporting News*, 23 April 1942, 4. The editors included the results from a Gallup poll conducted shortly before the publication of the April 23 issue. According to the editors, the poll showed overwhelming support by Americans for the continuation of professional baseball, at 64 percent.

47. Quoted in "Editorial Comment," *Baseball Magazine*, January 1942, 305.

48. "The Game and the Old Navy Spirit," editorial, *The Sporting News*, 2 April 1942, 4.

49. Dan Daniel, "Veterans of Front Line Have No Kicks about 4-F's," *The Sporting News*, 6 April 1944, 13. Long quotation from a Private Mansfield, quoted in "Baseball Is Morale-Builder and Source of Enjoyment," *The Sporting News*, 16 April 1942, 2.

50. See as a typical example, "Service Men Are Aching for Some News of the Game," *The Sporting News*, 5 August 1943, 10.

51. Lt. Howard Roberts, "Fans on Flattop Strike Out Japs, but Yearn for More News of Game," *The Sporting News*, 9 November 1944, 12.

52. Edgar G. Brands, "'Keep 'Em Playing,' Men in Service Chorus to Query: 'Should Game Go on During War,'" *The Sporting News*, 16 April 1942, 2.

53. "Servicemen Overseas Want Game to Go On," editorial, *The Sporting*

News, 18 January 1945, 8. "And in the United States, What?," editorial, *The Sporting News*, 3 February 1944, 8.

54. Cpl. Bill McElwais, quoted in "Another Form of Strike for Higher Pay," editorial, *The Sporting News*, 23 March 1944, 10.

55. Quoted from the *Norfolk Seabag* in "Service Men's Views," *The Sporting News*, 18 February, 1943, 6.

56. "Game Helpful, but Not Essential," editorial, *The Sporting News*, 25 November 1943, 10.

57. "'Baseball Genuine Incentive,' Says Naval Training Chieftain," *The Sporting News*, 6 July 1944, 17.

58. Tom Fergusson, "Padgett, D. DiMaggio, McCoy, Rizzuto among Players on Training Station Squad," *The Sporting News*, 22 April 1943, 13.

59. Tommy Holmes, "'*The Sporting News* Like Letter from Home to Boys Overseas,' Says Rickey, Pointing to Wartime Value of Game and News about It to Fighting Forces," *The Sporting News*, 18 February 1943, 1.

60. "Service Men Are Aching for Some News," 10. Pvt. Ed Williams, "'More!' Ask Soldiers, Lining Up for No. 1 Paper at Pacific Base," *The Sporting News*, 18 May 1944, 11.

61. See as an example the advertisement on page 8 of *The Sporting News* of 27 May 1943.

62. "Brief Pause for Elimination," cartoon, *The Sporting News*, 23 November 1944, 11.

63. Maier, interview.

64. Woodling, interview.

65. Nowak, interview.

66. Two soldiers interviewed, Jim Burnett and Jack Krejci, did not recall listening to radio broadcasts of games. Both, however, spent time in German POW camps during the final stages of the war with no access to radios. Both interviewed by author, April 27 and 25, respectively, Omaha NE.

67. Barney McCosky, interview by William Marshall, 16 March 1988, Vero Beach FL. Part of the A. B. Chandler Oral History Project, University of Kentucky, Margaret I. King Library, Special Collections, Lexington.

68. Several accounts of radio broadcasts supplied to American troops can be found in "In the Service," *The Sporting News*, 13 August 1942, 6. "Series Broadcast Thrilled Bob Feller in the South Pacific," *The Sporting News*, 4 November 1943, 12. An account of Eisenhower's request for more radio broadcasts for his men can be found in "World Coverage for Series," *The Sporting News*, 14 October 1943, 14. "In the Service," *The Sporting News*, 13 August 1942, 6.

69. John Lardner, "Bookings Blamed As Stars Fail to Twinkle for Yanks," publication unidentified, 3 April 1944, located in Major Leon T. David Papers, newspaper clippings file.

70. "Take Game to the Men Overseas," *The Sporting News*, editorial, 25 March 1943, 4. "Tour of Army Camps Grand Scheme," *The Sporting News*, editorial, 26 August 1943, 8.

71. "Game Goes Along at Oran," *The Sporting News*, 1 April 1943, 6.

72. "Six Answer, Opportunity for Hundreds," *The Sporting News*, editorial, 16 December 1943, 8.

73. "Pacific Diamond Fans See Major Stars," *Marine Corps Chevron*, 17 March 1945, 8.

74. "Weekly Roundup," *Stars and Stripes* (Mediterranean Edition), 15 January 1944, 14.

75. Quoted in Mead, *Baseball Goes to War*, 8.

76. "Time to Plan for Overseas Tours," *The Sporting News*, editorial, 7 September 1944, 10.

77. "A Trio of Typical Rookies," *The Sporting News*, 9 April 1942, 6.

78. "Baseball Genuine Incentive," 17. Great Lakes' baseball program will be dealt with extensively in chapter 5.

79. "DiMaggio Packs Stands As Army Wallops Marines," *Marine Corps Chevron*, 1 May 1943, 15.

80. "Stars Go to Bat for Buddies—Help Joe E. Brown Hit Jackpot on Coast," *The Sporting News*, 26 August 1943, 9.

81. "Fliers Trip Navy in Hawaii," *The Sporting News*, 27 July 1944, 13.

82. Jim Britt, "The Year the Navy Won the World Series," *Downtown Athletic Club News*, April 1969, 67–68.

83. Lewis was "piloting aircraft in a far-away theatre," while both DiMaggio and Greenberg were in the States on leave at the time of the series. Britt, "The Year the Navy Won the World Series," 68.

84. Estimated attendance for each game was fifteen thousand. Tabulation found in Britt, "The Year the Navy Won the World Series," 67. There is some discrepancy among sources. A number indicate that eleven games were played between the two clubs while others mention only nine. Regardless, the scores and specifics of the final two contests, if played, could not be located.

85. Mead, *Baseball Goes to War*, 197–98. The scores of the first nine games were 5–0, 8–2, 4–3, 10–5, 12–2, 6–4, 3–5, 5–6, and 11–0, as reported in "Navy Captures Seven of Nine in Pacific Set," *The Sporting News*, 12 October 1944.

86. Quoted in Mead, *Baseball Goes to War*, 199.

87. Quoted in Mead, *Baseball Goes to War*, 199. Slaughter confirmed the extremely spirited nature of the games in the South Pacific in a separate interview found in Donald Honig, *Baseball between the Lines: Baseball in the Forties and Fifties As Told by the Men Who Played It* (Lincoln and London: University of Nebraska Press, 1976), 164.

88. Account of the games found in 1998 exhibit "Changing Times," Negro Leagues Museum, Kansas City MO; and Gary Bedingfield, *Baseball in World War II Europe* (Charleston SC: Arcadia, 1999). The issue of African Americans' role in military baseball will be dealt with in more detail in chapter 3.

2. YOUR DUTY, OUR DUTY

1. "Scribbled by Scribes," *The Sporting News*, 27 August 1942, 4.

2. David Q. Voigt, "The Crisis of World War II," *www.totalbaseball.com/history/voigt/mlbh18.html*, p. 3; Internet; accessed 11 August 1999.

3. "From Service Front," *The Sporting News*, 6 May 1943, 8. Similar announcements offering servicemen admission can be found throughout *The Sporting News* and military newspapers, such as the notice "Free Baseball Game Today" in *Jefferson Barracks Hub*, 19 September 1942, 6.

4. The one exception was the 1945 All-Star Game, which was not held because of travel restrictions.

5. For a detailed breakdown of donations by game and situation, see "$1,377,000 Game's Total Gift under W.S. Plans," *The Sporting News*, 3 September 1942, 3. For more information regarding the total contributions of the 1942 World Series, see Daniel M. Daniel, "Major Leagues Have Proud Record in War and Relief Enterprises," *Baseball Magazine*, September 1943, 327–28.

6. Virtually all of the Major League teams donated the gate receipts to the Army and Navy Relief Fund, which aided the families of servicemen. This charity was necessary for many families because of the specific way in which the government remunerated servicemen and their dependents. For example, as soon as a soldier or sailor was deemed missing, the government put a temporary hold on his salary, yet pension benefits could not be awarded to the family until the exact fate of the individual could be determined. In some cases, the bodies of deceased servicemen could not be recovered, and the family might have to wait years for money owed them. Many teams also held separate fund-raising contests to benefit other agencies and war-related entities in addition to the official relief games.

7. Account of game in Tommy Holmes, "Brooklyn Benefit Game Tribute to Larry's Promotional Genius," *The Sporting News*, 14 May 1942, 1. The exact amount of money raised by relief games is difficult to calculate precisely because of the conflicting though similar figures cited not only between sources but within sources. Furthermore, straight donations from fans, owners, or players also caused the final numbers to fluctuate even weeks after a particular exhibition game had been held.

8. "MacPhail and Brooklyn Again Show the Way," *The Sporting News*, editorial, 14 May 1942, 4.

9. For details of the game and the surrounding activities, see Dan Daniel, "Babe Goes to Bat Again and Scores for Uncle Sam," *The Sporting News*, 27 August 1942, 5; "69,316 See Yanks Split Twin Bill; Gate for Service Funds Exceeds $80,000," *New York Times*, 24 August 1942, 19; and Mead, *Baseball Goes to War*, 2–3.

10. Tallies for individual teams given in "$523,229 for Relief," *The Sporting News*, 27 August 1942, 5.

11. "Service Fund Games Sound Call to All Fans," *The Sporting News*, editorial, 21 May 1942, 4.

12. For the weekly's reaction to the poor showing of some Major League teams during their relief games and its suggestions for addressing the problem, see "Magnates Learn Relief Games Need Promotion," *The Sporting News*, editorial, 4 June 1942, 4.

13. "Army-Navy Series Close in Blaze of Dollars," *The Sporting News*, editorial, 27 August 1942, 4.

14. Data given in Mead, *Baseball Goes to War*, 3.

15. Information found in letter of 29 August 1943 from CPA firm of Lybrand, Ross Bros. and Montgomery of Pittsburgh, Pennsylvania, to *The Sporting News*. *The Sporting News* archives, St. Louis MO.

16. Figures given in Mead, *Baseball Goes to War*, 6.

17. Numbers cited in "Sparking Bond Sales through the Game," *The Sporting News*, editorial, 3 June 1943, 4.

18. A description of the efforts by Major League teams to promote war-bond sales can be found in Mead, *Baseball Goes to War*, 5–7.

19. An account of Walker's resistance to Robinson joining the Dodgers can be found in Jules Tygiel, *Baseball's Great Experiment: Jackie Robinson and His Legacy* (New York: Vintage Books, 1984), 169–72.

20. The organization and the specifics of the Baseball Writers Association game will be discussed later in this chapter. Information regarding the player auction can be found in Kingsley Childs, "War Bond Drive Here for Billion Projected by Baseball Writers," *New York Times*, 6 June 1943, 2s; and also within a brochure labeled "War Baseball" produced by the New York War Bond Sports Committee to promote a three-game all-New York exhibition series in 1944. The brochure, located in a file at the Major League Baseball Hall of Fame archives, contains a series of articles by local writers, many of whom mention the previous year's war-bond drive. The most extensive discussion of the auction can be found in one of these articles, "The Bond Box Score," by Arthur Patterson. See also "Baseball Fans Buy $123,850,000 Bonds," *New York Times*, 9 June 1943, 22. Other sources for supplementary information regarding the auction can be found in Mead, *Baseball Goes to War*, 5; and "War Bond Player Auction," *The Sporting News*, 10 June 1943, 8.

21. Shirley Povich, "Griffith and Military Official Praise Value of Publication for Boys in Service," *The Sporting News*, 8 January 1942, 2.

22. Citations regarding this topic are numerous in *The Sporting News*, even for minor league teams. For examples, see "In the Service," *The Sporting News*, 23 April 1942, 10; and "Toss Back Ball for Service Men," *The Sporting News*, editorial, 22 January 1942, 4.

23. The difficulty the American military encountered equipping servicemen adequately with athletic equipment will be dealt with in chapter 3. For information regarding the organization of the Ball and Bat Fund and the acquisition of tax-free status, see "File 5—Ball and Bat File—Ford Frick" at the National Archives and Records Administration, College Park, Maryland.

24. Data found in "Game's Gift to Fighters," *The Sporting News*, 4 June 1942, 6; "160 Dozen Balls to Army," *The Sporting News*, 18 June 1942, 6; and "Majors Give 1,134,229," *The Sporting News*, 15 October 1942, 6.

25. Sgt. Ed Nixon, "It Sez Here," *Stars and Stripes* (Mediterranean Edition), 3 March 1943, 7.

26. The Ball and Bat Fund was a government-organized entity designed strictly to utilize public and private finances to purchase baseball equipment for soldiers.

27. "Athletic Gear May Be Harder to Get," *The Sporting News*, 15 May 1943, 14. Although it is not clear if every armed forces base employed an Athletic Officer, many with sizable numbers of military personnel, such as Marine Corps Base, did maintain individuals with that title.

28. "In the Service," *The Sporting News*, 16 April 1942, 6.

29. "In the Service," *The Sporting News*, 9 April 1942, 6.

30. "How Clubs Can Aid Service Teams," *The Sporting News*, 8 April 1943, 4.

31. "Game Acts to Equip U.S. Service Teams," *The Sporting News*, 25 December 1941, 6.

32. "Landis Almost Gave Griffith 28 Night Games, Instead of 21," *The Sporting News*, 12 February 1942, 5.

33. Daniel M. Daniel, "Game Broadens Its Aid to War Effort," *The Sporting News*, 23 April 1942, 9.

34. "Baseball Becomes Vibrant in the War Effort," *The Sporting News*, editorial, 23 April 1942, 4.

35. Mulcahy was unable to play because the game conflicted with his scheduled arrival at Officers Candidate School. Hank Greenberg was also unable to compete because of a brief bout of appendicitis that did not require surgery.

36. Military and baseball officials funneled the first $100,000 into Clark W. Griffith's Ball and Bat Fund, which was primarily focused on purchasing baseball equipment for soldiers and sailors. The remaining monies filled the cof-

fers of the Army and Navy relief funds and also went to purchase war bonds and victory stamps. For more information on the two games and the allocation of funds, see John Drebinger, "American League 5–6 Choice to Win," *New York Times*, 6 July 1943, 20; John Drebinger, "Junior Loop Victor for 7th Time, 3 to 1," *New York Times*, 7 July 1942, 23; and James P. Dawson, "American League Turns Back Service All-Stars before 62,094 in Cleveland," *New York Times*, 8 July 1942, 28.

37. A detailed account of the game can be found in "War Bond Game Glitters before 2,000,000 Gate," *The Sporting News*, 3 June 1943, 5. For a brief discussion of and additional information about the exhibition contest, see Mead, *Baseball Goes to War*, 4–5.

38. For a detailed account of the financial campaign and the game itself, see John Drebinger, "40,000 War Bond Buyers Thrill to Baseball Spectacle and Variety Programs," *New York Times*, 27 August 1943, 11; and "Bond Game Again Proves Baseball Ace Salesman," *The Sporting News*, 2 September 1943, 3. For additional information on the game and the stunning amount of war bonds sold as a result of it, see Mead, *Baseball Goes to War*, 5.

39. For specific information regarding the contest and its promoters see both "Weekly Roundup," *Stars and Stripes* (Africa Edition), 28 August 1943, 7; and John B. Old, "DiMaggio's Bat Roars in Win," *The Sporting News*, 26 August 1943, 10.

40. "Benefit Game in 'Frisco," *The Sporting News*, 22 July 1943, 11.

41. "Armoraiders Annex 31 in Row, Eye Service 'World Series,'" *The Sporting News*, 13 July 1944, 12.

42. Fay Young, "Paige and Smith Tame Dizzy Dean's All-Stars," *Chicago Defender*, 30 May 1942, 19. Dean initially received permission to employ Feller in the contest, but the former Indian could not attend the game because of last-minute military obligations. Although the final tally donated to the Navy Relief Fund was not mentioned in the *Defender* article, one can assume the amount was substantial given the large attendance.

43. Bonura, as we will see in chapter 3, was one of the most important individuals associated with military baseball. However, at this point, July 1942, he had not yet been deployed overseas where he would eventually win the Legion of Merit for his role in promoting baseball among servicemen.

44. "In the Service," *The Sporting News*, 30 July 1942, 6. The exact monetary contribution generated by the game was not revealed, but since the article makes no mention of it, it most likely was not particularly impressive. *The Sporting News* consistently trumpeted any connection between baseball and the war effort and would surely have focused on the amount if it were significant.

45. "In the Service," *The Sporting News*, 11 June 1942, 6.

46. For a detailed account of the game, see Dave Camerer, "Feller Steams

Navy to 4 to 0 Win over Army in Relief Game," *The Sporting News*, 18 June 1942, 6. For further details on Mulcahy's attempt to gain exemption from the game, see "In the Service," *The Sporting News*, 9 July 1942, 6.

47. "Armoraiders Annex 31 in Row," 12.

48. Jim Ridge, "In the Service," *The Sporting News*, 7 January 1943.

49. For information on the game and the Britons' negative reaction to American and Canadian spectators, see "In the Service," *The Sporting News*, 13 August 1942, 6. For more financial information and supplementary data on the contest see Bedingfield, *Baseball in World War II Europe*, 87. Bedingfield's work, though interesting, is not as informative as one would hope in that its contents consist primarily of photographs and captions. The limited space devoted to text does contain important data, however.

50. "Service Diamond Stars Invade Sanctity of Wembley Stadium," *The Sporting News*, 2 September 1943, 9. Also see Bedingfield, *Baseball in World War II Europe*, 54 and 74.

51. Bedingfield, *Baseball in World War II Europe*, 54.

52. Accounts of the game can be found in Bedingfield, *Baseball in World War II Europe*, 50; and "In the Service," *The Sporting News*, 6 July 1944, 9.

53. Bedingfield, *Baseball in World War II Europe*, 102.

3. THE GAME'S THE THING

1. "The Commissioners Say," *Stars and Stripes* (African Edition), 10 July 1943, 7. Bonura was one of dozens of former Major Leaguers who became athletic officers or supervisors—a topic that will be addressed in chapter 5. However, because Bonura was so instrumental to the organization and promotion of military athletics, his efforts are also discussed in this chapter.

2. "From Army Front," *The Sporting News*, 8 January 1942, 8.

3. Bonura was sure handed but notoriously slow afoot. Many balls therefore got through to right field that other players might have fielded, which contributed to Bonura's reputation as a poor defensive player.

4. "Back in the Service," *The Sporting News*, 29 January 1942, 8.

5. For information on both Bonura's acquisition of equipment and the new diamond, see "In the Service," *The Sporting News*, 9 and 16 April 1942, both on page 6.

6. "In the Service," *The Sporting News*, 13 August 1942, 6.

7. Wakefield, *Playing to Win*, 88.

8. "In the Service," *The Sporting News*, 2 April 1943, 13.

9. Ed Rumill, "Battle Action," *Baseball Magazine*, January 1946, 256.

10. "In the Service," *The Sporting News*, 13 July 1944, 13. "The Commissioners Say," *Stars and Stripes* (African Edition), 24 July 1943. The comparison

to "Judge Landis" is a reference to Major League Baseball commissioner Kenesaw Mountain Landis, who served from 1920 to 1944.

11. "In the Service," *The Sporting News*, 20 January 1944, 10.

12. "Bonura Gets Award," *Stars and Stripes* (African Edition), 27 October 1943, 3.

13. Quoted in Rumill, "Battle Action," 256.

14. For information regarding the series, see "Sports: The Yankees Win in North Africa Too," *Yank: The Army Weekly*, 7 November 1943, 20; and Wakefield, *Playing to Win*, 88–89.

15. Pat Purcell, "Zeke Bonura: Keeps Word with Kelley, Signs G. I. Prospects," *The Sporting News*, 22 June 1944, 13. The article revealed that Bonura had signed five players but only revealed the fate of two of those individuals.

16. "Sports Service Record," *Yank: The Army Weekly*, 17 September 1944, 21.

17. "In the Service," *The Sporting News*, 24 June 1943, 6.

18. "Sports Service Record," *Yank: The Army Weekly*, 15 August 1943, 18; and "Bonura Teaching Game to Arabs in North Africa," *The Sporting News*, 5 August 1943, 10.

19. "The Commissioners Say," *Stars and Stripes* (African Edition), 10 July 1943, 7.

20. "Sports Parade," *Stars and Stripes* (Mediterranean Edition), 13 May 1944, 14.

21. "Zeke Directs Game in Liberated France," and "French Sports Editors Laud MPs 'Remarkable Swings,'" *The Sporting News*, 26 October 1944, 12.

22. It is unclear when Bonura began editing *Sports Lights*. The 3 April 1944 edition can be found in the newspaper clippings file of the Major Leon T. David Papers.

23. Wakefield, *Playing to Win*, 89–90. A promotional flyer for the Mustard Bowl, with Bonura's name and signature on the cover, can be found in the 601st Ordinance Battalion papers, Carlisle Military Barracks archives, Carlisle, Pennsylvania.

24. Sgt. Francis H. Barr, "Leathernecks Form 30 Teams in Three South Pacific Leagues," *The Sporting News*, 27 April 1944, 10.

25. "Pacific Marines Plan Baseball Careers," *Marine Corps Chevron*, 10 February 1945, 8; Sgt. Phil H. Storch, "Baseball Teams Again Invade Japan," *Marine Corps Chevron*, 19 May 1945, 8.

26. Royal Brougham, "Services to Provide Many Crack Prospects, Maj. Torrance Reports after Hitch in the Pacific," *The Sporting News*, 1 February 1945, 13. The article never states directly the cause of Torrance's hospital stay but implies it had something to do with his bout with jungle fever.

27. For an example of player transactions, see "Torrance and Veeck Pull Player Deal in Jungle," *The Sporting News*, 27 April 1944, 10.

28. "Game Given Impetus by Service Teams," *The Sporting News*, editorial, 24 September 1942, 4.

29. "Soldiers Are Sports Minded," *What the Soldier Thinks*, January 1944, 12. This was a quarterly report published by the Special Services, the branch of the Army responsible for recreational activities and monitoring the moods, tendencies, and morale of soldiers.

30. Chuck Maier, interview.

31. Joseph Whitehorne III Questionnaire, World War II surveys, Military History Institute Archives, Carlisle Barracks, Pennsylvania.

32. Herbert P. Bell Jr. Questionnaire, World War II surveys, Military History Institute Archives, Carlisle Barracks, Pennsylvania.

33. Sam Sambasile, interview by author, 23 April 2000, Omaha, Nebraska.

34. Joseph C. Donnelly Questionnaire, World War II surveys, Military History Institute Archives, Carlisle Barracks, Pennsylvania.

35. "In the Service," *The Sporting News*, 9 April 1942, 6.

36. For the organization of teams see "Baseball Tryouts to Begin Monday; Eligibility Rules," *Jefferson Barracks Hub*, 28 March 1942, 6; and "In the Service," *The Sporting News*, 9 April 1942, 6. The Jefferson Barracks select team was particularly talented, as we will see in chapter 4.

37. "Our Athletic Program." *Jefferson Barracks Hub*, editorial, 24 July 1942, 2.

38. "In the Service," *The Sporting News*, 2 July 1942, 8A.

39. "In the Service," *The Sporting News*, 18 June 1942, 6.

40. Information on Robinson's military service, which he found disappointing, can be found in Tygiel, *Baseball's Great Experiment*, 61–62.

41. An account of the game can be found in the exhibit "Changing Times," at the Negro Leagues Museum, Kansas City MO.

42. "Army Wins New Caledonia Title," *The Sporting News*, 28 June 1945, 11. Accounts of Doby's participation in integrated contests can be found in Honig, *Baseball between the Lines*, 117–18.

43. Buck O'Neill, *I Was Right on Time: My Journey from the Negro Leagues to the Majors*, with Steve Wulf and David Conrads (New York: Simon and Schuster, 1997), 159.

44. Most, if not all, of the publications featuring military athletics advertised regularly for umpires and informed readers of instruction schools in their area. For examples see "9th AF Conducts Official's School," *Stars and Stripes* (Paris Edition), 22 July 1945, 7; and "Seabee in Solomons Gets Tips on How to Call 'Em," *The Sporting News*, 29 June 1944, 12.

45. "The Commissioners Say," *Stars and Stripes* (Africa Edition), 26 June 1943, 7.

46. "The Commissioners Say," *Stars and Stripes* (Africa Edition), 22 May 1943, 7.

47. "In the Service," *The Sporting News*, 18 June 1942, 6.

48. A summary of Stimson's declaration can be found in "Restrict Service Games," *The Sporting News*, 25 June 1942, 6.

49. "In the Service," *The Sporting News*, 18 June 1942, 6.

50. "Round Robin Service League," *The Sporting News*, 27 April 1944, 10.

51. Wakefield, *Playing to Win*, 70–71.

52. "In the Service," *The Sporting News*, 30 April 1942, 6.

53. "In the Service," *The Sporting News*, 21 May 1942, 6.

54. Paulson, interview.

55. Maier, interview.

56. Earl Peak Questionnaire, World War II surveys, Military History Institute Archives, Carlisle Barracks, Pennsylvania.

57. Earl Peak, "War Diary of Col. Earl W. Peak," page 6, Military History Institute Archives, Carlisle Barracks, Pennsylvania.

58. William E. Faust Questionnaire, World War II surveys, Military History Institute Archives, Carlisle Barracks, Pennsylvania.

59. Special Service Survey, 13–24 September 1943, 8–9. Found in the Major Leon T. David Papers, box 1.

60. "Army Sports in the Tropics," *What the Soldier Thinks*, January 1944, 14.

61. "Sports Service Record," *Yank: The Army Weekly*, 3 October 1943, 18.

62. "Al Milnar Conducting Big Sports Program on Island" and "65 Diamonds, 10 Leagues on One Isle in Marianas," *The Sporting News*, 28 June 1945, 11.

63. Gary Bedingfield, "Baseball in Wartime: Veteran's Stories," [on-line document] (accessed 17 October 2000); available from *http://baseballinwartime .freeservers.com/veteran_stories.htm*, 3; Internet.

64. "Boys Take Game with Them in S. Pacific, Writes High," *The Sporting News*, 30 December 1943. The article did not reveal the exact area of the league though this circumspection was not uncommon in publications during World War II for obvious security reasons.

65. "Tarawa Air Strip Serves As Diamond," *The Sporting News*, 20 April 1944, 15.

66. Cpl. E. J. Williams Jr. "Navy Edges Army in New Hebrides Series," *The Sporting News*, 22 February 1945, 13.

67. "Army Wins New Caledonia Title," *The Sporting News*, 28 June 1945, 11.

68. For a detailed account of the game, see Sam Blumenfeld, "New Rules Wed Beer to CPA-GI Baseball," *MidPacifician* (Army newspaper in Hawaii), 1 May 1944, 11. It was not at all uncommon for military officials to integrate the consumption of alcohol, under controlled circumstances, with athletics.

Beer was often the prize for winning a contest, tournament, or league title. Indeed, the connection between baseball and beer in the military was quite strong and is discussed in Wakefield, *Playing to Win*, 107.

69. "Game in India Draws 3,000," *The Sporting News*, 11 November 1943, 11.

70. "Game Played in Russian Port under Difficulties," *The Sporting News*, 10 February 1944, 10.

71. Ralph Allen, "Plane Crash, Search for Mines Mere Interruptions in Play," *The Sporting News*, 31 August 1944, 13.

72. Dorothy Still Danner, "Oral Histories—U.S. Navy Nurse Prisoner of War in the Philippines, 1942–1945," [on-line document] (accessed 11 December 2000); available from *http://www.history.Navy.mil/faqs/faq87–3f.htm*; Internet.

73. Jack Kreicji, interview by author, 25 April 2000, Omaha NE.

74. Quoted from official War Department evaluation of Milag Nord POW camp, found in "Merchant Mariners at Milag Nord Prisoner of War Camp in Germany during World War II" [on-line document] (accessed 27 December 2001); available from *http://www.usmm.org/milag.html*; Internet.

75. Information located in ""Bill Goodall's Diaries: Autumn / Winter 1944" [on-line document] (accessed 15 April 2002); available from *http://www .goodall.net/Diaries/28.html*; Internet. This website is a fabulously comprehensive collection containing a diary digitized by the son of former RAF flier William Goodall in which Goodall recounts, among other things, his more than two years as a German POW.

76. "As Seen by New Zealanders," *The Sporting News*, 20 April 1944, 15.

77. For a description of the MacArthur Cup, see "In the Service," *The Sporting News*, 11 June 1942, 6. For an account of the Spalding tour, see "First Games 'Down Under'" *The Sporting News*, 13 August 1942, 6. For a reproduction of a promotional flyer advertising the 1945 contest, see "Game Promotes Allied Good Will," *The Sporting News*, 28 June 1945, 11.

78. Bedingfield, *Baseball in World War II Europe*, 23.

79. "As Seen by Irish Scribe," *The Sporting News*, 6 August 1942, 6.

80. "In the Service," *The Sporting News*, 2 July 1942, 8A.

81. Entire story regarding the game and the incident involving the Queen found at Bart Bachman, "A Photo, A War, A Missing Finger and What Might Have Been," [on-line document] (accessed 14 December 2000); available from *http://www.mutha.com/ ww2 memorabilia/index.html*; Internet.

82. Bedingfield, *Baseball in World War II Europe*, 25–26.

83. "ETO Sports Mirror," *Stars and Stripes* (Paris Edition), 14 July 1945, 6.

84. "75th Blanks XVIth, 4–0 for Second League Win," *Stars and Stripes* (Paris Edition), 23 July 1945, 7.

85. "Raiders Drop Orly Field," *Stars and Stripes* (Paris Edition), 18 July 1945, 7.

86. Bedingfield, *Baseball in World War II Europe*, 124.

87. "First Kits Go to Camps," *The Sporting News*, 26 February 1942, 6. The exact materials contained in each type of kit are described in a letter from the chief of the Bureau of Navigation to the commanding officer of the Naval Air Station, Argentina, Newfoundland, in "File 5—Ball and Bat File—Ford Frick" at the National Archives and Records Administration, College Park, Maryland.

88. As reported by Sgt. Ed Nixon, "It Sez Here," *Stars and Stripes* (Mediterranean Edition), 3 March 1943, 7.

89. Figures given in "Army, Navy Take 90 Per Cent of U.S. Sports Gear," *Stars and Stripes* (Western Europe Edition), 30 August 1944, 3.

90. Bedingfield, *Baseball in World War II Europe*, 11.

91. "Batter Up," *Jefferson Barracks Hub*, 2 May 1942, 3.

92. *What the Soldier Thinks*, August 1943, 71.

93. United States Army, *Special Services Companies*, 5.

94. Minutes of Faculty and Staff Conference. In "Faculty Minutes of Special Services Branch School March 3 to November 21, 1942," Major Leon T. David Papers.

95. Special Service Survey, 13–24 September 1943, 5. Found in the Major Leon T. David Papers, box 1.

96. Special Service Survey, 13–24 September 1943, 9.

97. "Capt. Robert R. M. Emmet No. 1 Man in Baseball to Great Lakes Trainees," *The Sporting News*, 6 July 1944, 17.

98. Lt. T. J. Flanagan Jr., "Baseball in the Air at Reception Center," *Jefferson Barracks Hub*, 31 January 1942, 3.

99. "Name Field after Player," *The Sporting News*, 11 June 1942, 6.

100. "Army Seeks Arc Plants," *The Sporting News*, 11 February 1942, 6; "Camp Grant Seeks Arcs," *The Sporting News*, 15 March 1943, 13; "Lighted Park for Night Games at Fort Sheridan," *The Sporting News*, 6 April 1944, 13.

101. "In the Service," *The Sporting News*, 22 June 1944, 12.

102. Sgt. Francis H. Barr, "Leathernecks Form 30 Teams in Three South Pacific Leagues," *The Sporting News*, 27 April 1944, 10.

103. Quoted in Mead, *Baseball Goes to War*, 199.

104. Hugh Mulcahy, questionnaire completed for author, 10 October 1998.

105. Shirley Povich, "Big Leaguers Romp in Jap-Made Parks," *The Sporting News*, 15 March 1945, 11.

106. "In the Service," *The Sporting News*, 4 June 1942, 6.

107. "Camp Field," *The Sporting News*, 5 April 1945, 11.

108. Gary Bedingfield, "James 'Jimmie' Trimble III," [on-line document]

(accessed 18 May 2000); available from *http://baseballinwartime.freeservers.com/mem_trimble.htm*; Internet.

109. "Ball Field on Guadalcanal Dedicated to Minor Hurler," *The Sporting News*, 4 January 1945, 13.

4. FINEST TEAM ASSEMBLED

1. "Admiral's Message," *The Sporting News*, 24 December 1942, 6.

2. Richard Ben Cramer, *Joe DiMaggio: The Hero's Life* (New York: Simon and Schuster, 2000), 208.

3. Frank Baumholtz, interview by William Marshall, 10 December 1992, Cleveland, Ohio. The taped interview is part of the A. B. Chandler Oral History Project and is available at the University of Kentucky Library, Special Collections, Lexington.

4. That Tebbetts had an unusual amount of influence on Army officials is suggested in Bob Savage, "Bob Savage Tells His Story," [on-line document] (accessed 26 December 2000) available from *http://philadelphiaathletics.org/a8.html*; Internet.

5. All-star military teams assembled for just one game or a short series of games are not discussed in this chapter. Instead, only teams from specific military installations or teams that were organized for extended periods will be examined.

6. Quoted in "The Game and the Old Navy Spirit," *The Sporting News*, editorial, 2 April 1942, 4.

7. "Baseball Genuine Incentive Says Naval Training Chieftain," *The Sporting News*, 6 July 1944, 17. The Great Lakes facility was the largest of its kind in the world during the war, and, although other naval training stations trained large numbers of sailors, the sheer size of Great Lakes is the most obvious reason for the dominance of its baseball team.

8. Sgt. Dan Polier, "Sports: The Great Lakes Ball Team has a Major League Line-up," *Yank: The Army Weekly*, 8 August 1943, 18.

9. For an account of scattered games of the 1942 season and end-of-the year discussion of the team's accomplishments, see "In the Service," *The Sporting News*, 11 June 1942, 6; "In the Service," *The Sporting News*, 27 August 1942, 6; "In the Service," *The Sporting News*, 31 December 1942, 14.

10. For information on the players on the 1943 team see "Special Letter from the Athletic Office of the United States Naval Training Station at Great Lakes, Illinois to *The Sporting News*," dated 15 April 1943, located at *The Sporting News* archives, St. Louis MO. For an account of games and overall performances, see "In the Service," *The Sporting News*, 22 July 1943, 9; Polier, "Sports: The Great Lakes Ball Team," *Yank: The Army Weekly*, 18; and "Baseball

Dope," *Marine Corps Chevron*, 3 July 1943, 15. For Cochrane's comparison of the three teams, see "No Sparring on 1944 Tars! Mickey Says They're the Best," *The Sporting News*, 17 August 1944, 12.

11. Letter, the Athletic Office of the U.S. Naval Training Station, Great Lakes, Illinois, to *The Sporting News*, 1 September 1944, *The Sporting News* archives, St. Louis MO.

12. Harrington E. Crissey, "Baseball and World War II," [on-line document] (accessed 14 December 2000); available from *http://www.totalbaseball .com/leagues/military/armed.htm*; Internet.

13. "No Sparring on 1944 Tars! Mickey Says They're Best," *The Sporting News*, 17 August 1944, 12. Their two losses came against the Dodgers and, ironically, a Detroit semipro team.

14. Although Rowe also played for the Dodgers and Phillies during his stellar thirteen-year career, he is most remembered for his tenure in Detroit where he led the American League in wins with twenty-four in 1934 and also winning percentage in 1940 with a 16–3 record.

15. Woodling, interview.

16. "Sports Service Record," *Yank: The Army Weekly*, 3 September 1944, 21.

17. "Rowe's Broadside for Cochrane Tars Sinks Phillies, 3–1," *The Sporting News*, 18 May 1944, 12. "Bluejackets Ride over Bosox, 3–1, on Trucks' Fire Ball," *The Sporting News*, 1 June 1944, 13. "Great Lakes 8, Browns 2," *Stars and Stripes* (Mediterranean Edition), 17 June 1944, 14.

18. "Rowe May Become Outfielder," *The Sporting News*, 20 April 1944, 15.

19. "Rowe's Broadside for Cochrane Tars Sinks Phillies, 3–1," *The Sporting News*, 18 May 1944, 12.

20. "Sports Service Record," *Yank: The Army Weekly*, 22 October, 1944, 21.

21. "Navy Kayoes All-Star Clubs," *The Sporting News*, 12 April 1945, 11.

22. Tunney's program included extensive training in organizing base athletic programs. This topic will be discussed more extensively in chapter 4.

23. Information regarding McClure located in Mead, *Baseball Goes to War*, 189–91.

24. "Norfolk Sailors Set Pace for Service Teams," *The Sporting News*, 1 October 1942, 16. "In the Service," *The Sporting News*, 16 April 1942, 6.

25. "Sixteen Guns from Majors Give Power to Norfolk's Two Service-Star Teams," *The Sporting News*, 2 April 1943, 13.

26. "In the Service," *The Sporting News*, 8 April 1942, 6.

27. For information regarding rosters and lineups, see Mead, *Baseball Goes to War*, 189–91; Harrington E. Crissey, "Baseball and World War II," [on-line document] (accessed 14 December 2000); available from *http://www .totalbaseball.com/leagues/military/armed.htm*; Internet; and "The Navy's Great-

est Team," [on-line document] (accessed 11 December 2000); available from *http://www.hrnm.Navy.mil/baseball.htm*; Internet.

28. "Sports Service Record," *Yank: The Army Weekly*, 20 June 1943, 18.

29. For information on this topic and an account of naval regulations, see "In the Service," *The Sporting News*, 29 July 1943, 9.

30. "Eight Major Leaguers on 1945 Roster," *The Sporting News*, spring 1945. Exact date and page number unknown. Clipping is available in file #1 of "Armed Services Baseball" at *The Sporting News* Archives, St. Louis MO.

31. "Sampson Splits Strong Team," *The Sporting News*, 1 June 1944, 13.

32. "Sampson's 24-Hit Barrage Crushes Boston Hose, 20–7," *The Sporting News*, 15 June 1944, 12.

33. Al Cartwright, "Crack Bainbridge, Md., Outfit Stakes Claim to Eastern Toga," *The Sporting News*, 7 September 1944, 12.

34. "Ted and Teammates on Bronson Field Fliers," *The Sporting News*, 22 June 1944, 6.

35. "High-Flying Wings Clip Four Big League Foes," *The Sporting News*, 9 September 1943, 6.

36. For information on the roster and performances of the McClellan squad see "Turns Heat on in Winter," *The Sporting News*, 21 January 1943, 6; "Major-Minor Stars Twinkling for McClellan," *The Sporting News*, 20 May 1943, 6; and accounts by Rugger Ardizoia and Charlie Silvera in Gary Bedingfield, "Baseball in Wartime: Veteran's Stories," [on-line document] (accessed 17 October 2000); available from *http://baseballinwartime.freeservers.com/veteran_stories.htm*; Internet.

37. For information about the two teams and their fierce competition, see "Battery at Randolph Field," *The Sporting News*, 16 April 1942, 6; G. H. Scherwitz, "Pollett, Slaughter and Wilber Lead San Antonio to G.I Title," *The Sporting News*, 28 September 1944, 12. See also Mead, *Baseball Goes to War*, 196; and Honig, *Baseball between the Lines*, 162.

38. "Lt. Tebbetts' Waco Wolves Winners of Houston Title," *The Sporting News*, 14 September 1944, 12.

39. "Stars in Texas Camp," *The Sporting News*, 30 July 1942, 6; and "Weekly Roundup," *Stars and Stripes* (African Edition), 16 October 1943, 7.

40. Cpl. Dick Peebles, "Hughes, Mullin among Talent Giving Sparkle to Army's New Cumberland Diamond Entry," *The Sporting News*, 13 May 1943, 6.

41. Lt. Thomas J. Flanagan Jr., "Major Leaguers Now Play Ball at Reception Center," *Jefferson Barracks Hub*, 4 April 1942, 6.

42. "Sislers at Bat for Army and Navy," *The Sporting News*, 8 July 1943, 14.

43. See "Camp Pickett Busy on Diamond," *The Sporting News*, 1 July 1943, 9; and "Help Line Up Pickett Lineups," *The Sporting News*, 1 June 1944, 13.

44. "76th Infantry Division Fields Formidable Team," *The Sporting News*, 10 August 1944, 12.

45. "Armoraiders Annex 31 in Row, Eye Service World's Series," *The Sporting News*, 13 July 1942, 12.

46. For roster information and details concerning the 1942 season, see "Marines Hit As Straight As They Shoot," *The Sporting News*, 13 August 1942, 6; Pvt. Wade Lucas, "The Sports Front," *Marine Corps Chevron*, 20 February 1943, 14; and a letter, from the Athletic Officer, Marine Corps Base, San Diego CA, to *The Sporting News*, 23 July 1942, located in folder "Armed Services Baseball," *The Sporting News* archives, St. Louis MO.

47. Information found in a publicity pamphlet entitled "The Mare Island Marines Baseball Team," located in file "Armed Services Baseball," *The Sporting News* Archives, St. Louis MO.

48. "Major Leaguers Win for Beach," *Marine Corps Chevron*, 5 June 1943, 26.

49. Milton Gross, "Maryland Team's 50 Victims include Major League Outfits," *The Sporting News*, 4 October 1945, 10.

50. "Ex-O.B Stars Shine in Panama Play," *The Sporting News*, 26 April 1945, 11.

51. For information on the lineups of some of the exceptional service teams and specific games in Hawaii, see "Fliers Win 16 in Row," *The Sporting News*, 17 August 1944, 12; Cramer, *Joe DiMaggio*, 211; Honig, *Baseball between the Lines*, 116–18; Mead, *Baseball Goes to War*, 195; Harrington E. Crissey, "Baseball and World War II"; and comments from Rugger Ardizoia in Gary Bedingfield, "Baseball in Wartime: Veteran's Stories."

52. Quoted in Honig, *Baseball between the Lines*, 163.

53. For information on the struggle for diamond supremacy in Hawaii and the relocation of players to the South Pacific, see Honig, *Baseball between the Lines*, 117, 163–64; and Mead, *Baseball Goes to War*, 197–98.

54. "Clark Gable As First Sacker," *The Sporting News*, 23 December 1943, 10.

55. Information on baseball in England and quotations regarding specific teams can be found in Bedingfield, *Baseball in World War II Europe*, 26–27, 45, 70–71, 78.

56. Information regarding the Seventy-first Infantry team found in Bedingfield, *Baseball in World War II Europe*, 124; and interview, Harry Walker, by William Marshall, 11 May 1988, Leeds, Alabama. The taped interview is part of A. B. Chandler Oral History Project and is available at the University of Kentucky Library, Special Collections.

1. Identifying the exact number who served is difficult since various sources cite different numbers, although the figures are similar. For these calculations, see Douglas A. Noverr and Lawrence E. Ziewacz, *The Games They Played: Sports in American History, 1865–1980* (Chicago: Nelson Hall, 1983), 151; David Quentin Voigt, *Baseball: An Illustrated History* (University Park: Penn State University Press, 1987), 189; and Harrington E. Crissey, "Baseball and World War II."

2. John Underwood, "War Bond," *The 1992 Information Please Sports Almanac* (Boston: Houghton Mifflin, 1991), 53.

3. "Keeps 'Em Playing in the Navy," *The Sporting News*, 9 April 1942, 6.

4. Polier, "Sports: The Great Lakes Ball Team," *Yank: The Army Weekly*, 18.

5. Carter Latimer, as quoted in "Scribbled by Scribes," *The Sporting News*, 2 April 1942, 4.

6. "Pfc. Masi Gets Fill of Being Mistaken for Braves' Phil," *The Sporting News*, 15 June 1945, 13.

7. Sgt. Dan Polier, "Sports: Critics Put the Blast on Navy Big Leaguers," *Yank: The Army Weekly*, 6 February 1944, 20.

8. Kreicji, interview.

9. Sambasile, interview.

10. Maier, interview.

11. Paulson, interview.

12. Polier, "Sports: Critics Put the Blast on Navy Big Leaguers," 20. Robert Smith, *Baseball* (New York: Simon and Schuster, 1970), 299.

13. G. Edward White, *Creating the National Pastime* (Princeton NJ: Princeton University Press, 1996), 270.

14. For DiMaggio's reaction to his treatment by fans, see Cramer, *Joe DiMaggio*, 203.

15. "Through Mill with Joe," *The Sporting News*, 25 February 1943, 6.

16. For DiMaggio's Army experience while in California and Hawaii, see Cramer, *Joe DiMaggio*, 208–13.

17. "Sports Service Record," *Yank: The Army Weekly*, 12 September 1943, 18.

18. Cramer, *Joe DiMaggio*, 208.

19. "Weekly Roundup," *Stars and Stripes* (Africa Edition), 28 August 1943, 7.

20. "DiMag Leads Major Stars to 4–1 Victory," *The Sporting News*, 17 February 1944, 18.

21. "Sports Service Record," *Yank: The Army Weekly*, 23 July 1944, 21.

22. Sam Elkins, "I Remember DiMaggio," in *The DiMaggio Albums: Volume II*, ed. Richard Whittingham (New York: G. P. Putnam's Sons, 1989), 462–63.

23. For information on the latter portion of DiMaggio's military career, see "Service World's Series in October for Hawaii," *The Sporting News*, 7 September 1944, 12; "DiMag on Kilmer Tour," *The Sporting News*, 18 January 1945, 9; and selected articles in Whittingham, *The DiMaggio Albums*, 455–69.

24. "Hugh and Hank—Teammates," *The Sporting News*, 9 July 1942, 6.

25. Mulcahy, questionnaire.

26. "In the Service" *The Sporting News*, 21 May 1942, 6.

27. "Old Heads Assist Mulcahy," *The Sporting News*, 28 May 1942, 6.

28. Mulcahy, Questionnaire.

29. For an account of several of Mulcahy's games in the Northeast, including the exhibition contest, see "In the Service," *The Sporting News*, 9 July 1942, 6.

30. For information on Mulcahy's South Carolina and Memphis stints, see "In the Service," *The Sporting News*, 6 May 1943, 7; and "In the Service," *The Sporting News*, 6 July 1944, 9. For details concerning Mulcahy's performance in the championship game, see Henry Reynolds, "Mulcahy Pitches Second Army Club to Southern Title," *The Sporting News*, 7 October 1943, 9.

31. Mulcahy, Questionnaire.

32. Data regarding Mulcahy's performances leading up to the series can be found in "Hugh Mulcahy Gets Army Discharge," *Stars and Stripes*, 7 August 1945, 6; and "Hugh Delays Trip Home: Rain Blocks P. I. Series," *The Sporting News*, 19 July 1945, 13.

33. "In the Service," *The Sporting News*, 29 October 1942, 8.

34. Rizzuto, Questionnaire.

35. "In the Service," *The Sporting News*, 26 November 1942, 8.

36. For Rizzuto's success as a war-bond salesman, see "In the Service," *The Sporting News*, 24 December 1942, 6; and "The Navy's Greatest Team," [online document] (accessed 11 December 2000); available from *http://www .hrnm.Navy.mil/baseball.htm*; Internet.

37. Information about all-star games in Hawaii and the "Stumpy" club found in Blues Romeo, "Phil Rizzuto, Navy's Lend-Lease Star, Flashed Yankee Form in GI Series," *The Sporting News*, 23 November 1944, 11. Details concerning the Australian all-star game located in WAC Cpl. Jessie Stearns, "Ex-Big Leaguers Star for Navy in Australian Game," *The Sporting News*, 23 November 1944, 11. For his general observations about the war and his experiences, see Rizzuto, questionnaire.

38. For Slaughter's early experiences in the Army, see "This Is the Army," *Stars and Stripes* (Africa Edition), 5 June 1943, 7; and Honig, *Baseball between the Lines*, 162.

39. Information regarding Rizzuto's time in San Antonio can be found in G. H. Scherwitz, "Pollett, Slaughter and Wilber Lead San Antonio to G.I.

Title," *The Sporting News*, 23 September 1944, 12; and Honig, *Baseball between the Lines*, 162.

40. Statistics located in "Sports Service Record," *Yank: The Army Weekly*, 3 September 1944, 21. Quotations from "Seaman Vandy Believes He's Better Hurler Now," *The Sporting News*, 13 July 1944, 13.

41. "Vander Meer Wins, 8–2," *Stars and Stripes* (Western Europe Edition), 26 September 1944, 3.

42. "Pacific Diamond Fans See Major Stars," *Marine Corps Chevron*, 17 March 1945, 8; and "Vander Meer Heftier," *The Sporting News*, 18 October 1945, 14.

43. Statistics found in letter from Athletic Office of the Great Lakes Naval Training Station to *The Sporting News*, 1 September 1944, located at *The Sporting News* archives, St. Louis MO.

44. "Fireman Trucks Whiffs 19," *The Sporting News*, 27 July 1944, 12.

45. For details regarding Trucks's performance, see "Navy Guns Blast Army Four Straight to Romp in Pacific World's Series," *The Sporting News*, 5 October 1944, 19; and "Honolulu Navy Team Sweeps World Series," *Stars and Stripes* (Western Europe Edition), 29 September 1944, 3.

46. Reactions to Gordon's ill-timed photograph is found in "A Time for Players to Be Circumspect," *The Sporting News*, editorial, 23 March 1944, 10. A summary of unofficial restrictions placed upon players is provided in Mead, *Baseball Goes to War*, 14.

47. For details on Gordon's performance in the series see "Navy Guns Blast Army Four Straight," *The Sporting News*, 19; and Britt, "The Year the Navy Won the World Series," 67–68.

48. For Gordon's South Pacific experiences, see "Star-Studded Army Clubs Stage Series in Marianas" and "Gordon Used As Ringer in Pacific Softball Game," both in *The Sporting News*, 9 August 1945, 13; and also Mead, *Baseball Goes to War*, 198–99.

49. For information concerning Tebbetts see "In the Service," *The Sporting News*, 24 December 1942, 6; and "Tebbetts Receives Promotion," *The Sporting News*, 1 February 1945, 13. See also note 4 in chapter 4.

50. Ed Burns, "Watch Out for Ted the Tartar," *The Sporting News*, 27 August 1942, 4.

51. Quoted in "In the Service," *The Sporting News*, 22 October 1942, 6.

52. Lt. Louis Olszyk, "Old Ted Makes Baseball Talk in Teaching Sport to Natives," *The Sporting News*, 1 March 1945, 13.

53. "Lyons Says Career Not Over," *The Sporting News*, 21 October 1943, 11.

54. Dickey's role in naval athletic programs and the Servicemen's World Series are described in "Service World's Series in October for Hawaii," *The*

Sporting News, 7 September 1944, 12; and Britt, "The Year the Navy Won the World Series," 67–68.

55. Britt, "The Year the Navy Won the World Series," 67.

56. Underwood, "War Bond," 55.

57. For Williams's classification issues, see "Ted In and Out of Draft," *The Sporting News*, 21 May 1942, 6.

58. Ted Williams, with John Underwood, *My Turn at Bat: The Story of My Life* (New York: Simon and Schuster, 1969), 144.

59. For accounts of the games and Williams's performance, see "N. L. Navy Stars Lead," *The Sporting News*, 4 October 1945, 19; and "Few Hits for Stars," *The Sporting News*, 18 October 1945, 14.

60. "Kids Collect around These Cloudbuster Cadets," *The Sporting News*, 18 July 1943, 11; and "Ted and Teammates on Bronson Field Fliers," *The Sporting News*, 22 June 1944, 12.

61. "In the Service," *The Sporting News*, 10 December 1942, 10.

62. Vincent X. Flaherty, "When Navy Ordered Williams to Take Diamond Bow," *The Sporting News*, 23 November 1944, 11.

63. "Ted Williams Proves He Can Take It," *The Sporting News*, editorial, 16 December 1943, 8.

64. "Ted Disputes Captain," *The Sporting News*, 24 June 1943, 6.

65. "In the Service," *The Sporting News*, 25 March 1943, 6.

66. "In the Service," *The Sporting News*, 24 February 1944, 10.

67. For information on Greenberg's various assignments early in his military career see "Hank in New Job," *The Sporting News*, 20 August 1942, 8; "In the Service," *The Sporting News*, 26 November 1942, 8; and "In the Service," *The Sporting News*, 11 March 1943, 8.

68. For Greenberg's views on the difficulty of playing baseball in the military see "Short Sports Stories: Hank Greenberg Says Goodbye to Baseball and an Ump Confesses," *Yank: The Army Weekly* (British Edition), 23 May 1943, 9. Earnshaw's quotation given in "Keep 'Em Flying in the Navy," *The Sporting News*, 9 April 1942, 6.

69. Underwood, "War Bond," 55.

70. "Greenberg Escapes Injury in Bomb Blast on Plane," *The Sporting News*, 27 July 1944, 13.

71. Quoted in Tim Ponaccio, "War Ball," *Philadelphia Enquirer*, 8 August 1976, 1–2E.

72. Information on Feller's 1942 performances found in "Back in Strike-Out Stride," *The Sporting News*, 7 May 1942, 6; and "In the Service," *The Sporting News*, 21 May 1942, 6.

73. Underwood, "War Bond," 55.

74. Descriptions of Feller's combat experiences in Mead, *Baseball Goes to War*, 192–94.

75. Mead, *Baseball Goes to War*, 194.

76. Harry Dwyer, "Sparks from the Sports Wheel," *Our Navy*, 1 August 1944, 59.

77. "Sports Service Record," *Yank: The Army Weekly*, 13 August 1944, 21.

78. Bob Feller with Bill Gilbert, *Now Pitching, Bob Feller* (New York: Harper Perennial, 1990), 120.

79. "Bobby Feller Fans 12 As Great Lakes Tops A's," *Stars and Stripes* (Paris Edition), 11 July 1945, 6.

80. "Feller Hurls a No-Hitter against Ford's All-Stars," *The Sporting News*, 26 July 1945, 11.

81. Mead (*Baseball Goes to War*, 26–27) indicates that the Army may have given preferential treatment to Lewis in granting a deferment because of the close relationship between Army officials and Clark Griffith, the owner of the Washington Senators.

82. "Hitting High in Tough Loop," *The Sporting News*, 16 April 1942, 6.

83. "From Army Front," *The Sporting News*, 1 January 1942, 10.

84. "In the Service," *The Sporting News*, 2 July 1942, 8A.

85. Quoted in Honig, *Baseball between the Lines*, 76.

86. Ed Rumill, "Battle Action," *Baseball Magazine*, January 1946, 255.

87. Berg occasionally even dabbled in espionage during the Cold War. For an encompassing account of Berg's amazing activities during the 1930s and 1940s, see Nicholas Davidoff, *The Catcher Was a Spy: The Mysterious Life of Moe Berg* (New York: Vintage Books, 1994), 76–217. Supplementary information can be found in "Morris 'Moe' Berg," [on-line document] (accessed 16 June 2001); available from *http://www. baseballreliquary.org/berg.htm*; Internet.

88. For accounts of Walker's experiences in Europe, see "Harry Walker, Ex-Cardinal Bagged 29 Nazi Soldiers," *The Sporting News*, 9 August 1945, 13; "Harry Walker Decorated with Bronze Star in ETO," *The Sporting News*, 16 August 1945, 13; and A. L. Marder, "350 Youths Attend Clinic Held by 71st Division Diamond Stars," *The Sporting News*, 18 October 1945, 14. For Walker's own recollections of his time in Europe, see Walker, interview.

89. For brief discussions of Travis's experiences, see Mead, *Baseball Goes to War*, 201; and Bedingfield, *Baseball in World War II Europe*, 124.

90. Information on Shepard's military and baseball experiences in "Bert Shepard" [on-line document] (accessed 17 June 2001); *http://web.indstate .edu/community/vchs/wvp/!SHEPARD.pdf*; Internet.

91. Mead, *Baseball Goes to War*, 200.

92. Bob Savage, "Bob Savage Tells His Story," [on-line document] (accessed December 26, 2000); *http://philadelphiaathletics.org/a8.html*; Internet.

93. Bedingfield, *Baseball in World War II Europe*, 128.

94. Gary Bedingfield, "Harry O'Neill," [on-line document] (Accessed May 28, 2001); *http://baseballinwartime.freeservers.com/mem_oneill.htm*; Internet.

95. Quoted in "In the Service," *The Sporting News*, 4 March 1943, 8. Additional information regarding Gedeon's heroic effort and his recovery can be found in "In the Service," *The Sporting News*, 20 August 1942, 8; and "Gedeon Gets Promotion," *The Sporting News*, 24 December 1942, 6.

96. Gary Bedingfield, "Elmer Gedeon," [on-line document] (accessed 28 May 2001); *http://baseballinwartime.freeservers.com/mem_gedeon.htm*; Internet.

6. WHAT MIGHT HAVE BEEN

1. Although Greenberg's postwar statistics do not rival his prewar numbers, he was instrumental in Detroit's World Series victory in the 1945 season, which he contributed to in the final weeks after winning release from the Army. Also, the Tiger star did lead the American League in home runs and RBIs in his first full season back but had a batting average much below his norm. After the war, Greenberg never again hit over .300 and had retired within two years of his return.

2. Though at the time of Musial's retirement, only Babe Ruth had surpassed that total, Hank Aaron eventually accomplished the feat as well.

3. Total Player Rating is a statistic compiled by the editors of *Total Baseball* that considers not only traditional statistical categories such as batting average, home runs, RBIs, and fielding percentage, but also such measures as home-park advantage and a player's performance against others at the same position. Numbers in the positive range indicate progressively increased effectiveness, while larger negative numbers indicate the opposite. For the exact method for calculating TPR see John Thorn, Pete Palmer, Michael Gershman, Matthew Silverman, and Sean Lahman, eds., *Total Baseball* (New York: Total Sports, 1999), 655.

4. Only players who completed a full season before their military service and one year after returning were included in this analysis of position players who served. My analysis of pitchers who served utilized the same criteria.

5. Information provided in a memorandum listing Feller's personal achievements and milestones, from Bob Feller to the author, 30 August 1998.

6. "Walker Cooper Thinks Bob Feller Will Reach New Heights after War," *Janesville (Wisconsin) Daily Gazette*, 15 August 1945, 12.

7. Sec Taylor, "Behind the Sports Headlines," *Stars and Stripes* (Paris Edition), 3 August 1945, 7.

8. Total pitcher index, which is similar to TPR for position players, calculates a pitcher's performance above a statistically average counterpart (tabu-

lated as zero) based on both traditional statistical categories such as wins, losses, and ERA and other factors such as the home park and defensive strength of the pitcher's team. The more positive the TPR number, the greater the pitcher's effectiveness; larger negative numbers indicate the opposite. For the exact method for calculating TPI see Thorn et al., *Total Baseball*, 1386.

9. For a description of Lyons' employment as a "Sunday pitcher" see Thorn et al., *Total Baseball*, 172.

Name Index

Index contains names of Major League, Minor League, Negro League, and other individuals directly related to professional baseball. Numbers in italics refer to the photographic insert; the first number is the text page preceding the insert, the second is the photograph number in the insert. See subject index for all other names.

Subject Index

See Name Index for all names of Major League, Minor League, Negro League, and other individuals directly related to professional baseball. All other military, political, celebrity, or historical names are in this index.

"ghost" baseball, 3

Glenn, John, 114

"Golden Age" of baseball, 1

goodwill tours, professional player, 19–21

government policy, wartime baseball and, 12–13

Grable, Betty, 20

Great Britian, baseball in, 68–69, 94–95

Great Lakes Naval Training Station (IL): baseball teams of the, 76–84, 161n7; Bob Feller and, 118; exhibition games, 22; Gordon "Mickey" Cochrane and, 112; military baseball and, 4, 17; playing field conditions at, 72; segregated baseball and, 60–61; treatment of professional players at, 98

"green light" letter, 12–13, 16–17

Griffith, John L., 8–9

Hannegan, Robert, 13

health and medical care: athletic injuries and, 9, 85, 98; Cecil Travis, 131; combat injuries and death, 53–54, 57, 90, 105, 121–24; Joe DiMaggio, 100–101; player post-war performance and, 126; Ted Williams, 114; veneral disease and, 6–7

Heisenberg, Werner, 121

Hollywood Stars, 22, 44

India, baseball in, 66

injuries, athletic. *See under* health and medical care

integration: Bill Veeck and Major League, 57; Larry Doby and Major League, 61, 94; opposition to, 36; overseas military teams, 26–27, 60–61, 96; Truman and armed forces, 60. *See also* Negro League; segregation

interservice rivalry, 76

Ireland, Northern, baseball in, 69

Italy, baseball in, 54–55, 64, 71

Japan: baseball in, x; defamation of Babe Ruth, 3–4; 1934 All-Star tour, 120–21; POW baseball and, 67; soldiers at exhibition games, 25–26

Kansas City Monarchs, 45, 61

Korean War, 114–15, 129

LaGuardia, Fiorella, 12

Langer, William, 15

leadership, baseball and military, 8–9

Little World Series, 113

Los Angeles Angels, 22, 44

Lucas, Scott, 16

Major League baseball: Ball and Bat Fund, 37–38; combat service record of, 97–100; fundraising and support of war effort, 28–35, 151n6; goodwill tours, 19–21; night games, 34; players in the military, 21–22; rivalry with military teams, 81–83; uniform and equipment donations, 51, 72–73; war bond sales, 35–37; wartime continuation of, 12–17. *See also* Negro League; professional players; *specific team by name*

Marine Corps baseball teams, 91, 110–11

McArthur, Douglas, 8

medical care. *See* health and medical care

military baseball teams, domestic: availability to servicemen, 58–60; Bronson Field (FL) Fliers, 87, 113; Camp Campbell (KY) Armoraiders, 46, 90; Camp Edwards (MA), 103; Camp Grant (IL), 59, 72–73; Camp McCoy (WI), 90; Camp Pickett (VA), 90; Camp Roberts (CA), 72, 91; Camp Shelby (MS), 38, 46, 51; Camp Sibert (GA), 46; Chico Flyers, 46; Cochrane Field (GA), 59; Curtis Bay (MD) Cutters, 91; Fort Custer (MI), 59–60; Fort Jackson (SC), 103; Fort Riley

military baseball teams (*continued*)
(KS), 60; Fort Rosecrans (CA), 38–39;
Fort Sheridan (IL), 72–73; fundraising
by, 45–49; Great Lakes Bluejackets, 23–
25, 51, 77–84; interservice rivalry, 76;
Jacksonville Naval Air Station (FL), 98,
116; Jefferson Barracks (MO), 59, 71–
72, 90; Lambert Field Wings, 87–88;
league organization and competition,
62–63; Long Beach Army Ferry Command (CA), 91; Mare Island (CA) Leathernecks, 91; Mather Field (CA), 91; Mc-
Clellan Field (CA) Commanders, 88, 91,
109; Naval Reserve Base Sailors, 46;
Navy Pre-Flight Cloudbusters, 113; New
Cumberland Reception Center (PA), 89;
1942 All-Star Game and, 39–41; 1943
exhibition game, 43; Norfolk (VA) Sailors, 42–43, 84–85, 105, 117; playing
field conditions, 72–73; Randolph Field
(TX) Ramblers, 88–89; Sampson (NY)
Bluejackets, 87, 107–8; San Antonio
Aviation Cadet Center (TX) Warhawks,
88–89, 106–7; San Diego (CA) Devildogs, 91; Santa Ana Army Air Base (CA),
22; segregation in, 60–61; Serviceman's
World Series, 23–25; Sheppard Field
(TX) Mechanics, 89, 106; Twentieth Armored Division Armoraiders, 44–45;
umpires for military, 61–62; Waco Army
Air Field (TX) Wolves, 77, 89, 110. *See
also* athletic programs; military baseball
teams, overseas
military baseball teams, overseas: Algiers
Streetwalkers, 53; Army Air Force, 48–
49; Canadian, 47–48, 95; Casablanca
Yankees, 53; Central Base Section
Clowns, 69, 95; Eighth Army Chicks,
104; Ground Forces, 48; Hickman Field
(HI) Flyers, 92–93; integration of, 60–
61; international rivalry in, 47–49;

league organization and competition,
63–66, 70–71; Ninth Army Air Force,
48; Overseas Invasion Services Expedition All-Stars, 26–27, 96; Panama Canal
Zone, 46–47, 92; playing field conditions of, 73–74; segregation in, 60–61;
Seventy-First Infantry Division, 26–27,
95–96; South Pacific, 56–58; umpires
for, 61–62. *See also* athletic programs;
military baseball teams, domestic; *country or region by name*
Milwaukee Brewers, 58
Minneapolis Millers, 53, 56
Minor League baseball: Chattanooga Lookouts, 44–45; fundraising for, 44–45;
Milwaukee Brewers, 58; Minneapolis
Millers, 53, 56; New Orleans Pelicans,
38, 51, 74; players in the military, 48,
85, 88–90, 92, 95–96, 122; uniform
and equipment donations, 38–39, 51,
72–73. *See also* Pacific Coast League;
Southern Association
mobilization, World War II, 1–2
morale: baseball goodwill tours and, 19–
21; Branch Rickey on baseball and,
17–18; importance to military success,
145n3; interservice rivalry and, 76;
military effectiveness and, 2–6; organized team sports and, xi, 7; servicemen
bonding and, 11–12; wartime baseball
and, 14–15

National Basketball Association, 77
National Semi-Pro Congress, 62
Navy Relief Fund, 32–35, 39, 45–46,
151n6
Negro League: Bill Beeck and the, 57; ETO
World Series, 26–27, 96; exhibition
games, 45; players in the military, 60–
61. *See also* integration
New Caledonia World Series, 61, 65

New Guinea, baseball in, 73

New Orleans Pelicans, 38, 51, 74

New York Giants, 32, 38, 48, 139

New York Yankees: morale and public relations of, 21; and 1942 World Series, 31–32; players in the military, 24, 85, 109, 111, 135; relief games, 32–33

New Zealand, baseball in, 68

night games: fundraising and, 34; importance of, 12; lighting for, 64, 72–73; 1942 All-Star Game, 40

Nimitz, Chester, 23, 93

Norfolk Naval Training Station (VA), 5, 17, 42, 84–87

North Africa, baseball in, 50–55, 64

Oakland Oaks, 44

Office of Strategic Services (OSS), 120–21

owners, Major League, 13, 28–34, 37–42, 57

owners, Minor League, 39, 53, 56–58

Pacific, War in the, 14. See also South Pacific

Pacific Coast League: exhibition games, 44–45; Herman, Floyd "Babe," and, 30; Hollywood Stars, 22, 44; Los Angeles Angels, 22, 44; Oakland Oaks, 44; players in the military, 48, 88, 95; San Diego Padres, 8, 91; San Francisco Seals, 44; Seattle Rainers, 56. See also Minor League baseball

Panama Canal Zone, 46–47, 92

Patton, George S., 2–3, 146n4

Philadelphia Athletics, 25, 33, 40, 78

Philadelphia Phillies: bankruptcy of, 31, 57; exhibitions with military teams, 81–83; players in the military, 41, 46, 90; relief games, 34

Philippines, baseball in the, 64–65, 67, 104

pick-up games, 3, 7, 101–2

Pittsburgh Pirates, 33, 85

politics, wartime baseball and, 12–13, 15

Povich, Shirley, 13, 37, 41–43, 73

prisoners of war (POW), baseball and, 67–68, 123

professional players: auction for war bond sales, 36–37; combat injuries of, 90; combat service of, 97–100; decline in wartime talent of, 29–30; draft deferments for, 17; exhibition games, 19; goodwill tours, 20–21; in the military, 21–27; post-war performance of, 126, 131–33, 140–41; Total Pitcher Index (TPI) defined, 135–36, 170n8; Total Player Rating (TPR) defined, 130, 170n1. See also Major League baseball; Minor League baseball; Negro League; specific players by name

Pyle, Ernie, 6

racism. See integration; segregation

radio broadcasts, baseball, 2, 18–19, 53

recreation, baseball for morale and, 2–6, 12, 16

recruitment, baseball and military, 28

Red Cross, 31–32, 39, 47–49, 67–68

relief games, 32–35, 151n7

Richardson, Robert, Jr., 23, 93

Rickenbacker, Eddie, 12

Rommel, Erwin, 14

Roosevelt, Franklin D., 12–13, 16–17, 60

Russia, baseball in, 66

Sampson Naval Training Center (NY), 87

San Diego Padres, 8

San Francisco Seals, 44

scouting, talent, 53, 56–58

Seattle Rainers, 56

segregation, xiii, 60–61. See also integration

Serviceman's World Series: attendance, 150n84; Bill Dickey and, 111; Enos

104; radio broadcasts, 18–19. *See also*
Serviceman's World Series
World War I, baseball in, 9, 12, 14, 37
World War II, baseball prior to, 1

Yankee Clipper. *See* DiMaggio, Joe "Yankee
Clipper"